THE NEW AMERICAN DILEMMA

To Mike and Amy—
With best regards,
[illegible]
10/1/84

THE NEW AMERICAN DILEMMA

Liberal Democracy and School Desegregation

JENNIFER L. HOCHSCHILD

Yale University Press
New Haven and London

Published with assistance from the foundation established in memory of Philip Hamilton McMillan of the Class of 1894, Yale College.

Copyright © 1984 by Yale University. All rights reserved. This book may not be reproduced, in whole or in part, in any form (beyond that copying permitted by Sections 107 and 108 of the U.S. Copyright Law and except by reviewers for the public press), without written permission from the publishers.

Designed by Nancy Ovedovitz and set in Highland type by Ro-Mark Typographic. Printed in the United States of America by Alpine Press, Inc., Stoughton, Massachusetts.

Library of Congress Cataloging in Publication Data

Hochschild, Jennifer L., 1950–
  The new American dilemma.
  Bibliography: p.
  Includes index.
  1. School integration—Government policy—United States—
Citizen participation. I. Title.
LC214.2.H63 1984 370.19′342 84-40196
ISBN 0-300-03113-0 (alk. paper)
ISBN 0-300-03114-9 (pbk. : alk. paper)

The paper in this book meets the guidelines for permanence and durability of the Committee on Production Guidelines for Book Longevity of the Council on Library Resources.

10 9 8 7 6 5 4 3 2 1

To
Barbara and George Hochschild,
who teach by example

Liberalism that is sincere must will the condition of achieving its ends.

—John Dewey, *Liberalism and Social Action*, 1933

What the best and wisest parent wants for his own child, that must the community want for all its children. Any other ideal for our schools is narrow and unlovely; acted upon, it destroys our democracy.

—John Dewey, *The School and Society*, 1900

CONTENTS

PREFACE

This book grew out of a policy observation, an empirical theory, and a normative concern. The policy observation is that the apparent contradictions that are the hallmark of the voluminous research on desegregation fit into an important and sensible pattern. In brief, the bit of conventional wisdom "Half a loaf is better than none" is mistaken in the case of school desegregation. Slight or partial movements to desegregate schools do little good (and considerable harm) to minorities *and* to Anglos. Drastic desegregative change does a lot of good for minorities and—more controversial—for Anglos as well. Most controversial, *either* sweeping change *or* no desegregation at all (assuming something else is done instead to achieve racial justice) is better for virtually everyone than the partial change that minorities prefer to none and resistant whites prefer to much. That observation was the beginning of my work, but the empirical theory and normative issues soon threatened to take over.

The empirical theory is the idea that incremental change responsive to popular wishes is a key element of both any description of American politics and any prescription for liberal democracy. Two of its progenitors, Robert Dahl and Charles E. Lindblom (both of whom, not so coincidentally, are now less certain of its veracity than they used to be) teach at Yale University, where I was a student. So much of my political science world view revolves around issues of incrementalism and pluralism and their implications. And yet I am a child of the 1960s, and share its mistrust of and distaste for cautious middle-class-oriented change in the face of serious, even desperate, problems. Are incrementalism and pluralism the only tools the United States has to promote racial justice? I hoped not, but had no clear alternative to offer.

My normative concern was that old chestnut, "Why is there no socialism in the United States?" Anyone who addresses that question must deal with the issue of race, which has permeated our society and confounded our class structure since Europeans landed. The socialism question was linked to another, even more problematic. How could a society that purports to guarantee the rights and opportunities promised by liberalism, and the political sovereignty and equality promised by democracy, countenance racism in its midst? I could answer neither question, but needed answers to both.

This book seeks to weave these threads into a coherent pattern. My hope is that it demonstrates and explains the policy observation, addresses and responds to the empirical theory, and points the way toward solving the normative concern.

More precisely, it seeks to show how school desegregation can foster excellence rather than exacerbate shoddiness. Note that I do not assert that desegregation, overall, does either. Thoughtful observers of school desegregation, no matter their ideological or institutional position, now agree that to ask "Does school desegregation work?" is about as useful as asking "Is personality shaped by nature or nurture?" The useful questions are: "How well does desegregation work under specified conditions?" "What do we mean by 'work well'?" "Why does it work better in some places, and along some dimensions, and for some people, than in others?" "What can we do to make it work better?"

This set of questions leads me to focus on variations along a particular dimension among many school districts that also vary along particular dimensions; they do not lead me to focus on global questions of total success or failure, or on particular cases. Thus I cannot conclude, "Desegregation works" (or "doesn't work"), or even, "Desegregation is successful in city X but not in city Y because it did Z." I *can* say, "City X did better for a given measure of success than city Y," or, "This type of student will be better served by desegregation if the plan follows that rule." The useful questions are complex, and so must the answers be, if school desegregation is to promote racial justice.

Finally, a word about school desegregation itself, or rather a word about schools. Research on education has fairly low prestige among social scientists, a fact I find hard to understand. After all, university professors are teachers. And education is big public business—it uses close to one-tenth of our gross national product; New York City's school budget approaches $3 million. It employs three and one-half million people, and it is among the most salient experiences outside the family for all children. It prepares us for our occupations, helps to determine our income, and shapes our view of the world.

More important than all of that is schools' role in fostering and maintaining liberal democracy. According to Thomas Jefferson, only through public schools are "worth and genius . . . sought out from every condition of life," and only universal public education will "raise the mass of people to the high ground of moral responsibility necessary to their own safety and to orderly government." Horace Mann insisted that universal public education would eradicate class conflict, as well as the "obdurate and dark mass of avarice and ignorance and prejudice." John Dewey saw schools as "the democratic password"; when each school becomes "an embryonic community . . . saturating [the child] with the spirit of service," we will have "the deepest and best guarantee of a larger society which is worthy, lovely, and harmonious."

Today, we worry that schools are not doing their liberal democratic job. Public schools are floating on "a rising tide of mediocrity" (whatever that is), says the National Commission on Excellence in Education. Educational mediocrity "threatens our very future as a nation and as a people." Schools must be made excellent again.

Schools matter, a lot. Ask any parent, or child. And therefore school desegregation matters a lot, not because it contributes to schools' current shoddiness as so many people fear but because it can, and sometimes does, contribute to their excellence. Properly implemented, it fosters Jefferson's goal of "rais[ing] the mass of people to the high ground" of political, social, economic, and intellectual quality. If school desegregation is permitted to fail, then American liberal democracy may be in even worse shape than the most purple prose of a national commission can conjure up.

But it need not fail. This book is offered in the hope that our history may profit our future. We can use the lessons of policy analysis and empirical theory to address our normative problems. That is, we can promote racial justice and liberal democracy through the schools by taking the steps everywhere that a few school districts have already taken to make desegregation work. Effective school desegregation in the 1980s is a matter of moral and political will, not of either revolutionary apocalypse or better policy analysis. If we Americans can overcome our predilection for incremental change through popular control, if we can muster the courage and political will to desegregate successfully, Anglos and minorities alike will benefit.

If we cannot, we had better do something else. School desegregation is not the only route to racial justice and liberal democracy; alternatives are numerous and compelling. The big danger is that we will *neither* desegregate successfully *nor* pursue other ways to fulfill the promise of *Brown*. In that case, minorities and Anglos alike will suffer the consequences of our political, theoretical, and moral failings.

The length of my list of people and institutions to thank would be embarrassing if it were not an indication of the breadth and depth of the community of scholars. First, I would like to thank Willis Hawley and John McConahay for piquing and supporting my interest in school desegregation, and John Witte for making the connection between the policy problem and the empirical theory. In addition, the following students, teachers, colleagues, and friends (many play several of those roles at once) have been invaluable intellectually and emotionally: Deborah Baumgold, Robert Bradley, David Braybrooke, Valerie Broadie, Elizabeth Bussiere, Robert Dahl, Fred Greenstein, Judith Hanna, David Hirsch, Stanley Katz, David Kirp, Lucy Knight, Charles E. Lindblom, Duane Lockard, David Mayhew, Daniel Monti, Richard Nathan, Gary Orfield, Paul Peterson, Sarah Rosen, Christine Rossell, Leonard Stevens, Clarence Stone, Dennis Thompson, Amanda Thornton, Jeffrey Tulis, Mary von Euler, Clement Vose, Stephen Wasby, Gibson Winter, and an anonymous reader for Yale University Press. I could not have done without their help—both substantive and affective—even if I sometimes did not heed their wisdom.

I would also like to thank several collectivities, which are of course shorthand for the people in them. The Department of Politics and the Woodrow Wilson School of Princeton University have given me three stimulating, enjoyable, and productive years in which to work out my argument; I hope for many more such years. The Institute of Policy Sciences at Duke University, the Political Science Department of Columbia University, the Desegregation Studies Unit of the

National Institute of Education (which provided research grant NIE-G-79-0185), the Office for Civil Rights of the Department of Health, Education and Welfare, the Joint Center for Political Studies, the American Philosophical Society, the Andrew W. Mellon Preceptorship of Princeton University—all provided institutional, financial, and other types of support. Faculty-student seminars at Princeton, the University of Chicago, and Wesleyan University, chaired respectively by Manfred Halpern, Russell Hardin, and Donald Moon, asked me tough questions that I did not wish to hear but that forced me to sharpen (or modulate) my arguments. My students in a policy conference on school desegregation in Chicago, chaired by David Martland, not only asked tough questions but also did the research needed to answer them, and I have relied heavily on their work and insights. My thanks also to the American Political Science Association for awarding an early draft of this book the Franklin L. Burdette Pi Sigma Alpha Award for the best paper at the 1982 American Political Science Association meeting.

Marian Ash of Yale University Press has been a superb and unfailingly encouraging editor, a point I recognized even when struggling against her good advice. Becky Saletan has been all that one could ask for in a manuscript editor, whether one needs a sharp grammarian, astute political observer, or morale booster at a given moment. Suzanne Cox, Connie Dent, Joanne George, Linda Iannucci, and Pat Skowronek were astonishingly even-tempered and helpful, even when urged to type faster to make up for my missing deadlines. Claire Laporte, Colette Shabbott, Regina Thomas, Amanda Thornton, and Marjorie Wilkes were equally good-natured and reliable in their research assistance. The administrators of the Woodrow Wilson School—Dean Donald Stokes, Dean Charles Berry, Dean Ingrid Reed, Agnes Pearson, and Joyce Mix—have all been wonderful.

The many people I have interviewed and buttonholed give me hope that this book breathes something other than the proverbial rarified atmosphere of the ivory tower. I could not have written it without them; their insights and experience permeate every page. I hope that I have been true to their views and respectful of their lives.

Last but hardly least are my family. Tony Broh shares my frustration and joy in scholarship. More important, he shares my life. The book is dedicated to my parents, Barbara and George Hochschild.

They taught their children to respect others, to strive for integrity and excellence, and to pick up and try again when striving fails. And they give us the love that does not care about success and failure.

ONE

Racism and Liberal Democracy

The Negro problem in America represents a moral lag in the development of the nation and a study of it must record nearly everything which is bad and wrong in America. . . . However, . . . not since Reconstruction has there been more reason to anticipate fundamental changes in American race relations, changes which will involve a development toward the American ideals.

—Gunnar Myrdal, *An American Dilemma*, 1944[1]

Racism and liberalism are as intertwined in American history as they are antithetical. Since the English settled Jamestown, our politics have simultaneously affirmed the natural rights of all persons and legitimated the oppression of non-Caucasians. The plantation economy of the South flourished from the work of black slaves. Slaves produced many of the goods which paid France for its invaluable help in our war for independence. The Constitution was shaped by disputes over whether slaves were persons or property. The boundaries and cultures of Western states grew out of the "free soil" battles of the early nineteenth century. We fought our only internecine, and most vicious, war partly over slavery. The presidential election of 1876 was decided on racial grounds. The anemia of working-class consciousness and the absence of class conflict result partly from racial antagonism. In short, the economy of the South, the Revolution, the Constitution, the Western frontier, the Civil War, the labor movement—these facets of American history and others have been molded by the juxtaposition of racism and liberalism.

Two more different concepts can hardly be imagined, however, than racism and liberalism (or more appropriately in the United

States, liberal democracy). Liberalism asserts the unique value of all persons, political equality of all citizens, liberty of all humans. It insists on natural rights, autonomy, opportunity, dignity. Since the 1820s, Americans have used majoritarian democracy to translate liberalism's assertions into mass governance. Democracy calls for the sovereignty of citizens over government action through collective choice of policies or leaders. All citizens have an equal right to express their political wishes and equal opportunity to act politically. Freedom is assured by keeping government responsible to the citizenry and channeled within constitutional bounds of rights and laws, which are themselves shaped through democratic processes. Thus in common American parlance, liberalism and democracy are inextricably entwined; the phrase *liberal democracy* embraces that vast corpus of philosophy and ideology.

But racism, whether in the virulent form of slavery or the less pernicious form of prejudice and discrimination,* is profoundly antiliberal and antidemocratic. It is antiliberal in its assertion of the unequal worth of persons, of civil—not natural—determinations of rights, of the legitimacy of denying liberty and opportunity to some. And it distinguishes among people not by what they have done (indeed, even liberals will disfranchise and imprison criminals) but by what group they were born into. It uses ascriptive characteristics, not achieved character, to determine people's fate, and it proclaims that some groups should not partake of liberalism's promises.

Racism is also undemocratic. Slavery obviously denies political sovereignty to slaves, and a slave society typically develops a steep political hierarchy even among its free members. Discrimination is also antidemocratic, though more subtly; it prohibits or inhibits some members of the polity from expressing their political wishes and

*By racism, I do not mean personal dislike or denigration of another race or ethnic group. Individual prejudice is neither necessary nor sufficient for racism to exist. It is not necessary because of the phenomenon of "institutional racism"; a society or part of it may act in ways that severely and systematically discriminate against members of one race without anyone so intending or realizing. Prejudice is not sufficient for racism because it is possible to dislike another race yet treat its members without harm. Thus to assert that American history and contemporary politics are deeply racist is not to accuse individuals of harboring evil thoughts; it is to say that our society is shaped by actions in consequence of racial differences—actions that usually elevate whites and subordinate blacks.

from running for office. Thus the government remains unresponsive to some citizens. Their rights, liberties, and opportunities are thereby curtailed, liberalism's promises are unredeemed—and the circle is closed. The antiliberal and antidemocratic qualities of racism are as entwined as liberalism and democracy are.

How, then, can racism coëxist with liberal democracy? This is not a new question for Americans, and they have typically given one of two answers. One response assumes that slavery, or more generally racial separatism, is a terrible and inexplicable anomaly stuck in the middle of our liberal democratic ethos. It must be eradicated for that ethos to thrive. Thomas Jefferson indicted the hapless King George III in an early draft of the Declaration of Independence for having "waged cruel war against human nature itself, violating it's most sacred rights of life and liberty in the persons of a distant people . . . captivating and carrying them into slavery. . . . [H]e has prostituted his negative for suppressing every legislative attempt to prohibit . . . this execrable commerce . . . this assemblage of horrors."[2]* Patrick Henry made explicit the implicit contradiction between Jefferson's words and his life as a plantation owner:

> Is it not amazing that at a time, when the rights of humanity are defined and understood with precision, in a country above all others fond of liberty, that . . . we find men . . . adopting a principle as repugnant to humanity as it is inconsistent with the Bible and destructive to liberty? . . . Would anyone believe I am the master of slaves of my own purchase! I am drawn along by the general inconvenience of living here without them. I will not, I can not justify it. However culpable my conduct, I will so far pay my devoir to virtue, as to own the excellence and rectitude of her precepts, and lament my want of conformity to them. I believe a time will come when an opportunity will be offered to abolish this lamentable evil. Everything we can do is to improve it, if it happens in our day, if not, let us transmit to our descendants, together with our slaves, a pity for their unhappy lot, and an abhorrence of slavery.[3]

Sixty years later, people were still lamenting the evil of slavery in a liberal and increasingly democratic society. But the level of frustra-

*This paragraph was struck by the Continental Congress, "in complaisance to . . . [those who] felt a little tender under those censures" and "whose reflections were not yet matured to the full abhorrence of that [slave] traffic," as Jefferson put it. See Becker, *Declaration of Independence*, pp. 171–72.

tion and fury was mounting: William Lloyd Garrison "repudiate[d]" the Declaration of Independence as "a rotten and dangerous instrument" and saw the Fourth of July as a "great carnival of republican despotism" consecrated "to bombast, to falsehood, to impudence, to hypocrisy."[4] Even the cautious Abraham Lincoln came to assert with increasing vehemence that practically, "A house divided against itself cannot stand," and that normatively, "The plain unmistakable language of the Declaration [of Independence] . . . intended to include *all* men."[5]

The most famous modern statement of the anomaly thesis is Gunnar Myrdal's *An American Dilemma*. He described "the subordinate position of Negroes [as] perhaps the most glaring conflict in the American conscience and the greatest unsolved task for American democracy."[6] The dilemma is neither a structural problem of some uniting to repress others, nor an ideological battle between good and evil people or regions. Rather, it is a conflict *within* "the heart of the American," a struggle within each person between high ideals and base actions. Myrdal's depiction of the American dilemma explains the pathos in Patrick Henry's *cri de coeur*:

> [It] is the ever-raging conflict between, on the one hand, the valuations preserved on the general plane . . . [of] the "American Creed," where the American thinks, talks, and acts under the influence of high national and Christian precepts, and, on the other hand, the valuations on specific planes of individual and group living, where personal and local interests; economic, social, and sexual jealousies; considerations of community prestige and conformity; group prejudice against particular persons or types of people; and all sorts of miscellaneous wants, impulses, and habits dominate his outlook. (p. xlvii; italicized in original)

Myrdal, like the nation he so admired, was optimistic, and his optimism is a distinguishing feature of the anomaly thesis. Americans "are all good people"; whites are slowly changing their ways; Negroes are slowly coming into full possession of their liberal democratic heritage. He cautioned against complacency and inertia, insisting that "if America wants to make the . . . choice [admit Negroes into full citizenship] she cannot wait and see. She has to do something big, and do it soon" (p. 1022). But America *could* do it, without violence and without destroying the nation as we knew it. In the midst of World War II, Myrdal concluded his masterpiece by affirming that "America is constantly reaching for . . . democracy at home and abroad. The main trend in its history is the gradual realization of the American Creed. . . . America can demonstrate that justice, equality and cooperation are possible between white and colored people. . . . *America is free to choose whether the Negro shall remain her liability or become her opportunity*" (pp. 1021–22; emphasis Myrdal's).

However, the anomaly thesis and its hopeful prognosis are themselves embattled. Some argue that racism is not simply an excrescence on a fundamentally healthy liberal democratic body but is part of what shapes and energizes the body. In this view, liberal democracy and racism in the United States are historically, even inherently, reinforcing; American society as we know it exists only because of its foundation in racially based slavery, and it thrives only because racial discrimination continues. The apparent anomaly is an actual symbiosis.

This argument has spawned several variations, each of which gained prominence during a particular historical era. Edmund Morgan has recently argued that slavery permitted the republican ideology of freedom and rights to flourish among eighteenth-century Virginian aristocrats. Only the ability to keep the poorest colonists totally controlled, and the next-to-poorest allied with the well-off rather than the worst-off, made the dangerous new ideas safe enough to develop:

> "The Virginians," he [Sir Augustus John Foster] said, "can profess an unbounded love of liberty and of democracy in consequence of the mass of the people, who in other countries might become mobs, being there nearly altogether composed of their own Negro slaves. . . ." There it was. Aristocrats could more safely preach equality in a slave society than in a free one. Slaves did not become leveling mobs, because their owners would see to it that they had no chance to. The apostrophes to equality were not addressed to them. And . . . the remaining free laborers . . . were too few in number to constitute a serious threat to the superiority of the men who assured them of their equality. Moreover . . . small farmers could perceive a common identity with the large. . . . Neither was a slave. And both were equal in not being slaves.[7]

Nineteenth-century Southerners defended slavery on grounds ironically similar to Morgan's attack on it. The very emergence of the

American nation from wilderness depended on forced labor: "Labour is pain, . . . and the nature of man is averse to pain. . . . The coercion of Slavery alone is adequate to form man to habits of labour. Without it, there can be no accumulation of property, no providence for the future, no taste for comforts or elegancies, which are the characteristics and essentials of civilization."[8] Furthermore, they argued, slavery is as necessary to liberty and equality as it is to culture. The existence of black slaves "cause[s] . . . the perfect spirit of equality so prevalent among the whites of all the slave-holding states. . . . The man to the north will not shake hands familiarly with his servant, and converse, and laugh, and dine with him. . . . But go to the south, and you will find that no white man feels such inferiority of rank as to be unworthy of association with those around him. . . . And it is this spirit of equality which is both the generator and preserver of the genuine spirit of liberty."[9] In a final confirmation of Morgan's analysis, Southerners claimed that majoritarian democracy itself requires slavery:

> Universal suffrage, though not essential in theory, seems to be in fact a necessary appendage to a republican system. . . . [But] it is a wretched and insecure government which is administered by its most ignorant citizens, and those who have the least at stake under it. . . . These are rapidly usurping all power in the non-slaveholding States, and threaten a fearful crisis in republican institutions there at no remote period. In the slaveholding States, however, . . . the poorest and most ignorant have no political influence whatever, because they are slaves. Of the other[s] . . . a large proportion are both educated and independent in their circumstances, while those who unfortunately are not so, being still elevated far above the mass, are higher toned and more deeply interested in preserving a stable and well ordered government, than the same class in any other country. Hence, Slavery is truly the "corner-stone" and foundation of every well-designed and durable "republican edifice."[10]

In the twentieth century, arguments about the unity of racism and liberal democracy have often grown out of Marxist political economy. This thesis has several steps. First, the capitalist economy of the United States is closely linked with its liberal democratic polity. Second, one task of political leaders is to foster economic prosperity, which means fostering capitalism. Up to this point, Ronald Reagan and Marxists agree. Third, say Marxists (but not Reaganites), a capitalist economy thrives on racial hostility and employment discrimination. Racial hostility among workers keeps them divided and inhibits working-class consciousness. Employment discrimination permits employers to hire some workers more cheaply and for less attractive jobs than others will accept. It also provides a cushion for economic fluctuations by keeping some workers unemployed or underemployed, reduces competition for scarce higher-level jobs, and creates a class of dependent consumers for the surplus goods of ever-expanding producers. Political actors become implicated in these economic practices because they want the economy to succeed. Thus "dominant class actors [commercial farmers, businessmen, and trade unionists] . . . depend on the racial order and the racial state to dislodge subordinate labor from the subsistence economy, to help organize a labor force, . . . [and] to help insure labor's continuing cheapness, immobility, and political impotence."[11]

Furthermore, the Marxists continue, political leaders are not only instruments of the economic order but also independent actors whose politics and policies are as tainted by racism as their economic acts. Racist ideology develops a life of its own. White politicians run for office on the strength of overt or covert appeals to whites against blacks. George Wallace's "Segregation Forever" is an obvious example, but more recent slogans of white candidates facing black opponents are similar, if more subtle. Consider, for example, Atlanta, 1973: "Atlanta Is Too Young to Die"; Birmingham, 1979: "Don't Let Birmingham Become Another Atlanta" [a black candidate had won in Atlanta]; second congressional district, Mississippi, 1982: "Elect Webb Franklin to Congress. He's One of Us"; and Chicago, 1983: "Epton. Before It's Too Late." Legislators' calls for "law and order" or for "getting welfare mothers off the dole and onto the payroll" can also be signals that they favor white constituents at the expense of blacks.

Policies, continue exponents of the symbiosis thesis, are similarly laced with racial implications. Programs of urban redevelopment and gentrification, labor unions' insistence on seniority, hiring police and firefighters on the strength of high scores on (perhaps irrelevant) tests—all have the effect if not the intention of favoring whites over blacks. Some even argue that blacks' main role in American policymaking is to serve as a bargaining chip between competing whites.

In "a conflict between segments of white society, . . . [the] resolution of their differences . . . [is] facilitated and often made possible by arrangements that seriously disadvantage blacks."[12] The Tilden-Hayes compromise of 1876 that ended Reconstruction and Tom Watson's embrace of racism in the early 1900s in order to unite poor and wealthy white Southerners are clear historical examples. The movement of the Office for Civil Rights (OCR) away from desegregation and toward a focus on sex discrimination and aid to the handicapped, and the 1981 educational block grant, which gave most school districts more federal funds but eliminated desegregation spending, may be contemporary examples of the same phenomenon.

Finally, claim symbiosis exponents, liberal norms themselves reinforce racism that is already in place, even if liberalism is antithetical to the establishment of racial separatism. Hallowed liberal principles of symmetry in treatment ("To be valid for you this law must be valid for them"), of focus on individuals rather than ascriptive groups or classes, of tolerance for all viewpoints—all permit, even encourage, racism to continue. Thus, this argument concludes, capitalists build upon and benefit from racism; the liberal democratic state is partly driven by the exigencies of a capitalist economy; and a liberal democratic state develops racist principles, practices, and structures of its own.

We have, at this point, one agreed-upon fact and two divergent explanations for it. Racial problems have profoundly shaped United States history, and the philosophy of racism is antithetical to the philosophy of liberal democracy. But some see racism as anomalous: the dilemma of Americans is our continued weakness in (to change the metaphor) weeding out our shame so that our true creed may flourish. Once we bring ourselves to pull the weeds, American idealism will bloom all the better. Others see racism as symbiotic: the American garden is rooted in and nurtured by blacks' second-class status. To eradicate it, we must be willing and able to change the whole shape and ecology of the American landscape. Only then can the American creed blossom. This book examines these two arguments by asking whether the United States wishes to, and can, end racism without severe dislocation. If so, then the anomaly thesis gains support, and Myrdal's optimism was justified. If not, then the symbiosis thesis gains support, and we face a dilemma much less tractable than the one he so eloquently described.

Myrdal's prescription for resolving the American dilemma actually implies two claims, each of which I will examine. First is an argument that we can abolish racism and its consequences through conventional forms of political action. We do not need radically uprooting techniques of policy-making to improve the condition of blacks; we need only to apply standard practices. Myrdal was not naive on this point; he did not expect painless progress or complete success. But nowhere did he suggest that normal processes of policy-making stood in the way of resolving the American dilemma. I will examine this assumption by analyzing the recent effects of *incremental policy-making* (or *incrementalism*) on segregation in America.

Incremental policy-making occurs when governments change existing policies and practices in small steps. Such steps imply marginal adjustment from a given base and presumably permit policy-makers to experiment, rethink, and retract while stopping short of wholesale reformulation. Most observers see incremental change as the standard—indeed almost ubiquitous—mode of policy enactment in the United States and perhaps in most nations. Examples range from raising the property tax rate a few mills, to sending a few more soldiers to Vietnam, to adding one more stop to the Washington, D.C., subway system. Proponents argue that incremental change is the best way to change or create policies while maintaining the stability and consensus essential to liberal democracy. Opponents argue that incrementalism cannot produce sufficient change, that it generates the wrong changes, and that a stable polity need not (or even must not) be so cautious.

Chapter 4 looks at the effects of incremental policy-making to see if, in fact, it moves us with reasonable promptness in the direction of eradicating racism. Anomaly theorists argue that it can—that a garden can be rejuvenated by pulling one weed at a time. Symbiosis theorists argue that it cannot—if the soil and layout of a garden are unsuited to their intended crops, pulling a few weeds does no good and actually does harm by deluding us into false perceptions of progress.

The second claim derived from *An American Dilemma* is that

Americans, white and black, *want* to eradicate racism and its consequences. Again, Myrdal was no Pollyanna; he recognized the strength of whites' prejudice, self-interest, and social pressure. But he asserted that the American creed is even stronger, and that liberal ideology and an innate sense of justice lead whites to want to overcome their own base preferences. Given the chance, and an external push, they would choose creed over practice. I will examine this assumption by looking at Americans' recent political choices regarding segregation; when policies are formulated through *popular control*, do they help or hinder the cause of racial justice?

Popular control occurs when citizens determine the overall direction for policies to proceed. They may be involved directly in shaping and carrying out policies, or indirectly through electing leaders who shape policies for them and are held accountable in the next round of voting. Most observers see popular control as the standard, although not ubiquitous, mode of policy choice in the United States. It is not ubiquitous because, at the broadest level, the popular will is constrained by constitutional guarantees of rights and problems of feasibility, and, at the most specific level, experts or bureaucrats shape details of the public mandate. Nevertheless, proponents describe popular control as a defining characteristic of liberal democracy in general and American politics in particular. The value itself has few opponents (unlike the concept of incremental change); controversy occurs instead over how extensive it is and ought to be.

Chapter 5 looks at the effects of popular control to see if, in fact, Americans are choosing to move with reasonable promptness in the direction of eradicating racism. If we can fulfill the American creed through politics as usual (that is, incremental policy-making), do we seek to do so? Anomaly theorists argue that we do—that all Americans (except imbeciles, idiots, and Ku Klux Klansmen) would prefer a garden blooming with racial equity to one choking in the weeds of discrimination. Symbiosis theorists argue that we do not—that whites (and perhaps some blacks) benefit from a landscape that includes racial discrimination and will resist the bulldozing needed to reshape it.

School desegregation is my test case for examining the racial effects of incremental policy-making and popular control of policy choice. Desegregating elementary and secondary public schools is perhaps the most important means our generation has used to eradicate racism. Has school desegregation, as it was intended to, eliminated prejudice, provided equal opportunity, guaranteed rights to all? Is it moving acceptably fast in that direction? Or has the way we have gone about desegregating schools caused more harm than good, for blacks as well as whites? The limits of our success, their causes and implications, and our choices for the future are the substantive focus of this book.

Thus, knowing how well incrementalism and popular control work to desegregate schools will enable us to understand better how racism can persist in a liberal democracy. The history of school desegregation will support one of the two theses more strongly than the other. If I find that incrementalism and popular control are successfully desegregating schools, the anomaly thesis gains support. In that case, our task is clear: we have only to find the political will and policy-making skill to rid ourselves of the rest of the weeds in our fundamentally thriving garden. If, however, incrementalism and popular control work poorly to desegregate schools, then the symbiosis thesis gains support. In that case, we face a new dilemma, and our task is not at all clear. Should we maintain practices that are normally effective and attractive but fail in this case to reach the roots of the problem, or should we use risky, even undesirable, means that can dig deep enough to achieve our goal? We face a contradiction, in short, between good policy-making practices and good outcomes, and between most citizens' preferences and more citizens' benefits.

If (as I will argue) this new formulation of the American dilemma in fact encapsulates American race relations more accurately than Myrdal's formulation, we have three choices for the 1980s, which I analyze in Chapter 6. We can (1) continue to use flawed practices in a well-intentioned but futile effort to desegregate our schools; (2) abandon school desegregation in favor of some other goal that is more likely to succeed through incremental policy-making and popular choice; or (3) choose more effective but less palatable methods of desegregating schools.* I believe that the first is the most likely

*The strongest symbiosis proponents describe a fourth choice which I will not consider further. They claim that all policy options short of revolution are futile, that

outcome; either the second or the third offers a more desirable future for whites as well as blacks. The new American dilemma is soluble but perhaps only at a price that most Americans are unwilling to pay. If that is the case, we are a much less liberal and democratic society than we would like to think.

---

no means can eradicate racism and still preserve liberal democratic society as we know it. Only a radical restructuring of society or a radical transformation of individual psychology can succeed. I disagree, but at any rate that is not a very useful path for a book on American public policy to pursue.

There is, of course, a fifth choice—to give up any effort to eradicate racism. That alternative is politically impossible and morally impermissible, so it too will not be considered further.

TWO

Eradicating Racism

Since the law was made clear on last May 17, it would seem that completed desegregation by September 1955 would work no real hardship and would create no substantial administrative problems.
—Spottswood Robinson, Memo to NAACP, Summer 1954[1]

Before we can decide whether school desegregation poses a new American dilemma for the 1980s, we need a few facts about the 1950s, 1960s, and 1970s. That is, we need to know where we are and how we got here, for both school desegregation and, more generally, the status of blacks in American society.

THE RISE AND FALL OF CIVIL RIGHTS FERVOR

In 1954, *Brown v. Board of Education of Topeka, Kansas* made public school desegregation the keystone of modern efforts to eradicate racism. *Brown* overturned the 1896 Supreme Court ruling in *Plessy v. Ferguson* that blacks could legitimately be given "equal but separate accommodations" in railroad cars, restaurants, schools, and other public places. *Plessy* had found it a "fallacy" to assume "that the enforced separation of the two races stamps the colored race with a badge of inferiority" and could "not accept [the] proposition[s] . . . that social prejudices may be overcome by legislation, and that equal rights cannot be secured to the negro except by an enforced commingling of the two races." *Brown* repudiated all three of these points. It held that "separate educational facilities are inherently unequal; . . . to separate [children in schools] from others of similar age and qualifications solely because of their race generates a feeling of inferiority as to their status in the community that may affect their hearts and minds in a way unlikely ever to be undone." Furthermore, the implementation ruling a year later (*Brown II*) held that school systems must, sooner or later, change their structures and practices to admit blacks "on a nondiscriminatory basis." It thus implied, *contra Plessy,* that legislation *can* "overcome social prejudices" and that legislation may, even must, "enforce the commingling of the two races" in order to "secure equal rights to the negro."[2]

At least since Reconstruction, blacks and their white supporters have debated whether racial integration is necessarily preferable to truly equal, voluntarily separate accommodations. Justice John H. Harlan pointed out in his famous dissent to *Plessy* that "a colored citizen . . . does not . . . perhaps . . . object to separate [railroad] coaches for his race, if his rights under the law were recognized." Marcus Garvey's separatist Universal Negro Improvement Association captured the imaginations of thousands of blacks in the early 1900s. The National Association for the Advancement of Colored People (NAACP) debated throughout its march to the Supreme Court in the 1940s and 1950s whether to pursue truly equal, separate schools instead of desegregation. Most arguments for separate equality were strategic—it was a demand whose gratification seemed more likely than a reversal of the sixty-year-old precedent of *Plessy*.[3] But a few people argued substantively, not just strategically, for the worth of separate equality. Columbia University law professor Herbert Wechsler, for example, asked Thurgood Marshall in 1951 if it "was so plain . . . that a Negro child attending a segregated school was worse off than a Negro child attending a non-segregated school where he might feel the full brunt of white prejudice? Could it not reasonably be argued that . . . [the latter child] would be doubly frustrated by the limited economic and social opportunity that would later confront him in a world where *de facto* segregation prevailed?"[4] Such views were held by a distinct minority; they matter much more as harbingers of arguments to come two decades later (and four chapters from now) than as roles in the *Brown* drama.

Response to the *Brown* decision "was predictable: all hell broke loose."[5] People were exultant or outraged, fearful or hopeful; few who heard of the decision were indifferent. Here I wish to focus on only one, perhaps the most puzzling, of the many responses. This was the upsurge of fellowship and goodwill between white and black Americans during the decade after *Brown,* followed by an equal but opposite reaction in the succeeding two decades. Why were so many so quick to take up the cause of integration and then so quick to drop it just when it began to take hold?

Two comments voiced the day after *Brown* set the tone of high-minded optimism for liberals in the decade to come. "What the Justices have done," editorialized the *Cincinnati Enquirer,* "is simply to act as the conscience of the American nation." Thurgood Marshall predicted "up to five years" for all schools to be integrated, and nine for all of American society.[6] Carrying out the promise of *Brown* through civil rights activity might be dangerous and difficult, but it was nevertheless virtuous and efficacious. One could know the right course of action, take it, and expect good results.

It is hard to recreate the moral fervor and communal spirit that grew in one segment of the population during the late 1950s and that culminated in the passage of the Civil Rights Act of 1964 and the Voting Rights Act of 1965. But we can try. Remember President Kennedy's speech in June 1963, after the Birmingham protest marchers had been met with police dogs and fire hoses:

> We are confronted primarily with a moral issue. It is as old as the scriptures and is as clear as the American Constitution. The heart of the question is whether all Americans are to be afforded equal rights and equal opportunities. . . . We face therefore a moral crisis as a country and as a people. . . . It cannot be quieted by token moves or talk. It is a time to act. . . . Those who do nothing are inviting shame as well as violence. Those who act boldly are recognizing right as well as reality.[7]

Remember Martin Luther King's "I have a dream" speech and blacks and whites crossing their arms, holding hands, and singing "We Shall Overcome." Finally, consider a more obscure capsule of the times. Robert Goheen, then president of Princeton University, spoke before a conference of the newly formed Association of Black Collegians in 1967. Princeton's sole black administrator and organizer of both the association and the conference described Goheen's speech of welcome:

> Something had happened; . . . this was no perfunctory greeting. . . . He [Goheen] had taken off! For the next 30 minutes, he held the audience in rapt

> attention as he spelled out his own convictions about the necessity of equality of opportunity at all levels of society and especially in the sphere of education. He acknowledged the inequities of the past, but urged the students to look forward to the future, to make the most of their opportunity to gain an education that would help them to be in the vanguard of new achievements and progress for their people and for the nation as a whole. Every eye was glued on him. They were taking in every word. When he finished, there was an outpouring of applause. In one spontaneous motion, the audience rose to its feet and rocked the Wilson School Auditorium with a tribute. . . . It was from the heart and expressed appreciation for not the mere words but the feelings from the heart and soul of the man. . . . The black students of Princeton watched him with pride as he moved out of the auditorium. He was their President! They were Princeton![8]

Goheen's words perfectly capture the heady mix of *noblesse oblige*, *mea culpa*, and sheer excitement of the 1960s civil rights movement. And the students' (and recorder's) response capture the equally heady sense of "making it."

But just as an integrated edifice seemed near completion, it began to crack at the base. By 1964, Malcolm X was telling white Harvard students that "there's nothing in our backgrounds nor anything around us which in any way gives either of us reason to love each other." James Baldwin was asking, "Do I really *want* to be integrated into a burning house?" Norman Podhoretz was responding with another question: "Why, *why* [are] . . . white and black . . . enemies beyond any possibility of reconciliation? . . . We white Americans are—for whatever reason, it no longer matters—so twisted and sick in our feelings about Negroes that I despair of the present push toward integration."[9] A federal district court charged New Rochelle, New York—a Northern school district—with deliberate school segregation. And as the 1960s continued, they brought Black Power, riots, "forced busing"—and liberal confusion, doubt, panic, and retreat. Eventually, white liberals split into three groups. A tiny proportion have been radicalized by the juxtaposition of hope and frustration and seek to end racism by ending American society as we know it; some continue to pursue the old goals of integration; and most have moved to the suburbs and taken up ecology, declaring sadly that desegregation does not work.

What happened? Why commitment and intensity in one decade and disillusionment and withdrawal in the next two? The crux of the matter is: desegregation, never mind integration, upsets the apple cart. One's children are one's most precious possessions; schooling is one of the most important early influences outside the family. Parents are not—indeed, must not be—willing to sacrifice their children to an ideal. In the ten years after *Brown*, white liberals did not think they had to do anything of the kind. They believed that black students could be brought into the classroom (or black voters into the polling places) without white students (or voters) being severely disrupted. If nothing but prejudice and narrow self-interest must be sacrificed and if virtue and community can be gained, then Gunnar Myrdal could be proven right. All whites had to do was encourage, or even require, their best instincts to come to the fore and our national shame would be redeemed. Gordon Allport wrote just before the *Brown* decision that

> most Americans have a deep inner conviction that discrimination is wrong and unpatriotic. While their own prejudices may make them squirm and protest in opposition to proposed laws, they may also sigh with relief if the law, in accord with their "better natures," is passed—and enforced. People need and want their consciences bolstered by law, and this is nowhere more true than in the area of group relations.[10]

The law *was* changed, and Americans trapped in Myrdal's dilemma eagerly started down the path to escape.

But a decade later, the situation looked much more complicated and Myrdal began to seem naive. Blacks did not necessarily want to join white society. The agonizingly slow, even murderous, process of desegregating the South and the absence of much stomach for change in the North taught some blacks that the game of integration was not worth the candle. Perhaps desegregation was not the only or best route to equality; perhaps the old formula of "separate but equal" would work better in wrenching some concessions from "the white devil." Whites, for their part, did not want their children to, as they saw it, sink to the level of ghetto life. They began to fear that segregation and its attendant evils could not be abolished without at least short-term sacrifices and, more seriously, the possibility of lasting harm to their children.

Few white liberals or Black Panthers thought through the question of whether racism is intrinsic to our society and their position in it or merely an anomalous shame. But everyone learned that its eradication would entail much more fundamental change than the nation had bargained for. So most have withdrawn to their own kind and now either ignore the whole problem or regretfully proclaim *Brown*'s failure. Those who remain in the fray continue to insist that conventional politics can suffice to eradicate racism through the schools. This book questions both the proclamation of failure and the efficacy of conventional means to success.

THE STATUS OF BLACKS IN AMERICAN SOCIETY

Thirty years after the *Brown* decision, in the wake of this flow and ebb of integrationist idealism, what are the contours of the American racial terrain? We have evidence to support claims ranging from "Racism is as virulent and destructive as ever" to "Race is no longer a useful category for differentiating winners from losers." Let us pause to consider a few illustrative data on blacks' status in American society.

Attitudes have changed but perhaps less than initially meets the eye. On the one hand, overt prejudice has declined: given a choice among "desegregation, strict segregation, and something in between," the proportion of the population choosing "strict segregation" decreased from 23 percent in 1964 to 5 percent in 1978.[11] Whites report more black co-workers, friends, and even employers and subscribe to fewer racial stereotypes than twenty years ago.[12] On the other hand, enthusiasm for integration is weak. Support for desegregation *declined* between 1972 and 1978 from 41 to 34 percent; endorsement of the wishy-washy "something in between" increased in the same period from 45 to 54 percent. Fewer blacks than whites find integrated work relations "pleasant and easy," in the stilted phrase of the pollster, and most whites still oppose relationships any closer than friendship across racial lines.[13] Even in 1982, 57 percent of Americans (of both races) with an opinion agreed that "blacks shouldn't push themselves where they're not wanted" (no question was asked about pushy whites).[14]

The picture is as mixed politically as it is psychologically. More blacks are now registered to vote than ever before, but black registration and participation still lag behind those of whites.[15] The number of black elected officials has increased fourfold since 1970 (when data were first collected), but blacks still hold barely more than 1 percent of elected offices.[16] Blacks are mayors of our second, third, fourth, and sixth largest cities, among others, but black city-dwellers at all income levels "are less likely to receive minimum service levels [and] . . . are more likely to be dissatisfied with these services" than urban whites with similar incomes.[17] More people (77 percent) would vote for a black presidential candidate than for a female one (68 percent); nevertheless one-fourth of the population find the idea of a black president—even a male one—untenable.[18] Black political participation is unquestionably greater than it has been since the 1860s; equally unquestionable is the gap between black and white political power.

Blacks' economic situation is even harder to characterize briefly. The progress of some is astonishing: young blacks who complete college, stay married to another earner, move north or west, and hold a white-collar job now earn *more* than their white counterparts.[19] Since 1955, the median earnings of black female full-time workers has increased from 57 percent to 99 percent of the earnings of white female full-time workers.[20] For others, progress is a bitter myth: close to half of black children live in poverty, and one-fifth live below 50 percent of the poverty level (compared to 17 percent and 5 percent of white children, respectively).[21] Twice as many blacks as whites are unemployed, a datum that has not changed since 1950. However, black male participation in the labor market has declined drastically since 1960, so actual racial disparities in unemployment are much greater than the official figures indicate. Black youth unemployment is ludicrously high—48 percent in 1982, compared to 20 percent among white teens.[22]

Controversies rage around whether and why black incomes are lower than white incomes. On the face of it, the answer to "whether" appears to be "yes": median black family income in 1982 was 55 percent of median white family income, down from 59 percent in 1967 (when the Census Bureau first collected data separately for blacks).[23] This global figure, however, obscures variations among categories of people that affect their income but have nothing to do with race. For example, young people earn less than old people; if more blacks than whites are young, then apparently malignant income disparities between races are actually benign income disparities between age groups. Thus we must divide income data into finer categories and control for racially irrelevant variables in order to decide whether racial discrimination exists and how extensive it is. Such disaggregation, to sum up an enormous and enormously complex literature, shows two things. First, slightly more than half of the apparent racial disparity in incomes stems from differences in age, sex, or experience (which have no connotations of racism) or from differences in education, seniority, labor market participation, family structure, or background (which may or may not have connotations of racism, depending on how one explains the differences). Second, the rest of the apparent racial disparity in incomes—10 to 20 percent difference between blacks and whites—can be explained by nothing except difference in race—which leaves us with a finding of continuing, extensive employment and wage discrimination. Thus, to cite only one datum, even if the races were identical in their education, work experience, hours worked per year, occupation, and region of residence, black men would still have earned 88 percent of white men's earnings, and black women only 64 percent of white men's earnings in 1979.[24]

Whether racial discrimination in employment and earnings is lessening is a question as controversial as and even more complex than whether and how much it exists at one point in time. The literature permits only one definitive conclusion right now. Labor market discrimination has declined since 1950 but has not disappeared, and it has probably worsened in the past ten years. Again, I will cite only one set of representative data: the annual earnings of employed black men of all ages with less than a high school education increased from 67 percent of the earnings of similar white men in 1967 to 74 percent in 1978. For high school graduates, the black-white earnings ratio increased from 69 percent in 1967 to 77 percent in 1978. These figures suggest a decline in wage discrimination among workers with similar educations. However, the findings are reversed for young men (those out of school one to five years). Among them, black high school dropouts with jobs earned 79 percent of the wages of similarly situated whites in 1967, but only 69 percent in 1978. For employed high school graduates, the decline was from 81 percent to 76 percent. These figures suggest that black youth, who presumably would benefit most if racial discrimination in employment were declining, are actually experiencing *greater* problems in the labor market.[25]

The economics of race merit another book, but a few points are as clear as they are important. A small minority of blacks are doing extremely well; half of all black children and one-third of all black persons are poor. Blacks experience high unemployment, have worse jobs, and are paid less well in those jobs than whites. Progress is indisputable; so is the need for more.

In education, the story is similar: blacks are better off than they were three decades ago but a long way from parity with whites. Minority adults in 1950 averaged less than seven years of school (compared to almost ten years for whites); by 1980, both races averaged more than twelve years of education.[26] Illiteracy among blacks has declined from over one-tenth in 1947 to less than 2 percent today (the figure for whites in 1947), and black and white youth are equally (and almost totally) literate. Eight percent of blacks, compared to 18 percent of all persons (mainly whites), have completed college, a fourfold increase in black graduation since 1950.[27] Most important, black student achievement scores are improving relative to white scores—the average gap of 18 points in the early 1970s declined to 12 points by 1980.[28] Furthermore, the younger the students, the less the gap,* and the longer they have attended desegregated schools, the greater the rise in blacks' test scores.[29]

But the evidence is, once again, shot through with disheartening numbers. Over nine-tenths of white teenagers are functionally literate, compared to only 58 percent of blacks.[30] Even with their improving scores, blacks still average 9 to 22 percent fewer correct answers on tests of specific knowledge than whites, depending on age and subject tested.[31]† Virtually all whites (97 percent) eventually

*Optimists will view this datum as part of a time series, suggesting that schools now provide much more equality in educational outcomes than they used to, and that today's young black achievers will be tomorrow's adult black achievers. To pessimists, however, it suggests that schools provide less equality of educational outcomes for older than for younger students, and that today's young black achievers may fall behind whites as they become tomorrow's black adults.

†Home and neighborhood surely affect students' performance, but they are not the full explanation for blacks' lower achievement, since we know that test scores do not

passed minimum competency tests in one state; only three-quarters of blacks did so. After a semester of remedial teaching, "the racial gap in test scores actually increased."[32] Blacks continue disproportionately to attend two-year colleges and less prestigious four-year colleges.[33]

Most arresting, perhaps, are differences between the races' perceptions of the racial terrain I have just described. Blacks and whites appear to inhabit different countries when they consider the extent and effect of racism. Blacks perceive more racism and less racial progress and have less hope for the future than whites do. In 1946, two-thirds of the white population but only one-fourth of blacks thought "Negroes are treated fairly."[34] The number of blacks who saw "real change . . . in the position of blacks" declined from 60 percent in 1964 to 32 percent in 1976, exactly mirroring the *increase* in white perceptions of change (from 39 to 63 percent).[35] Only 8 percent of black leaders, but fully 41 percent of white leaders, think racism is declining,[36] and the number of blacks who think it will decline in the future dropped from half to one-third between 1968 and 1978.[37] To whites, race relations are fairly good and getting better; to blacks, race relations are fairly bad and getting worse.

Racial differences in assessing the effects of racism are just as striking as differences in assessing its extent. Whites are twice as likely to attribute blacks' disadvantaged state to personal faults as to discrimination; blacks are two and one-half times as likely to argue the reverse.[38] Up to 75 percent of blacks have felt discriminated against in at least one important aspect of their life; only one-fourth of whites see discrimination against blacks in those arenas. Over 40 percent of blacks see unemployment as blacks' biggest problem, and over half attribute job difficulties to discrimination. But only 11

---

perfectly reflect students' socioeconomic status. On average, whites do slightly better on assessment tests than one would predict from their socioeconomic status, and blacks do somewhat worse. See National Center for Education Statistics, *The Condition of Education, 1981*, p. 110.

The debate over whether blacks' lower scores are caused by cultural biases in the tests, lower IQ, poorer teaching, low expectations, greater problems at home, or something else, is voluminous, and one I cannot engage in here. Whatever else is occurring simultaneously, discriminatory treatment certainly does not help the situation.

percent of whites worry about black unemployment; over 90 percent think "blacks are getting a better break in getting jobs than they did ten years ago," and fewer than one-fifth perceive employment discrimination. Whites' concern about job discrimination declined from 1968 to 1978, while blacks' concern increased.* Even the generally upbeat report of these Harris poll data concedes that "whites have obviously missed the depths of both the urgency and despair that blacks feel about their troubles in getting work. . . . The white attitude about black joblessness is one of vague concern, tempered with some heavy doses of indifference."[39]

What, then, can we conclude? It is true but not very interesting to say that substantial progress has occurred on some fronts but not on others. There are, I think, more incisive patterns in the data that help us to set school desegregation in a general framework of American race relations.

First, the greatest racial equalization occurred soon after the only period during these three decades that a concerted national effort was made to eradicate racism and its consequences. The civil rights movement, culminating in the Civil Rights Act and the Voting Rights Act increased the number of black voters and elected black officials, access to universities and jobs, white perceptions of the illegitimacy of racism, and black perceptions of the possibility of success in a white world. Obviously many other things occurred simultaneously, but the close temporal connection between the only period of strong civil rights activity and the only period of strong improvements in the status of blacks permits me to assert that determined policy interventions can be efficacious.

A second pattern in the evidence is that some of these improvements have been slight or even partly reversed—suggesting the need for continued policy intervention. The number of black political leaders, for example, rose steadily before 1976, but the rate of increase slowed to a trickle between then and 1983. The black poverty level declined up to 1968 but has been rising since then.

*In 1978, one-fifth of a national sample believed unemployment to be higher for whites than for blacks—despite the fact that the black unemployment rate has been twice that of whites since the federal government started keeping records in the late 1940s. See John Herbers, "Changes in Society Holding Black Youth in Jobless Web," *New York Times*, March 11, 1979, p. 44.

Median family income ratios are poor explanatory but excellent illustrative data, and they suggest that blacks' incomes are declining relative to whites': the black-white median family income ratio rose from .59 in 1967 to .61 in 1970 and fell to .55 in 1982. White endorsement of desegregation rose steadily from 1964 to 1972 but has been declining since then; black endorsement of segregation declined

Fig. 1. Family Income in 1982, by Race

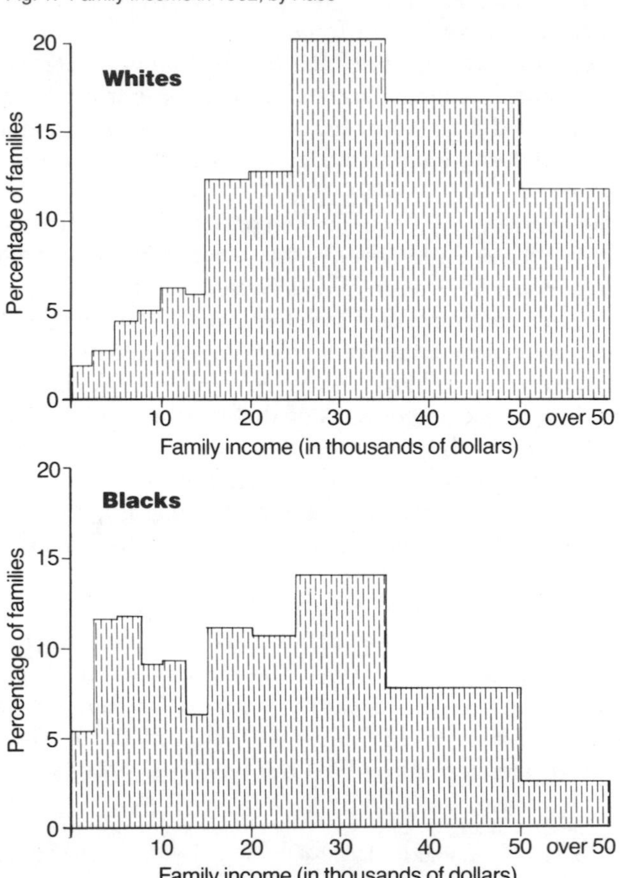

Source: U.S. Bureau of the Census, Current Population Reports, P-60, no. 140, *Money Income and Poverty Status of Families and Persons in the United States: 1982* (Washington, D.C.: U.S. Government Printing Office, 1983), p. 10.

from 1964 to 1972 but has *risen* since then.[40] Policies to eradicate racism and its effects are just as necessary in the 1980s as they were in the 1960s, if we are not to return to pre-*Brown* inequities.

A third pattern is the wide gap between blacks who have benefited from the recent improvements and those who have been left out—suggesting urgency in the need for further policy interventions. Averages obscure enormous variations, masking such troubling patterns as the tendency of blacks to split into a bipolar distribution rather than to array themselves along the bell-shaped curve that we normally assume to lie around an average. Consider figure 1.

The first graph shows that in 1982, as whites' incomes rose to $35,000, the number of families with that income also rose. As incomes rose beyond that point, the number of well-off families declined—a bell-shaped curve skewed to the right. But for blacks, the largest clusters of families are near the bottom (between $2,500 and $7,500) and top ($25,000 to $35,000) of the range of black incomes. The middle ranges have fewer occupants than any except the extremes of wealth and poverty—a bipolar distribution. Another way to describe this phenonemon is to point out that the poorest 20 percent of black families have a smaller share of total black income than the poorest 20 percent of white families have of total white income, and that the wealthiest fifth of black families have a larger share of black income than the wealthiest fifth of white families have of white income. That is, poor blacks are poorer and rich blacks are richer than the comparable sets of whites.[41]

This bifurcation in black family incomes did not exist in 1970 (the first year for which we have adequate data). White families exhibit the same bell-shaped curve along the income dimension that we see in figure 1. Black families show the beginnings of a bipolar distribution, but there is no dip in the middle income range. In short, as our society moves toward increasing interracial equality, we have at least a hint that we are maintaining if not increasing intraracial inequality.*

*As the evidence and data manipulations become more sophisticated, it becomes less and less clear whether polarization within the black community is increasing. In three of the strongest empirical investigations of this question, Frank Levy ("Have Black Men Gained in Employment?" Paper presented at the Brookings Panel on Economic Activity, Washington, D.C., October 1980) concludes that it is; Sar Levitan et al. (*Still a Dream* [Cambridge: Harvard University Press, 1975]) conclude that it is

One side of this phenomenon is illustrated by the fact that young, professional, urban black couples earn more than their white counterparts. The 1980 riots of Liberty City, Miami, are a frightening reminder of the other side. For the first time in the long history of American race riots, poor blacks exploded with focused hatred of whites. As one observer put it, "We're not dealing with the '60s. These rioters were different. [In the past] white people got hurt because they got in the way or because they provoked a confrontation. In this riot, the purpose was to kill white people. That's a whole new ballgame to deal with." Black youths fought over an ax with which to beat a white passerby; one white victim had his ears and tongue cut off; rioters prevented an ambulance from reaching three dying white teenagers. We suddenly saw the power of young blacks with no stake in society, no hope of one, and nothing to lose; "The white man ain't been doing us no good. So we didn't do him no good. The white man got the jobs and we don't got no jobs. The white man got everything and we got nothing. It ain't right."[42] The 1960s gave some blacks a foothold on, even a push up, the ladder of mobility—but it left too many dangling below the bottom step. The disparity between young black professionals and young black gangs is wide, deep, and a vital danger to a would-be liberal society.

SCHOOL DESEGREGATION

Policy interventions to abolish racism and its impacts, then, are sometimes effective; their continuation is clearly, even urgently, needed. School desegregation has been the centerpiece of such interventions ostensibly since 1954 and actually since 1968. In order to see what we should do next, we need to know what we have already done. How much desegregation has there been, where, and with what results?

The history of school desegregation resembles the history of the

---

not; and Reynolds Farley and Suzanne Bianchi ("Social and Economic Polarization: Is It Occurring among Blacks?" [Paper presented at the annual meeting of the American Sociological Association, San Francisco, September 1982]) find mixed results. Therefore I do not insist that polarization between wealthy and poor blacks is increasing, only that the successful black professional and the unemployed ghetto-dweller live in something close to entirely different worlds, and they are certainly not moving closer together.

more general civil rights movement, except that each step came several years later. Both movements had a slow but steady buildup, won a few dramatic and galvanizing legal victories, saw astonishing activity for about five years, then fell into a slow, steady decline punctuated by continued rearguard action and a few notable successes. *Brown* was seen as a Southern issue—it was aimed only at legislatively mandated dual school systems—for the first decade of its life. Some Border states and the rare Southern district responded immediately and effectively, if rather brutally, usually by closing black schools and incorporating black students into white schools. Most states and districts resisted in a variety of imaginative ways, ranging from "bribing" blacks into accepting segregation by channeling resources into their schools, to offering carefully constrained freedom-of-choice plans, to exhibiting mean-spirited defiance. In general, and with a few notable exceptions such as federal troops in Little Rock and *Goss v. Board of Education* (which struck down a "minority to majority transfer" plan),[43] the federal government did little to counter the resisters. The results were predictable; in 1964, barely 2 percent of Southern blacks attended desegregated schools.

By 1964, however, leaves began to stir. Presidents Kennedy and Johnson persuaded Congress to pass the Civil Rights Act, which forbade the use of federal funds in segregated institutions. The 1965 Elementary and Secondary Education Act put teeth into that provision by suddenly making considerable federal aid available but only to compliant school districts. At the same time, the judiciary and regulatory agencies began to move. The Supreme Court declared in *Griffin v. County School Board of Prince Edward County* (1964) that "the time for mere 'deliberate speed' has run out." Because the Civil Rights Act had authorized the Justice Department to sue segregated school districts or to join private suits, litigation expanded in amount and velocity. The Department of Health, Education and Welfare (HEW) began writing regulations and negotiating desegregation plans with hundreds of noncompliant Southern districts. The Supreme Court ruled in 1968 in *Green v. Board of Education of New Kent County* that passive "freedom of choice" plans no longer sufficed. Schools had "the affirmative duty to take whatever steps might be necessary to convert to a unitary system in which racial discrimination would be eliminated root and branch." If necessary, a unanimous Court declared several years later in *Swann v. Charlotte-Mecklenburg Board of Education* (1971), districts should bus children across town to achieve "the greatest possible degree of actual desegregation." Said the Court:

> All things being equal, . . . it might well be desirable to assign pupils to schools nearest their homes. But all things are not equal in a system that has been deliberately constructed and maintained to enforce racial segregation. The remedy for such segregation may be administratively awkward, inconvenient, and even bizarre in some situations and may impose burdens on some; but all awkwardness and inconvenience cannot be avoided in the interim period when remedial adjustments are being made to eliminate the dual school systems. . . . Desegregation plans cannot be limited to the walk-in school.[44]

The results of all of this activity were considerable but contradictory. Some gratified proponents of desegregation. By the early 1970s, OCR had investigated, negotiated with, and arm-twisted over 3000 districts in the South. Courts had handed down desegregation orders in over 150 districts. As a consequence, racial isolation in the South dropped considerably. In 1972, Congress passed the Emergency School Aid Act (ESAA), which provided funds ($300.5 million in 1978, its high-water mark) for schools implementing desegregation plans. Schools began to fund programs, buy materials, and employ staff to ease the transition to desegregated classes in (it was hoped) improved educational settings. Legislators, litigators, and regulators turned their attention to the North; the Supreme Court ruled in *Keyes v. School District No. 1 of Denver, Colorado* (1973) that Northern districts, even without a history of legislated dual school systems, could be found to have intentionally segregated their students and thus could be subject to the same mandates as the South.[45] The problem of racial isolation seemed on the way to being solved.

But actions generate reactions. Even as OCR was beginning its most active period, newly elected president Nixon sought (successfully) to restrain its scope and energy. Even as Congress was passing new civil rights legislation in the late 1960s and 1970s, it was proposing (and sometimes enacting) inhibitions on mandatory student busing. Even as Justice Department lawyers were becoming experienced in litigating desegregation cases, they were increasingly directed to argue for delay and caution. Most important, hard on the heels of *Keyes,* which opened the door to mandatory desegregation in Northern districts, came *Milliken v. Bradley* (1974), which almost closed the door on effective desegregation for most Northern blacks.[46] A split Supreme Court ruled in *Milliken* that courts could not order busing across school district boundaries unless all the affected districts were found guilty of de jure segregation. Such a finding is possible but extremely difficult legally and politically, and *Milliken* demoralized civil rights litigants.

This retreat from school desegregation had several causes. Northern liberals became wary when desegregation moved out of the distant South and onto their own suburban doorsteps. Simultaneously, civil rights activists increasingly claimed that desegregation required not only the abolition of legal separation but also positive action to remedy the effects of past segregation. Taken together, the move north (to large cities with segregated neighborhoods) and the drive for positive action added up to "forced busing" and the attendant specter of innocent white first-graders being subjected to the psychological, physical, and educational dangers of ghetto schools. Congress responded to these new fears, and even liberal Northern legislators began to talk of alternatives to mandatory transportation.[47] Ironically, Governor George Wallace reinforced the liberal retreat by encouraging white workers to forge their dislike of hippies and student radicals, their economic and social insecurities, and their racial hostility into a powerful conservative populist movement. In retrospect, Wallace seems more a symbol than a strong political force, but in the 1960s and 1970s he inspired or scared a lot of citizens and their representatives. More conservative presidents, more conservative justices and administrators, skittish constituents, populist challengers, and a responsive Congress combined with perenially resistant local elites and school officials to slow the pace of desegregation to a crawl by the end of the 1970s.

But the problem of racial isolation has only diminished; it has not gone away. In 1968, 77 percent of all black students were in schools with more than half non-Anglo students; in 1980, 63 percent were. More encouraging is the decline in the number of blacks in schools with virtually no Anglo students. Complete racial isolation has declined from two-thirds in 1968 to one-third in 1980. Table 1 shows

Table 1. Racial Composition of Schools, by Percent Minority Enrollment and Region, 1968–1980

Percentage of Black Students in Schools with More Than Half Minority Students	1968	1972	1976	1980	Change, 1968 to 1980
U.S. Average	76.6	63.6	62.4	62.9	−13.7
South	80.9	55.3	54.9	57.1	−23.8
Border States	71.6	67.2	60.1	59.2	−12.4
Northeast	66.8	69.9	72.5	79.9	+13.1
Midwest	77.3	75.3	70.3	69.5	−7.8
West	72.2	68.1	67.4	66.8	−5.4
Percentage of Black Students in Schools with 90–100 Percent Minority Students					
U.S. Average	64.3	38.7	35.9	33.2	−31.1
South	77.8	24.7	22.4	23.0	−54.8
Border States	60.2	54.7	42.5	37.0	−23.2
Northeast	42.7	46.9	51.4	48.7	+6.0
Midwest	58.0	57.4	51.1	43.6	−14.4
West	50.8	42.7	36.3	33.7	−17.1

SOURCE: Gary Orfield, *Public School Desegregation in the United States, 1968–1980* (Washington, D.C.: Joint Center for Political Studies, 1983), p. 4. "Minority" includes black, Hispanic, Asian, and all other non-Caucasian students.

regional and temporal variations underlying this overall change. Segregation, especially complete racial isolation, has fallen dramatically in the South and Border states, and considerably in the Midwest and West. But it has *increased* in the Northeast, where black student enrollment is rising as a proportion of white enrollment.[48] The races are now more separated in the Northeast than anywhere else, and least separated in the South. Furthermore, the disparity between North and South is greater for the extremely isolated than the partially isolated students.

Table 1 also gives evidence on the timing, pace, and trajectory of desegregation. Change in the South was concentrated between 1968 and 1972; some resegregation has occurred since OCR and court pressure eased. The Border states, Midwest, and West also accomplished most of their change before 1976, often in a single four-year period. Segregation has increased in the Northeast at a fairly steady rate over the same twelve years; the pace of partial separation is accelerating. Overall, segregation slightly increased between 1976 and 1980.

But table 1 does not show the full extent of school segregation. Classrooms are more segregated than schools—and students, of course, spend their days in rooms, not buildings or regions. On average, across the nation 5 percent more classrooms than schools have more than half non-Anglo students; 3 percent more classrooms than schools have over 90 percent non-Anglo students. Here the South has a slightly worse record than the rest of the country, and the Northeast is as good or better.[49]

This hint of a disparity between school desegregation levels and classroom segregation levels suggests the new problem of "second-generation discrimination." The term refers to the fact or suspicion of inequitable disciplinary practices and of "tracking" blacks into low-skill and whites into high-skill classes. It may be, of course, that "black students are disproportionately disciplined because they are disproportionately disruptive"[50] and that they are in low expectation classes because they have less capability or training. But such treatment may instead reflect racism. According to the former ESAA regulations, more than 20 percent overrepresentation of blacks in classes for the educable mentally retarded (EMR) or in suspensions and expulsions creates a presumption of discrimination. Using the 20 percent standard, in 1973 at least 92 percent of Southern districts discriminated in EMR placement, and over three-fourths had more than 100 percent overrepresentation of blacks in EMR classes.[51] And this skewness grew during the period for which we have data; blacks were 330 percent overrepresented in EMR classes in 1968, but 540 percent overrepresented in 1974.[52] Even when economic status and academic achievement are controlled for, blacks (and Hispanics) are disproportionately enrolled in compensatory education classes.[52] They are underenrolled in college preparatory programs and programs for the gifted and talented.[54]

Fewer Southern districts (those for which we have the best data) are presumptively discriminatory in student punishment. In 1973 over two-thirds exceeded the 20 percent standard, and from 35 to 85 percent (depending on the state) punished blacks more than twice as often as whites.[55] In the nation as a whole, blacks in elementary school are three times as likely to be suspended as their white peers, and secondary school blacks are twice as likely to be suspended. On average, blacks are suspended at a younger age, for a longer period, and more times than whites.[56]

So far, we have been looking at data aggregated across states, regions, or the whole nation and at a single figure that averages differences. But, as we saw in the discussion of economic status, aggregate data and averages obscure wide variations. Some school districts have dramatically reduced racial isolation: St. Petersburg (Florida), Winston-Salem (North Carolina), and Oklahoma City have increased the number of white students in the typical black's school by over 40 percent since 1968.[57] In five of the twenty largest districts, fewer than one-fourth of black students are in black-dominated schools.[58]

Other school districts are becoming more segregated: in Sacramento (California), Paterson (New Jersey), and New Haven (Connecticut), the number of whites in a typical black's school has declined by 14 percent or more.[59] In ten of the twenty largest school districts more than 70 percent of the black students are in predominantly black schools.[60] Three of the four largest—New York, Chicago, and Philadelphia—have never been subjects of a mandatory student desegregation plan (and the fourth, Los Angeles, had such a plan for only one semester and no longer does).

Segregation within school buildings varies as widely as segregation in school assignments: Broward County (Fort Lauderdale, Florida), Clark County (Las Vegas, Nevada), and Charlotte-Mecklenburg (North Carolina) have at least 220 percent more blacks in EMR classes than their numbers in the school system would indicate; New York, Cleveland, and St. Louis have only (!) 55 percent or less disproportionality.[61]

White enrollment losses—the dread disease "white flight"—varies as much as, but not in conjunction with, desegregation. In some desegregated districts, such as Dallas, Prince Georges County (Maryland), and Boston, the white proportion of enrollment has declined by 30 percent or more since 1968; in others, such as six of the eleven largest Florida districts, white enrollment has stayed the same or increased. Just to confuse matters, some of the greatest losses of whites have occurred in cities with no mandatory desegregation to flee from—such as New York, Chicago, and Houston.[62]

Quality of desegregation varies as much as quantity. Greenville (South Carolina), Charlotte-Mecklenburg, and Louisville (Kentucky) all report improved student scores on achievement tests since desegregation; test scores in Detroit (and by some accounts, Charlotte and Wilmington) have declined.[63] Some communities welcome, or at least accept gracefully, their desegregation plan. The school board of Seattle, Washington, imposed a mandatory plan in 1977; now, when asked by a journalist why students "take a bus all the way across town" to school, a nine-year-old can think of no better reason than "It's too far to walk."[64] Charlotte-Mecklenburg reluctantly desegregated under court order in 1970; now a white high school junior does not think that "segregated schools would be very interesting. Here you learn to work with different kinds of people."[65] But others continue to do battle: South Boston High School is still incendiary, and a judge in Cleveland has found it necessary to jail school board members for contempt of court.

Can I draw any conclusions at this point? A few. The South and Border states have progressed; the Northeast has regressed. The school districts yet to be desegregated are huge, overwhelmingly black and Hispanic, and increasingly racially unbalanced. Ending racial isolation at the level of schools does not imply desegregated classrooms or equitable treatment. In some districts, desegregation improves achievement and race relations; in others, it does not. The pace of desegregation has slowed almost to a standstill, and both whites and blacks increasingly question its value.

In 1984, then, we have the largest, most urban, and most heavily non-Anglo schools left to desegregate. We also must ask whether the trauma that so many people—white and black—have felt is worth it. We face the further question whether districts can move beyond "bean counting" to address the quality of their students' education and interaction. Most important, we need to examine why the pace of change has slowed. Can racism and its effects be eliminated through normal processes of political choice and policy implementation? If so, the pace may readily speed up again when the nation's temper and energy level change. Or must we discard some of our most cherished procedures to move away from our current stasis? If so, we face a new American dilemma, whose resolution is yet unknown.

THREE

Incrementalism and Popular Control

As we have seen, anomaly theorists, as exemplified by Myrdal's *American Dilemma,* claim that normal policy-making processes will suffice to eradicate racism once Americans choose to do so. Since policies in the United States are typically changed through small steps—incrementalism is engaged in "day by day in ordinary political circumstances by congressmen, executives, administrators, and party leaders"[1]—we need to understand its meaning and ramifications in order to test the anomaly thesis. It is also claimed that our preferred means for determining policy—popular choice within constitutional constraints—will lead the government to enact policies eradicating racism and its effects. That is, not only *can* we desegregate our schools through normal processes, but also we will *choose* to do so once our wisest leaders start us down the right path. I need, therefore, to explicate the meaning and ramifications of popular control to see if this feature of Myrdal's construction also holds up. Finally, I need to specify what "eradicating racism and its effects" means in the context of school desegregation. This chapter performs these three tasks.

INCREMENTALISM

Many policy analysts assert that, although any new policy may fail and displeases some people, incremental moves avoid disaster and gross offense. Taking small steps slowly also permits experimentation, response, and adjustment—all without policy-makers having to agree on exactly where they want to go or how, ultimately, to get there. More formally, incrementalism as I define it has six elements. It is "decision-making through *small or incremental moves on particular problems* rather than through a comprehensive reform program. It is also *endless*; it takes the form of an indefinite sequence of policy moves. Moreover, it is *exploratory* in that the goals of policy-making continue to change as new experience with policy throws new light on what is possible and desirable. . . . It . . . *mov[es] away from known social ills* rather than . . . moving toward a known and relatively stable goal" (p. 71; emphasis added). It has a temporal dimension: *slow moves and long periods of time* between moves are more incremental than rapid change and short periods between changes. Finally, it has a spatial dimension: a policy change that affects only *a small area or a few people* is more incremental than one that affects a large area or many people.[2]

Proponents of incremental change distinguish it from three other kinds of policy-making: "utopian reconstruction," administrative and technical decisions, and "revolutions and grand opportunities." Each entails larger changes and/or greater knowledge than incremental policy moves do. In fact, proponents claim, one of incrementalism's many virtues is that its three alternatives are almost always impossible, irrelevant, or serendipitous. "The information and comprehension requirements of synoptic problem-solving [i.e., a comprehensive analysis of all alternatives for achieving a given goal] simply cannot be met for large-scale social change" (p. 79); thus utopian reconstruction is impossible. For a few technical or administrative problems, synoptic decision-making is possible, but these situations exclude most policy dilemmas and certainly one as important and politicized as school desegregation. Extraordinary, once-only crises or grand opportunities call for heroic leaders and idiosyncratic methods for making decisions. We simply do not know enough to infer anything useful for ordinary decisions from such serendipitous events. If nothing else works, then incremental methods are by default the best.

Incrementalists make positive as well as negative claims for their namesake. Even in the face of ignorance, conflicts among actors over goals, and ambivalence within actors about goal priorities, incremental policy moves at least permit movement by "draw[ing] policies forward in the light of what recent policy steps have shown to be probably realizable" (p. 71). Furthermore, incremental politics can adjust to unforeseen consequences and new circumstances, respond to new political pressures, and head off new political threats. Above all, moving incrementally provides the minimal but absolutely essential ability to avoid disaster, to "leave institutional insurance in being."[3]

Most significant for our purpose is the claim that incrementalism is intrinsic to liberal democracy, even that "nonincremental alternatives usually do not lie within the range of choice possible in the . . . body politic" (p. 73). Democratic polities "can avoid dissolution or intolerable dislocation only by . . . [recognizing] that certain kinds of change are admissible only if they occur slowly. Political democracy is often greatly endangered by nonincremental change" (p. 73). Such strong language results from proponents' view that liberal democracy will survive only if all citizens agree on fundamental rights and rules, "avoid . . . social cleavage along ideological lines" (p. 74), and permit all interests to be expressed and to receive at least some gratification. Revolutionary change or futile efforts to reconstruct society synoptically violate these precepts; only incremental politics "reduces the stakes in each political controversy, [enough to] . . . encourag[e] losers to bear their losses without disrupting the political system . . . [and] maintain the vague general consensus on basic values . . . that many people believe is necessary for widespread voluntary acceptance of democratic government."[4]

Of the many issues that this concept raises, I will deal with only two especially important ones. The first is speed, or the lack thereof. Critics argue that incrementalism is inherently conservative in that it endorses slow over rapid change and uses the status quo as a touchstone for evaluating new proposals. Its progenitors Braybrooke and Lindblom, however, disagree. They assert correctly that an incremental policy-maker who relies on existing knowledge and settles for a short-term consensus will move more quickly than one who waits for a complete analysis of alternatives and complete agreement among political actors. They also claim that "a succession of small moves, if they follow quickly one upon the other, may lead to rapid overall change."[5] The tortoise, after all, beat the hare.

If the alternative to incremental change is no change, then incremental politics is not conservative. But that is a cheap victory, because these are not always the only alternatives. Authorities can, after all, impose substantial change over opposition and despite the absence of complete knowledge of all alternatives. Incrementalism does seem to me inherently conservative in the sense that its spirit militates against "rocking the boat," against pushing the actors involved farther or faster than they want to go. Its whole point is not to make changes that are irreversible, that disrupt too many things at once, that require a leap of faith. In addition, by starting from the status quo as at least a minimally acceptable alternative, it puts all the burden of proof on new ideas and thus uses a double standard for change versus stasis. It may conceivably lead to transformations, but only in spite of itself.

A thornier problem in the concept is the notion of size—how large can a change be and still be incremental? Who decides? On what criteria? Charles Lindblom argues that "all U.S. forms of desegregation have been what I'd call incremental."[6] David Braybrooke defines any move that "leaves institutional insurance in being"—that leaves the basic structures of society intact—as incremental. Perhaps so, but calling any move short of revolution an incremental change does not provide much analytic leverage. A concept that explains everything explains nothing because it cannot distinguish one thing from another. A concept that distinguishes some relatively common forms of change from others, and that addresses the implications of those distinctions, is more helpful. The question then becomes, What divides incremental from nonincremental change within a society engaged in nonrevolutionary activities?

Ultimately, one draws an arbitrary line between a move that is incremental and a slightly larger (or more encompassing, or more system-threatening, or less reversible) move that is not. Braybrooke and Lindblom suggest one way to draw that line: rely on what actors in the policy process think they are doing and what those acted upon think has happened to them (pp. 62–64). In the case of desegregation, most changes are designed to be marginal, but a few have sought to restructure relations between blacks and whites at least within the affected school district. And most citizens, if presented with a few carefully chosen alternatives, would concur that a given desegregation plan either is or is not incremental change.

But such a reliance on "participant judgments" is too often insufficient. What if "to blacks, an integration plan . . . seem[s] token and incremental, while to whites, it . . . seem[s] massive and disruptive?"[7] Or what if a judge sees his order as falling squarely within constitutional precedent, but a defendant school board sees it as a blatant example of judicial arrogance? If participants cannot agree on what is small, the analyst must turn elsewhere for a judgment.

Unfortunately, we have no safe haven; I can offer no absolute, abstract definition of a nonincremental change short of total revolution, and I have already argued that that is not a very useful position to take. The best we can do is to follow two criteria for judgment. The first is to weigh the many dimensions of incrementalism against one another. A change that involves everyone, takes place all at once, or cannot be reversed is in some sense comprehensive even if the change itself is fairly small. Alternatively, a "major" change—one that seeks an ideal rather than moving away from a known ill, that addresses many problems in an integrated fashion, that pursues a set goal regardless of the consequences of previous acts—is in some sense nonincremental even if it proceeds slowly in a small compass.

The second analytic criterion for judging size is even more vague—to compare a given change to politically feasible alternatives. One alternative is always no change, but that comparison leaves us once again unable to distinguish among all other possibilities. More useful is to consider the array of "plausible" policy proposals made by "responsible" actors, always recognizing the fuzziness of those terms. Given virtually any pair of options, actors and observers will agree that one choice is more comprehensive than the other. We can proceed with a series of such comparisons until we can at least array the various proposals along a continuum from less to more comprehensive. A given choice will be incremental compared to all the choices on one side of the continuum, and nonincremental compared to the choices on the other side. Unsatisfactory though this method may be, it is perhaps as much as we can do to distinguish comprehensive from incremental change. Perhaps we can comfort ourselves by looking at incrementalism as Justice Potter Stewart looked at hard-core pornography:

> I shall not attempt further to define the kinds of material I understand to be embraced within that shorthand description; and perhaps I never could succeed in intelligibly doing so. But I know it when I see it.[8]

POPULAR CONTROL

The concept of "popular control" explains how opinions are transformed into policy choice in the liberal democratic polity of the United States. It "refers to those activities by private citizens that are more or less directly aimed at influencing the selection of government personnel and/or the actions they take."[9] It is the naive, bedrock meaning of democracy—rule "of the people, by the people, and for the people." The basic premise of popular control is that citizens ought directly or indirectly to shape their government's goals and priorities among goals, the amount and kind of resources used to pursue them, and the means of getting there. A government thus subordinate and responsive to the sovereign citizenry, so the theory of democracy goes, is best suited to maintain both the political equality and the individual liberty that constitute liberalism.

Within these glittering generalities lies the phrase "directly or indirectly," which suggests varying methods of popular control. The first is citizens' direct influence on policy choice and execution. Informed and concerned citizens help to plan, implement, evaluate, and change policies that affect their lives. The second method is citizens' indirect influence over policy choice through the election of public officials who choose policies, execute them, and are held accountable for the results. Many more citizens participate in elections than in policy-making, but such participation is less informed and less intense and offers less influence to any one person.[10]

Thus the concept of popular control implies three points. First, it may occur through either direct policy choice or indirect electoral contests. Second, the populace doing the controlling may range from a few committed and knowledgeable partisans to many less informed and less concerned voters. Third, it carries a lot of normative baggage: to most Americans, the more participation there is, the more democracy and the better the government.

Popular control, like incrementalism, comes more sharply into focus when contrasted with what it is not. It is not complete participatory democracy or loosely controlled anarchy. It is also not rule by a natural aristocracy, special interests, ciphers for class or sectoral interests, experts and bureaucrats, or judges. In short, popular control lies somewhere between elite rule ratified by a quiescent citizenry and direct decision-making by all citizens on all subjects.

Proponents of popular control, unlike incrementalists, do not claim that alternative means of policy choice are usually impossible, trivial, or serendipitous. On the contrary, they fear that some are altogether too prevalent, important, and entrenched. Fears vary with ideology and interest; the two most relevant to desegregation policy are that the federal government is so far away that it cannot possibly be responsive to citizens' wishes, and that policy choices are dominated by unaccountable bureaucrats and judges.

The problems with central decision-making are that it permits only a tiny fraction of citizens to participate and that it must ignore special circumstances and local idiosyncracies. There is less popular control in two ways, then, in central as compared with local decision-making: less of the populace is involved, and less control is exercised. The same complaints apply to decision-making by bureaucrats and judges, even if the decisions are locally specific. Very few citizens can participate, and those who do are necessarily atypical because they have special expertise, connections, or interests. In addition, bureaucrats and federal judges are not accountable to the citizenry, so even the indirect control exercised through elections is unavailable. Thus administrative and judicial decisions, like centralized ones, involve fewer citizens and permit less control than direct involvement or elections.

But why is popular control such a good thing, in the eyes of its proponents? There are, after all, advantages to letting those who see the big picture, or who need not bow to public pressure to keep their jobs, make hard choices for us. But the virtues of popular control are many and varied. It ensures that people in power know and respond to the interests and preferences of the rest of us. The politician who must face the voters in a few years and the bureaucrat who must answer to a citizens' watchdog group will think twice about (at least overt) dishonesty or favoritism and will be more inclined to take into account concerns that they might otherwise ignore. Popular control not only binds rulers to the ruled, but also works in reverse, binding the ruled to rulers. People more willingly obey laws promulgated by leaders they chose and more enthusiastically implement plans they have helped to formulate. In addition, loyalty to an official for whom one votes or commitment to a policy that one helped to design generalizes, so the argument goes, to loyalty to the electoral system, the policy-making system, and ultimately the regime itself.

Popular control presumably also generates better policy choices than bureaucratic, judicial, or other forms of elite rule. Incrementalists point out (in the first of many connections between the two concepts) that the more people involved in shaping or executing a policy, the less the likelihood of its doing egregious harm to any significant group. In addition, they say, the cumulative effect of having a lot of people with a little knowledge focus on one problem is that a lot of knowledge is brought to bear. Only residents, for example, know the idiosyncracies of their own community, so they are uniquely suited to shape its plans or judge its officials.

Finally come pure normative arguments for popular control, and here we return to the connection between democracy and liberalism. Participation in governance is an element of freedom and autonomy, as well as the best means of keeping government attentive to the pursuit of private interests. There is much more to say here, of course, but we can at least agree that if one believes in "rule by the people" one begins by endorsing popular control of government activities and actors.

Like incrementalism, the concept of popular control raises a host of problems, of which I will mention only the two most relevant here. One grows out of the idea of popularity: what happens if some of the populace want one set of things and others another set, or even diametrically opposite sets? This problem has been recognized at least since the days of James Madison and is typically considered to be solved by encouraging crosscutting cleavages. This bit of jargon refers, not to an elaborate sun-dress, but to the belief (and fervent hope) that American society is not divided into fixed groups, some of which always win on every issue and others of which always lose. Instead, we have multiple identities which differ from others' multiple identities, so that my opponent today is my ally tomorrow, and my minority status today becomes my majority status tomorrow. Thus Madison proposed a large over a small republic, and Tocqueville praised individualism, as ways of fostering the dissolution of a few large, fixed groups into many small, fluid ones.

The other solution to the danger of permanent minorities ties in closely with the justification for small, incremental changes. The polity must ensure that no one loses a policy dispute too badly, so that everyone can and will come back to fight again tomorrow (when they presumably will be part of a victorious group).

The need to maintain two delicate balances, between ever-shifting groups and between winners and losers in any one contest, is one reason why race is such an explosive phenomenon in a would-be democratic polity. If all issues are defined in racial terms (so that cleavages no longer crosscut), and if one race has many fewer members and is denigrated by the other (so that one group always loses in policy disputes), then some citizens become permanent big-time losers. At that point, the polity is in danger of self-destructing. Desegregation—or better, integration—becomes an urgent necessity so that the rigid group identification across all issues is relinquished and so that racism does not entice the victors to squash the vanquished.

The other relevant problem of popular control grows out of the idea of control: what happens if the populace seeks a policy outcome that violates the boundaries of liberalism? This too is a problem at least as old as the framers and is typically solved by the invocation of constitutional rights. We believe (and fervently hope) that the Constitution, properly interpreted by the Supreme Court, specified by Congress, and administered by the president, ensures that some decisions will never be taken: individuals have rights, and rights trump interests.[11] We differ, of course, over just what rights consist of, how they are to be ordered when they conflict, and when they can be overruled, but few Americans would argue that popular control ought to supersede individual rights. In that sense, democracy is subordinate to liberalism.

Here too, race is an explosive phenomenon in a would-be liberal society. Slavery violates rights so flagrantly that the two can coincide only by denying that slaves are human and therefore rights-bearers. Institutional racism violates rights less flagrantly, so sometimes the disjunction between belief and practice can be ignored. Individual racism violates rights flagrantly and is typically punished by the courts (at least recently) when it is expressed in a specific action. The tension between majority rule and minority rights is perennial in a liberal polity that seeks to be democratic (or a democratic polity that seeks to be liberal), but it is greatly exacerbated when racial differences turn into racial discrimination.

GOALS OF DESEGREGATION

My final conceptual task is to clarify the phrase "eradicating racism and its consequences." Goals for school desegregation abound, from the minimalist "End de jure segregation" to the maximalist "Equalize race, class, and power relations in the United States." But a reasonably ambitious middle ground is a list of ten goals used by Willis Hawley and his associates.[12] The first, without which the others are impossible, is:

- End racial isolation (more strongly, achieve racial balance) in school districts, schools, classrooms, and work groups

Several others are constitutive elements of any policy to eradicate racism and its effects:

- Enhance or maintain minority self-esteem and self-confidence

- Improve race relations among students, between educators and students, and among parents
- Enhance low-income or minority students' opportunities to improve their economic and social status

Still others are probably necessary to accomplish the goals just cited:

- Give all students equal access to appropriate educational resources, effective teachers and administrators, and fair procedures

- Improve academic achievement of unsuccessful (predominantly but not solely minority) students without lowering the achievement of successful students
- Promote and maintain community and parental support for civil rights, desegregation, and public education

Finally, they add three "negative goals," since simply maintaining some aspects of the status quo is desirable. Many people fear deterioration of a school system as a consequence of desegregation; in some ways, then, continuity indicates success. Thus the final goals of school desegregation are:

- Avoid white and upper-status minority flight to private schools or segregated public schools
- Minimize disorder in schools and the community
- Avoid new forms of discrimination

These ten goals comprise a laundry list, not a coherent theory, but they will serve as indicators of whether desegregation "works" or not.[13] They are both broader and narrower than other possible definitions of desegregation success. They are narrower in two ways. They focus on students and ignore faculty and staff desegregation, and they do not deal with bilingual education, the main issue dividing Hispanics and other minorities from blacks.* They are also broader in two ways. They assume that positive actions beyond the abolition of de jure segregation are constitutionally, morally, and politically necessary. They also address concerns of any educational system, even one in a uniracial society. It is both analytically and politically important to remember that any worthwhile discussion of school desegregation very quickly moves beyond the first goal, the only purely desegregative one and probably the most controversial.

We have at this point a description of the past, the present, and the ideal future and two prescriptions for getting from here to there. Let us examine them closely; if we cannot get there from here along the prescribed roads, then Myrdal's dilemma pales beside the new dilemma of the 1980s.

*Here as elsewhere, "minorities" is too sloppy a term because it glosses over differences between blacks and Hispanics and within each group. Although this book does not address the special concerns of Hispanics, I shall note them where they diverge from conventionally defined desegregation success. •

The term "racial balance" also merits a word of explanation. This phrase is considered by some to have negative connotations, like "forced busing" or "quotas." My usage implies no positive or negative implications; it is simply shorthand for "reducing racial isolation in schools or classrooms as much as possible, given the racial composition of the school district."

FOUR

Incremental Policies vs. School Desegregation

I believe his motives are always pure, and his measures often able; but they are endless, and never done with that pedetentous pace and pedetentous mind in which it behoves the wise and virtuous improver to walk. He alarms the wise Liberals; and it is impossible to sleep soundly while he has the command of the watch.

—Sydney Smith, c. 1837[1]

The preliminaries are complete; the argument begins. The first claim of the anomaly thesis is that racism can be weeded out of the American garden through conventional policy-making processes. It is not easy or painless so to remove it, but normal politics—defined here as incrementalism—is powerful enough to do so. Let us examine how well this argument holds up for the case of school desegregation.

TEMPORAL INCREMENTALISM

Time is one element of an incremental policy action; changes that require more time are more incremental than changes that arrive at the same destination in less time.

Change can be slow for two reasons. There may be a long lag between announcement and event, or the change may be phased in a little at a time, with lags between each phase. Many desegregation analysts call for both types of slowness. School desegregation is a drastic step; it requires time for everything from buying new school buses[2] to permitting parents to absorb new norms. In this view, the ambiguities of *Brown II* were necessary

> to outwit subtly the black belt and its allies. "All deliberate speed" in the hands of southern federal judges meant that tokenism, in one form or another, would provide the alternative to massive resistance for a few years to come. That, the [Supreme] Court sensed, was the safest way to breach the principle. Over time it turned the diehard into an empty and ludicrous posturer, not just in the eyes of his less crazed fellow Southerner but in the eyes of the nation on whom the Court would have to depend for southern compliance.[3]

Not all cases involve diehard crazies, but most continue to have vehement opponents of mandatory student transfers. Therefore organizational imperatives unite with political calculation in an argument for moving slowly, one step at a time.

However, research shows that such caution is unnecessary and possibly counterproductive. On the one hand, when forced, school districts can change with astounding speed and success. Kansas City, Missouri, schools began to prepare for desegregating fifty-four thousand students in eighty-eight schools only two months before school opened. The district closed four schools, changed grade levels in thirty, and reassigned several thousand students "remarkably well"—perhaps better than anywhere else in the nation, according to desegregation expert Gordon Foster.[4] The Milwaukee school system restructured its educational offerings and desegregated sixty-seven schools (one-third of its system, and 126 percent of its court-ordered requirement) in two summer months.[5] Once the Greenville, South Carolina, school district "had run out of courts," it yielded to a court order and transferred nearly twelve thousand students and five hundred thirty teachers in less than two weeks. To accomplish such "a revolutionary move," it "marshall[ed] its volunteer army. Businesses volunteered trucks, equipment, and personnel to assist in moving desks, chairs, books and other necessities. . . . The Junior League, church groups, and other organizations [over two thousand people in all] volunteered to man telephones and perform other chores."[6] Apparently, once desegregation appears inevitable, "actions which would have been rejected as too innovative or too radical become simply necessary solutions to a problem which must be solved."[7]

On the other hand, long lead times and plans that phase in desegregation over several years work poorly. Twenty-six Georgia school districts took drastic steps to desegregate in one or two years and virtually eliminated racial isolation; three took small steps over many years and ended up with less than one-third as much racial balance.[8] Slow change not only inhibits racial mixing; it also increases white flight[9] since "phased-in plans usually publicize the desegregation expansion planned for the next stages. Many parents thus have more time to locate alternative schooling, housing, or jobs outside of the desegregating school district."[10] Slow change also heightens "uncertainty, tension, and conflict," especially when it results from hesitance by school authorities.[11] Power abhors a vacuum; if officials do not lead, self-appointed leaders emerge. Some seek to facilitate desegregation but inevitably add to the confusion. Others seek to derail it, and delay permits white opposition to coalesce and organize. Resisters may, as in Los Angeles, channel their energies into protests. They may, as in Richmond, California, mobilize voters to oust liberal school boards.[12] And given enough time, uncertainty, and incendiary news reports, they may do both, as in Boston.[13]*

Another reason why delay inhibits success is that attitudes toward busing are partly contextual. That is, "interaction over this highly politicized issue induces some movement . . . toward the position shared by the bulk of the people in [a person's] social environment." The longer people remain among neighbors and local leaders denouncing busing, the more they will be swayed. Therefore, those who seek to "maximize compliance will do well to . . . inhibit the appearance of seemingly unified . . . opposition."[14] Furthermore, not only is resistance inherently problematic, but it also has a strong independent impact on white flight.[15] White flight, in turn, worsens racial isolation and reduces community morale and support for desegregation. Thus slow, incremental change sets up patterns of behavior that interact to defeat several desegregation goals at once.

Phasing in school desegregation one grade level at a time produces another problem. Constant change maximizes instability, making

*Similarly, in three cities where OCR would "accept almost any plan" to desegregate faculty that swiftly met its statistical goals, prompt mandatory transfer plans succeeded, while New York's nonmandatory phased-in plan largely failed. Rebell and Block, *Equality and Education*.

several more desegregation goals difficult to reach. Phased-in change requires that every year, schools reroute buses, parents with several children plan new schedules, principals reorganize teaching assignments, teachers redesign classes, and students cope with a new social situation. Such instability erodes morale, achievement, interracial familiarity, and efficiency.

Finally there is the moral argument against delay: "It should go without saying that the vitality of these constitutional principles cannot be allowed to yield simply because of disagreement with them," wrote Chief Justice Warren in *Brown II* (although, of course, this is precisely what *Brown II* did allow). If desegregation is morally and constitutionally just, why postpone it and deny still more children its benefits and their rights? Theoretically, the benefits of slow change could outweigh its moral costs, but for once evidence supports ethics; except in peculiar circumstances, a desegregation plan should neither be phased in nor have a long lead time.

Other temporal variables are the age of children and the number of school grades affected. The fewer the grades, the more incremental the change and—the reason this issue belongs in a discussion on time—the fewer the grades affected, the less likely are the oldest and youngest children to be involved. Many plans exempt primary schools from mandatory transfers. For example, citing the Supreme Court's finding in *Swann v. Charlotte-Mecklenburg* that "the limits on time of travel will vary with many factors, but probably with none more than the age of the students," the court in Dallas, Texas, left kindergarten through third grade out of its desegregation order. It ruled as "sound in terms of age, health, and safety of children in grades K–3" the school superintendent's contention that "the children had not matured sufficiently to cope with the problems of safety and fatigue associated with significant transportation."[16] Court orders in Nashville and Los Angeles also exempted kindergarten through third or fourth grade. Courts may also (as in Los Angeles and Dayton, Ohio) leave out high schools on the grounds that it is educationally and psychologically disruptive to insist upon change among students so near the end of their schooling.

However, lesser movement causes problems that greater change could avoid. If students are to be transferred for only a few years, it is feasible for them to skirt desegregation by attending private school during those years. In Louisville, for example, white enrollment appears to decline for the few years in which whites are reassigned and then to return almost to previous levels during the years that whites attend their "home" school.[17] But if the transfer of white students is mandated for many years, flight to private schools or out of the city requires a much larger investment of money and effort. If economists are correct, higher costs will lead fewer whites to avoid public schools. Furthermore, students who are transferred for only a few years have little incentive to develop loyalty to their new, temporary schools, and teachers similarly have slight reason to change their teaching methods and outlooks. If, however, a child's entire school career will be in a desegregated setting, everyone is much more likely to be motivated to make it work.

This argument can be carried a step further to address the more clearly temporal issue of how old children should be before being desegregated: "If there is one thing about desegregation that can be said with certainty, it is that the younger the student is when first desegregated, the better the outcome." This claim holds for several desegregation goals. Consider race relations: "the earlier a child is brought into contact with children of other races the better."[18] To cite only two instances, a cooperative work group "promotes greater interpersonal attraction in elementary schools . . . than it does in secondary schools."[19] Newly desegregated Wilmington children in lower grades have more positive racial attitudes than children in higher grades, and the difference persists two years after desegregation. Parents show the same result; the younger their children, the better the parents' racial attitudes before and after desegregation.[20] The issue of self-esteem generates less clear results. One summary of studies finds segregation to have worse effects on younger than on older black students' self-esteem. Another study, however, finds that for Mexican-Americans, one year of desegregation lowers "self-attitudes" for children in kindergarten through third grade, but not for fourth and fifth grades, and it raises the older but not the younger children's perceptions of others' favorable attitudes toward them.[21] At this point, no conclusions about self-esteem seem warranted, except that it does not appear to be strongly affected at any age by degree of racial isolation. For relations between the races, however, the evidence unambiguously says the younger the better.

Next, consider academic achievement: positive "effects of desegregation are almost completely restricted to the early primary grades; . . . desegregation is successful as an early childhood intervention."[22] Conversely, "it is reasonable to expect desegregation to pose greatest problems at the junior high level"[23]—precisely the level at which *Tasby* and other plans mandate moving students. Eight of ten studies show positive effects of desegregation in the first two grades; none show negative effects. But only three of seven show achievement gains, and an equal number show losses, when grades seven through nine are desegregated. When grades are split above and below sixth, desegregated younger grades show less negative worst-case results, higher best-case results, greater overall achievement gains, and less variation among gains than the older grades.[24]

Finally, consider unrest in schools: the risk of being a victim of robbery or violence in any school is greatest in seventh grade and declines up to twelfth grade.[25] If desegregation increases tension, it seems safer to impose it in high schools than in junior high. And some data bear out this inference. Violence is associated with court-ordered desegregation in junior high schools, while they are linked only slightly or not at all in senior high schools.[26] In sum, desegregating many grades avoids problems that desegregating only a few grades causes, especially since it implies change among the youngest, those most likely to reach goals of desegregation beyond "bean counting."

The problem with desegregating the youngest students is that it violates another goal—minimizing white avoidance. "Greater white flight [is] produced by elementary than by secondary school desegregation reassignments."[27] Thus the issue of grade level in desegregation illustrates on a rather mundane level the fundamental conflict between preferred means and desired outcomes. The most incremental changes receive the greatest (white) support, but they produce the fewest good and most bad results.

A third temporal factor is speed of instituting remedies for problems caused by previous changes. Incrementalism's proponents tout its ability to "proceed through a sequence of approximations. A policy is directed at a problem; it is tried, altered, tried in its altered form, altered again, and so forth."[28] Thus the many small steps of incrementalism *can* produce rapid change, not as unilinear progress toward a fixed goal but as constant reactions to previous actions.

But for school desegregation, that virtue is a fault. Consider academic achievement: minority achievement scores improve only after desegregation has been in place for several years.[29] ESAA funding had no effect on elementary students' achievement in its first year of implementation, slight effects in its second year, and statistically significant and "educationally meaningful" effects in its third year. "The data from this and other studies appear to show that large new programs such as ESAA require at least two to three years to 'shake down,' and that evaluations prior to that time may do an injustice to the programs."[30]

Or consider white flight: even when many whites flee the system before or during the year desegregation starts, postimplementation white loss sometimes recedes to the levels of preimplementation loss.[31] Consider white resistance: residents of Louisville, Kentucky, reacted violently to both the prospect and the fact of mandatory busing, but active opposition and even the salience of the issue declined after two years.[32] By the third year after implementation, antibusing candidates for the Boston School Committee and the Charlotte-Mecklenburg school board were defeated in reelection bids.* Several years after implementation, Louisville's antibusing mayoral candidate was defeated by an apparently more liberal opponent. A black advocate for black causes was one of two (out of eight) candidates surviving a 1983 mayoral primary in Boston. In sum, "protest . . . rarely continues past the implementation year."[33]

Looking at community attitudes toward schools also reveals the flaws of too-rapid change in response to previous change. In New Castle County (Wilmington), 72 percent of public school parents rated the schools as "good or excellent" two years before desegregation. That figure plummeted to 44 percent one year after desegregation, but rose to 62 percent five years later. Parents' views of how smoothly the schools are running, how well schools handle discipline and bus safety, and how "school atmosphere" seems all improved considerably between the first and fifth years of desegregation.[34]

Finally, consider race relations within schools: the longer a school

*At the same time, Boston elected its first black School Committee member. He had, however, an Irish name—John O'Bryant—which may or may not have been significant.

is racially mixed, the better parents, teachers, and principals become at dealing with racial issues and members of the other race, and therefore the better are students' racial attitudes. In fact, length of integration has a greater effect on white grade school students' racial attitudes than any other variable. Students' racial attitudes improved from 1972 to 1974 in the same desegregated schools (although white achievement declined, perhaps because of white flight). Furthermore, improvements in students' attitudes toward the other race in 1974 were related to characteristics of their schools in 1972, suggesting long-term benefits of desegregation that do not show up immediately. Desegregated schools with poor racial attitudes improved during these two years, and schools with good racial attitudes did not weaken.[35]

Not all studies find good effects after long experience with desegregation. Race relations in one district apparently remained almost unchanged over five years,[36] although reanalysis of these data shows "that the likelihood of an Anglo choosing minority students as friends and schoolwork partners increased somewhat."[37] In other schools, the increase in interracial contact over time produces a greater likelihood of expressing hostility or resentment. "When this happens, trouble begins in earnest, not because desegregation has failed but because the honeymoon is over."[38] The trick here, as so often, is to ensure that other improvements are brought into play simultaneously, so that when tension eases enough for real views to be expressed, enough whites remain to preserve a racial mixture, and the desegregation experience has generated positive as well as negative "real views." Neither outcome is easy to attain, but in their absence, long-term effects may be as bad as incrementalists predict from short-term evidence.

Despite the mixed results, one conclusion seems warranted: policy changes that respond immediately to white opposition, to lack of minority accomplishments, or to unimproved race relations will mistakenly reduce the amount of desegregation. The rapid remedial change most typical (and most praised) of incrementalism has deleterious effects, whereas more ponderous, less flexible moves bring us closer to successful desegregation.

Thus incremental change leads policy-makers to move slowly when they should speed up and quickly when they should drag their heels. Slow implementation of a new policy increases instability, decreases commitment, and sacrifices the advantages of youthful malleability. It may cause greater harm than would no change at all, if it magnifies violence and white flight and diminishes minority achievement. Rapid modifications of a newly implemented policy are just as problematic. Incrementalism's vaunted remedial qualities do not allow enough time for short-term disruptions to be offset by long-term benefits. Immediate flexibility after implementation may simply add new disruptions to old.

The fly in this ointment is popular control. Many whites (and some blacks) resist involving young children; most opponents would remain unconvinced by the claim that everyone will be better off in a few years. I will address this problem later; for now, let us turn to other forms of incremental change and their consequences.

SPATIAL INCREMENTALISM

Space is another element of incremental policy choice. Changes that affect a large territory (and, presumably, more people) are less incremental than changes that affect a small territory (and fewer people).[39]

I define spatial incrementalism as reassigning students in only part of a school district or in geographically contiguous areas within a school district. Its virtues seem obvious; as one desegregation handbook pronounces, "The most desirable assignment patterns . . . keep distances that must be traveled to and from school to a minimum; the least desirable require extensive travel in either time or distance."[40] Pragmatically, the fewer transportation changes the school district must make, the more it can concentrate on doing them well, and the fewer resources it must draw from "truly educational" purposes. Politically, the fewer people disrupted and the smaller the disruption the greater the community acceptance.

However, as early as 1966 researchers found that Northern desegregation went better when all schools in a community were involved, rather than only a few.[41] Their findings for mostly white suburbs also hold for mostly non-Anglo cities, for several reasons. First, one of the best ways to improve students' achievement is to mix them with higher-status (and generally higher-achieving) peers.[42] Even if status itself has no direct effect on learning, a school's "climate" is better and expectations of its students are higher—both are variables that do affect achievement—if many have high-status backgrounds.[43] However, if only part of a school district is desegregated, poor students of both races are more likely to be involved than wealthy students. Thus the academic benefits of mixing socioeconomic classes are probably lost in a partial plan.

Pairing contiguous schools in order to minimize busing distances has the same drawbacks as involving only a few schools in order to minimize the amount of busing. Contiguous neighborhoods are often of similar socioeconomic status, so minimizing the distances students are moved generally mingles poor (and less successful) blacks and whites in some schools, and wealthier (and higher-achieving) blacks and whites in others. Schools in poor neighborhoods are likely to have fewer resources, newer teachers, and lower expectations for students; combining or trading among such schools does little to improve educational facilities, instructional quality, or school climate. In short, improving the quality of education—a deep concern for parents of desegregated children[44]—probably requires that low-status students attend school with high-status students, who usually live farther away than the next block. More busing may be necessary for better education.

Minimizing busing distances and involving only part of a district may not only fail to improve academic achievement, but actually harm race relations. If poor whites are racist, it is often because they (correctly) perceive that blacks threaten their precarious social, economic, and political positions. To a white slum-dweller, the black ghetto a few blocks away visibly, tangibly manifests that threat. Poor blacks, of course, are likely to see nearby whites in exactly the same light. Students with such backgrounds who are suddenly placed in the same school will find it hard to drop their defenses and embrace their rivals. Indeed, evidence shows that racial hostility is greatest in schools with students (especially whites) of low socioeconomic status.[45] As a classic of understatement puts it, "The Boston desegregation effort should be instructive in this regard."[46]

Another argument against striving to minimize busing distances and involving only part of a district is that such incremental changes may, over the long run, exacerbate rather than mitigate white flight. In the situation just described, parents perceive that their children have no better facilities, are not learning more, must sit next to their economic and social rivals, and (for whites) are in a school that is now "blacker" and therefore losing status. Parents whose economic means permit may move or find a private school—thereby destabilizing the neighborhood and the school. Minimizing busing distances has a further, more precisely identifiable effect on neighborhood transition. The existence of poor contiguous neighborhoods with schools dominated by different races probably reflects the presence of an expanding ghetto. The white neighborhood is thus already seriously unstable, in the sense that at some point most whites will try to move before their property values decline. (Whether or not such diminished valuation "really" occurs is beside the point, since enough people assuming that it will occur and therefore selling their homes in a panic make it happen.) Potential buyers judge a neighborhood partly by its schools. If the school is "more black" than the neighborhood and housing prices are declining, relatively well-off whites will not move in and relatively poor blacks will. In this fashion, contiguous pairing of poor schools speeds the transformation of transitional neighborhoods into ghettos.[47]

Conversely, changing the racial ratio of an entire district may actually stabilize the system, even if it produces more initial white flight. If all schools in a district are racially and economically similar, parents who remain in the public system cannot gravitate toward the whitest (and presumably best) school. Indeed, "if a plan reaches all groups in the community, . . . the success of the local school system requires the success of desegregation—and all groups will have an interest in that outcome."[48]

Some research directly supports this line of reasoning. Parents do indeed see higher-status schools as better[49] and do expect, correctly, that minority-dominated inner-city schools will receive fewer resources.[50] Reducing the proportion of blacks and avoiding busing in a few schools in Charlotte-Mecklenburg[51] and "uneven desegregation" in Georgia districts[52] produced movement of whites among schools within the same district, whereas equalizing racial composition among schools across an entire district for several years increased stability of enrollment in Florida.[53] In both Atlanta and

Dallas, whites in one neighborhood were assigned to a nearby black school although "other areas of the city remained untouched. . . . [T]he affected areas were quickly depopulated of school-age children." Parents apparently found ways to move a few blocks away, give false addresses to school officials, or send their children to relatives across town.[54] In Boston, whites (and blacks) living in one subdistrict sometimes moved a short distance to another subdistrict with a more desirable racial ratio, and the court's commitment not to bus across subdistrict lines left it unable to adjust attendance zones to compensate and thereby stabilize the system.[55] Thus the slight direct and rich indirect evidence concur in showing that spatial incrementalism may, to the detriment of everyone, destabilize neighborhoods.*

A final reason for extensive rather than minimal movement of students is equity. Much white resistance derives from the (accurate) perception that the wealthy and powerful, who often design and implement desegregation plans, escape them:

> The . . . problem . . . is not that Whites are forced to . . . integrate their schools but that *certain White people have to pay the costs of abolishing the ghetto, by having their children mixed into the ghetto*. To minimize costs of transportation and to accommodate legal distinctions between central city and suburb, the people who are supposed to pay this cost are those who live near the ghetto. . . . This is, of course, no more than the cost that the system of segregation has imposed on . . . Black people all along, . . . but that does not change the perception of the White people—that they are being asked to pay a new cost of increased risks of crime and lowered educational quality in order to solve a social problem that is not their fault.[56]

The charge of unfairness is not only politically potent but ethically unanswerable, so long as we compare among whites only. I can think

*Incrementalism should not be blamed for stupidity, but incrementalism run amok can have absurd effects. Computer programs have been designed to minimize the number of students bused, travel time, and the number of buses needed for a given level of racial balance. In Charlotte and Columbus, these programs have sent white students living in an integrated neighborhood in one direction to a black school, and black students from the same neighborhood in the other direction to a white school. This action, of course, destabilizes what could be a naturally integrated community and neighborhood school; it "amounts to punishment of those who actually believe in and practice integrated living." Gary Orfield, *Toward a Strategy*, pp. 19–20.

of no justification for exempting the powerful rich from a burden (as whites perceive it) that they impose on the powerless poor. This is *not* to say that whites need not desegregate with blacks; it is to say that if the worst-off should do so, all the more reason for the best-off to do likewise.

Opponents of long busing distances assert its high costs—financial, academic, psychological, and demographic. The costs are undoubtedly real, but not in the ways that their claimants generally perceive. Consider, for example, financial costs: buses and gas obviously cost money, but seldom have more than a marginal (incremental!) effect on a district's budget after their purchase. Among the sixteen recently desegregated school districts that responded to a Civil Rights Commission request for information, transportation costs remained the same or declined in five, increased less than 1 percent in seven, and increased 1 to 2 percent in four.[57] These were relatively small cities; huge districts such as Los Angeles are a different story. Large cities, however, can use mass transit systems to reduce and diffuse the expenses of increased transportation. New buses, if needed, are expensive, but some states have long-standing laws to reimburse most of their districts' transportation costs (for whatever purpose), and other states are under court order to fund new costs of mandatory transportation for desegregation purposes. These mechanisms do not eliminate expenditures, of course, but they do remove the burden from local taxpayers. And in no case do busing costs come remotely close to the public's perception of them as at least 25 percent of a school system's budget.[58]

Physical costs to children are apparently no more burdensome than financial costs to a district. Children who walk to school are two to three times more likely to have an accident than children who ride a bus.[59] Busing for desegregation purposes has a slight *negative* relationship to school violence—the more busing, the less violence—in four of six types of schools (rural junior and senior high schools, urban and suburban senior high schools). Only in suburban and, especially, urban junior high schools does increased busing for desegregation purposes increase school violence.[60]*

*Relationships between racial mixing and violence (as distinguished from busing and violence) are complex. Simple correlations show that urban junior and senior high

Nor are educational and psychological costs severe, at least as far as we can determine from the very limited data available. Being bused apparently does no or slight harm to white student achievement, with differences in findings depending on differences in statistical techniques and control variables.[61] White busing is associated with *lower* tension levels in the schools to which the students are bused. With this exception, neither being bused nor attending neighborhood schools has much effect on either blacks' or whites' perceptions of social tensions, personal or academic morale, or achievement. Busing of black students apparently generates slightly worse race relations among both blacks and whites, but busing of white students has no or positive race relations effect on either race. Attending neighborhood schools has a negative impact on both black and white students' racial attitudes and behaviors.[62] The main conclusion we can draw from these few studies is that busing per se has almost no effect. The same can be said for having students attend their neighborhood schools. In the most extensive study of busing, of thirty-five possible findings of an association between busing or attending neighborhood schools and student outcomes, twenty-seven showed virtually no correlation, four showed associations that

---

schools suffer more violent crime as their proportion of black students rises. Rural junior high schools, however, suffer more crime as the proportion of *white* students rises. But these data are incomplete. When other influences on school crime are controlled for, only urban senior high schools continue to show a strong relationship between the proportion of blacks and crime level. And two types of schools—suburban and rural junior high schools—show an even stronger relationship between the percentage of *white* students and crime, when all other factors are controlled for. Crime level is more strongly associated with whether the school is in a dangerous neighborhood, has a high proportion of males, lacks fair and strict discipline procedures, and has older students than with students' race. (National Institute of Education, *Violent Schools—Safe Schools*, p. A15.) Thus parents of both races might well resist sending their children into an increasingly black urban senior high school (particularly if it has a lot of boys) or an increasingly white suburban or rural junior high school. But whites cannot legitimately resist busing white children into a dangerous school and simultaneously accept without protest the idea of sending black children into the same school.

Vandalism is even more strongly associated with the proportion of whites than violence is. In four of six types of school, the more white students, the more property loss the school suffered. In only one of six types of school did a rise in black students imply a rise in vandalism (p. A47).

were spurious effects of urbanism or socioeconomic status, and the three "survivors" showed coefficients ranging from .13 to .28 in magnitude.[63] On average, busing is substantively a nonissue.

But it is hardly a nonissue emotionally. No reader needs to be reminded of the enormous psychic costs—to both perpetrator and victim—of stoning buses in Boston or bombing them in Pontiac. White hostility to busing is so great that even if it is groundless, in itself it becomes one of the greatest obstacles to successful desegregation, at least in the years immediately surrounding implementation.

The most severe long-term cost of busing is white flight. Yet even here the evidence is complex. Parents' decision to flee the public schools is only weakly related to whether their child will be bused at all. For example, just over half of *both* compliers and rejectors among white Floridians would have had to put their children on a bus; in other words, almost half of the rejectors would *not* have had children bused,[64] and half of the compliers accepted desegregation despite busing. Busing distance affects white flight only in the implementation year, or only for children being bused for the first time, or only if children are bused to predominantly minority schools.[65] In brief, busing per se influences but does not determine whether a white family will flee the public schools; all we can conclude is that the time, distance, and destination of bus rides combine with other factors such as income, alternatives, and racism to cause some whites to flee and others to stay.*

*In fact, much white resistance to desegregation may have little to do with any policy manipulations. Just as white flight is only loosely related to the imposition of busing on one's children, so general opposition to busing is only weakly related to its direct impact on one's life. Having children in public schools, even having one's children bused, and several other measures of self-interest have little influence on whites' view of busing. Instead, racial prejudice, general conservatism, and mistrust of the process by which desegregation is occurring determine opposition to desegregation or busing. These findings do not imply that policy manipulations are irrelevant, only that they matter less than we might think and that they may have more effect through their long-term influence on racial attitudes in general than through their short-term impact on individual lives. See David O. Sears, Carl P. Hensler, and Leslie K. Speer, "Whites' Opposition to 'Busing': Self-Interest or Symbolic Politics?" *American Political Science Review* 73, no. 2 (June 1979): 369–84; Douglas S. Gatlin, Michael Giles, and Everett F. Cataldo, "Policy Support within a Target Group: The Case of

Thus extensive busing has costs, but of an odd sort. The tangible costs are minimal. The intangible cost—white opposition—is severe and is made tangible as whites express hostility or flee the system. Not only is this phenomenon ironic in itself, but its explanation reveals a deeper irony. If we assume that white opponents are neither simply racist nor intrinsically opposed to large yellow vehicles—indeed, "voters in several St. Louis County school districts voted in 1978–79 to authorize [non-desegregation-related] busing for students who otherwise would be ineligible"[66]—we must ask why they are so vehement. A clue to one answer lies in the fact that whites urge, pay for, and use busing for other purposes—vocational or special education, school consolidation, safety for young children, and so on. If the school at the other end of the ride seems better than the neighborhood alternative, the costs of busing are acceptable; if not, they are not.* This observation is not new, but combining it with the arguments given earlier about the value of extensive busing yields a new policy twist. Extensive busing, if well done and combined with other changes, *does* enhance educational quality, school system stability, race relations, and feelings of equity. Minimal busing and slight change harms (or at least does not help) educational quality, decreases stability, exacerbates racial tensions, and fuels the fear of exploitation. Extensive busing can solve some of the prob-

---

School Desegregation," *American Political Science Review* 72, no. 3 (September 1978): 985–95; John B. McConahay, "Self-Interest versus Racial Attitudes as Correlates of Anti-Busing Attitudes in Louisville: Is It the Buses or the Blacks?" *Journal of Politics* 44, no. 3 (August 1982): 692–717.

*This economistic language of weighing costs against benefits does not apply to those whose response to busing is symbolic rather than self-interested, or to groups who oppose busing per se. Some communities, for religious, ethnic, or other reasons, reject transportation of students for any purpose into or out of their geographic bounds. In their view, busing for desegregation is simply one particularly upsetting type of intrusion and dilution. Such claims are hard for liberal policy-makers to deal with. On the one hand, loyalty to a close-knit community merits respect and abstention from interference, at least partly because it *is* such a nonliberal phenomenon. On the other hand, in-group allegiance too often becomes xenophobia, which a liberal state should not be expected (or permitted) to endorse. In either case, the cost-benefit calculus that I implicitly use throughout this book is inappropriate for people in these communities. My thanks to Elizabeth Bussiere for pointing out the dangers of a purely individualistic loss-vs.-gain analysis of school desegregation.

lems that minimal busing creates. But once again, public opinion pushes policy-makers toward undesirable incremental actions rather than beneficial full-scale change. Note, finally, that massive busing is not always necessary to eliminate racial isolation. In some districts it may be, but in most, intelligent shuffling of existing bus routes would generate (or has generated) significant change. In at least four Southern states, busing for desegregation *reduced* the time, mileage, or cost previously entailed by busing for segregation.[67] It is also worth pointing out the well-known fact that over 50 percent of all American schoolchildren are bused to school for nonracial reasons, whereas probably no more than an additional 5 percent are bused for desegregation.

This whole discussion of spatial incrementalism within a district has been shadowed by the larger question of metropolitan desegregation—reassigning students (across school district boundaries in the North) so as to incorporate suburbs and city in one educational arena. All of the arguments for and against full within-district reassignment recur, *mutatis mutandis*, for metropolitan plans.* The logistical problems of desegregating a large area—with perhaps several dozen school districts and as many quirks and standard operating procedures—are formidable. So are the political problems, given suburban outrage, congressional fulminations, and defensive actions by now unnecessary administrators and school boards. Metropolitan desegregation adds a new problem: the daunting prospect of "one mammoth school district covering the entire SMSA [region] and more," with attendant "massive . . . busing" and "usurp[ation of] all local educational authority."[68]

But the arguments *for* metropolitan desegregation are even more powerful. First and foremost is Judge Roth's question during Detroit's trial: "How do you desegregate a black city, or a black school system?" The appellate court agreed: "This court finds itself unable to give any direction to the district court which would accomplish

*Here I am ignoring the constitutional obstacles to metropolitan desegregation across district boundaries. *Milliken I* made it legally difficult for a court to impose a cross-district plan, but not impossible; courts in Indianapolis, Louisville, Nashville, and Wilmington have found grounds for doing so. In chapter 6 I discuss possible actions that could both fall within the guidelines of *Milliken I* and achieve the advantages of metropolitan desegregation.

the desegregation of the Detroit school system in light of the realities of the present racial composition of Detroit."[69] Detroit's 86 percent black enrollment is not unique; by 1980, only four of the nation's fifteen largest school districts had over 50 percent Anglo enrollment. In all of them, black enrollment has increased since 1968 between 1 and 35 percent; in all but one, white enrollment has declined between 8 and 39 percent. (The exception was Tampa, Florida, which gained 1 percent whites under a metropolitan desegregation plan.) All six of the largest metropolitan areas, containing one-sixth of the nation's students, have mostly black and Hispanic cities surrounded by white suburbs; none has a desegregation plan crossing urban-suburban boundaries. Simple arithmetic requires us to involve metropolitan regions if we wish to end racial isolation.

And the data for once confirm common sense. Across fifty large school districts, having a countywide system (that includes heavily minority cities and white suburbs) does more to influence the amount of desegregation in elementary schools than any other variable, and it is an important predictor for change in secondary schools.[70] Other studies confirm that racial isolation is reduced more in metropolitan or countywide plans than in central city or suburb-only plans.[71] Eight of fifteen large metropolitan areas in Southern and Border states which have a metropolitan school district (or which incorporate most of their suburbs within the "city" district) have more than 50 percent whites in the school attended by the typical black. In contrast, only two of the fourteen districts limited to the central city have that much racial balance. (Just to show that no argument is airtight, Dade County (Miami)—which has a countywide plan—is the most segregated of these fifteen districts and experienced the greatest increase in segregation from 1970 to 1980.)[72] In brief, racial isolation declines more in metropolitan than in city-only plans; for many large cities, racial mixing is simply impossible without suburban involvement.

Consider also other desegregation goals. First, achievement: if low-status children achieve more when mixed with high-status children (and the latter do not achieve less, as virtually every reputable study of white student achievement in desegregated schools shows),[73] then mingling inner-city and suburban students should, in general, improve the performance of the former without harming the latter. Transporting poor minorities out to the better facilities and stronger staffs of suburban schools should enhance their learning. And in the unlikely event that white suburban teachers and students are transported into city schools, more resources, higher expectations, and a better climate will follow quickly. It was this logic that led a white working-class community group in Baltimore simultaneously to oppose a city-only desegregation plan and to endorse a metropolitan approach. Their children too would benefit from access to the suburbs.[74]

Metropolitan plans do, in fact, "show the strongest [achievement] effect of [any type of] desegregation," followed by countywide, central city, and finally suburb-only plans. Furthermore, black achievement increases the most in schools with 10 to 30 percent black enrollment, a racial ratio that most cities can no longer produce by themselves.[75]

Next, consider white flight and residential and enrollment stability. The arguments for intradistrict desegregation apply here also. Furthermore, if "implementation . . . in a central city with a high minority enrollment and surrounding white suburbs *not* included in the plan produces an accelerated white withdrawal from public schools,"[76] the solution is more change, not less. "Countywide school districts have half the white enrollment decline of city school districts."[77] The *least* avoidance occurs in "urban school districts with full metropolitan desegregation plans, plans which put all children in predominantly white schools and leave no readily accessible all-white districts to which to flee."[78] Even busing distances have no relation to white flight in countywide plans, although they do in central-city-only plans.[79]

There are several reasons why more change dampens the white flight that less change calls forth. First, "the larger the percent minority in the school district the greater the white enrollment decline,"[80] but metropolitan plans can disperse minority (and poor) students among white and higher-status students. It is not clear how much dispersion is desirable, because problems occur at several points. Some researchers find that after a district's or school's minority enrollment reaches about 30 percent, white flight increases exponentially (although the effect is less in countywide than in city-only districts).[81] Others find no such "tipping point" and claim that white flight increases only proportionally with increased black enrollment.[82] On the other end of the scale, an overwhelmingly white school (with fewer than 15 percent blacks) is apparently such a hostile environment that blacks suffer academically and psychologically.[83] The same results could hold, of course, for a small proportion of whites in an overwhelmingly black school—a likely occurrence in a city-only plan, but not a problem in a metropolitan plan. The evidence on equal proportions of both races is ambiguous. One study finds that violent crime is greatest in schools that have a small proportion of either race, and least where the racial balance is most even.[84] However, others claim that racial hostility is greatest when neither race dominates; when the numbers of both races are equal, battles over turf seem winnable and therefore worth engaging in.[85] But regardless of the precise dynamics of "tipping," turf, and isolation, one general point is clear: metropolitan plans have much more leeway to disperse blacks and whites enough but not too much than do city-only or partial plans. At the very least, metropolitan plans can keep the concentration of blacks low enough to defuse white resistance and flight.

The very magnitude of a metropolitan plan may promote stability and reduce flight. A partial or temporary change cannot nudge reluctant participants into commitment. But a metropolitan plan is such a massive undertaking that it is bound to seem permanent and may induce parents to dig in and try to make it work for their children. More mundane, the costs of moving far from job and friends increase as desegregation reaches further. At some point, exit becomes more expensive than voice.[86]

Finally, metropolitan plans apparently enhance housing integration—surely one of the best ways to desegregate schools. "The racial composition of a school and its staff tends to stamp that identity on the surrounding neighborhood."[87] And even in neighborhoods that are temporarily integrated because they are transitional, "a significant number of whites continue to move in" until the faster immigration of blacks halts the flow of whites.[88] These two facts—that schools stamp neighborhoods, and that whites will move into an integrated neighborhood as long as it is not "too" black—suggest that a school that maintains a constantly high percentage of whites may promote white immigration to an otherwise ghettoizing neighborhood.[89] Such stable, predominantly white schools are much more feasible in metropolitan than in city-only plans.

We have a little indirect and direct evidence bearing on this hypothesis. For any given amount of residential desegregation in the South, more city-only than countywide districts lose white students.[90] This suggests that in countywide districts, whites are less quick to withdraw their children from public schools when they see blacks moving into the neighborhood, presumably because they are more confident than city-dwellers that the schools will not "tip" and decline.

The direct evidence on ties between school and housing desegregation is even clearer. "By the late 1970's, the cities that had experienced metropolitan school desegregation were showing much more rapid desegregation of housing than their counterpart cities that had not experienced metropolitan school desegregation."[91] In Riverside, California, for example, fifteen years of housing desegregation has reduced from twenty-one to four the number of elementary schools requiring busing in order to be balanced. Where schools are segregated, both newspaper advertisements and real estate agents steer clients accordingly, and buyers respond; where all area schools are desegregated, there is less racial steering. Buyers then use other criteria such as proximity to work or public transportation to locate new homes, and these criteria probably have a less segregative impact than schooling would.

Such evidence implies that the main way for metropolitan plans to foster housing desegregation is by exempting students in integrated neighborhoods from transfer to a nonlocal school. In theory, city-only plans can also incorporate such exemptions. In practice, however, most city plans are too small to encourage flexibility and variation at the neighborhood level without disrupting the whole plan, so in this way, too, metropolitan plans have advantages. If integrated neighborhoods can keep local schools, a powerful incentive system is established. "By . . . encouraging housing integration, the white families in such neighborhoods . . . reacquire [a] neighborhood school. For blacks, . . . a move out of the ghetto . . . both exempts minority children from busing, and by contributing to racial balance in their new neighborhood (which will eventually exempt the white children living there) makes them welcome there."[92]

Public officials can, if they choose, reinforce these incentives. In

Mecklenburg County, city and school authorities cooperate in locating scattered site public housing (predominantly for blacks) in white neighborhoods which are then exempted from busing.[93] In Jefferson County (Louisville), the Kentucky Human Rights Commission publicized school attendance zones that blacks could move into to avoid busing, and white neighborhoods began recruiting black families. City and county housing authorities also used rent subsidy programs to encourage residential desegregation. Enough blacks moved from the city to the suburbs between 1975 and 1981 that the number of children bused declined by 40 percent, their average time on buses was halved, and the number of schools exempted from transportation because of neighborhood desegregation increased from twenty-eight to thirty-two.[94]*

Metropolitan desegregation has further virtues that city-only plans lack. It may actually lower busing distances and costs or at least make bus use more efficient. Desegregation reduced the number of miles driven in four of nine Florida countywide districts studied and the cost of busing in eight.[95] Justice Thurgood Marshall pointed out in his dissent to *Milliken I* that desegregating only Detroit would require nine hundred new buses; "the tri-county area, in contrast, [would need] almost two-thirds fewer than a Detroit-only remedy." In Kansas City, Missouri, a school board plan of 1977 for pairing schools "calls for transporting pupils between the largely white eastern part of the district and the largely black south central section. . . . Black students are to be transported *across* a white suburban district, and some would then cross industrial centers with poor roads and congested traffic."[96] Figure 2 shows graphically how Kansas City needs more busing for a city-only plan than it would for a metropolitan plan. Similar absurdities occur in almost every city that is not highly compact and that has black neighborhoods bordering on white suburbs—in short, in virtually every large, old American city.

In addition, metropolitan plans could increase educational options by creating economies of scale that permit programs for the gifted or

*Of course, deliberate efforts to desegregate housing are not limited to the suburbs; gentrification suggests that some whites will move back to central cities. But given the powerful forty-year-old tendency of white families with money and children to move to the suburbs and the newer preference of middle-class blacks to do the same, housing patterns are much more malleable in the suburbs than in the central city.

Fig. 2. Proposal for Desegregation Plan in Kansas City Public Schools, 1977

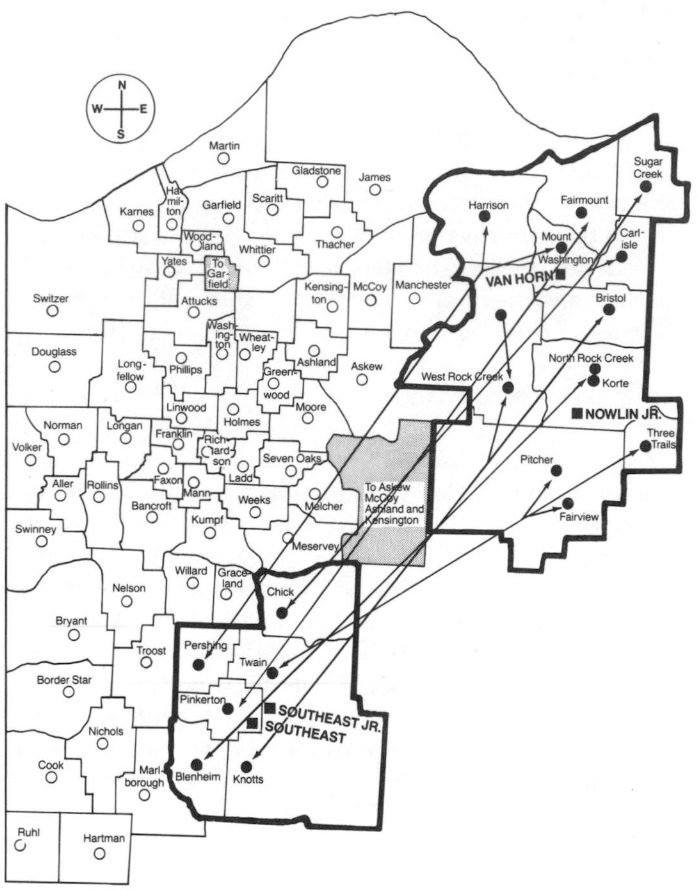

Note: The desegregation plan eventually adopted in Kansas City differed in some respects from this proposal.
Source: Daniel U. Levine and Rayna F. Levine, "The Social and Instructional Setting for Metropolitan Integration," in National Institute of Education, *School Desegregation in Metropolitan Areas: Choices and Prospects* (Washington, D.C.: U.S. Government Printing Office, 1977), p. 112.

handicapped, the purchase of computers and other equipment, schools of science or art, and so on.[97] Suburban districts could avoid closing schools and losing federal and state revenues because of declining enrollments—a point not lost on the administrators of twenty-three suburban St. Louis school districts who have joined with city school officials to promote a (voluntary) metropolitan plan. School districts could even become more accessible to local control; the metropolitan plan approved by the federal district court for the Richmond, Virginia, area (in a decision later overturned) called for six community districts of nine to twenty thousand students—each smaller than the smallest of the three existing districts they would have replaced. These districts would have hired faculty and staff and made budgetary and curriculum decisions on their own.[98] Central city school systems could alleviate budget problems with help from richer suburban districts—which may explain why school boards of Detroit, Richmond, and Kansas City (Missouri) have supported civil rights groups' suits against the suburbs.

Finally, there is again the issue of equity. White urban parents already resent their children's schooling being "disrupted":

> Now add the degree of perceived unfairness provided when the suburban residents near Boston and Los Angeles are exempt. Who caused the segregation? The suburbanites who fled the city, whose legislators refused state funds to the city, whose zoning policies kept blacks out of their towns, who consume the city's jobs and culture and widgets but not its public schools. Integration might have been salable as a positive constitutional duty of citizens and their representatives. . . . Here, however, the attenuations are too great: that child C be bused because politician P once offended; that parents F + M have their lives altered even though they did not vote for politician P, did not know P was misbehaving, did not themselves specifically benefit; all while other cities, and friends and relatives who had just enough money or initiative to move to the suburbs during the great migration, are spared.[99]

A constant and potent political attack against Senator Edward Kennedy and Judge Garrity, among others, is that their children are exempt from the plans they generate or support.[100] Again, to inner-city blacks who can charge whites as a whole with injustice, this lesser unfairness is irrelevant. But it cannot be justified to whites who "perceive school desegregation as another example of exploitation of the poor and the powerless by 'wealthy liberal suburbanites.'"[101]*

*A panel on Boston's desegregation decision "erupted into shouting and jeering from the audience when it was discovered during the question and answer period at the end that none of the four panelists, two blacks and two whites, lived in the city of Boston. After this revelation, their credibility appeared to be destroyed as far as the audience was concerned." Rossell, "The Mayor's Role," p. 267, note 1.

My point is now perhaps excessively clear: spatial incrementalism is a bad idea. More change solves problems that less change cannot, for whites as well as minorities. In addition, and more controversially, a little change is in many ways worse than no change at all. Limited or partial plans create new problems for both blacks and whites without solving the old ones of a segregated system.

There is a further paradox here: the plans that generate the least white resistance—partial or short-distance movement—do the least good and the most harm. Plans that generate an awesome furor—full-scale metropolitan movement—not only do the most good and least harm, but also produce the greatest community acceptance in the long run. Incremental policies resulting from the majority's preferences and policy-makers' caution have, at best, mixed results; sweeping changes that ignore opposition have, at worst, better results.

VOLUNTARY DESEGREGATION

One vaunted feature of incremental politics involves not the scope of its policies but the nature of the actions it results in: incremental changes are more voluntary than coercive. Indeed, the claim of a close association between incrementalism and liberal democracy rests on this feature. Liberal democratic polities have citizens with different opinions and the right to act on them. A well-designed policy will respect value and priority disagreements and protect citizens' freedom of action, by taking only steps that are essential or agreed upon and by leaving as much maneuvering room for individuals as possible. Incremental policies incorporate both of these forms of voluntarism; incrementalism calls for taking small steps that all actors consent to rather than large leaps that some abhor, and it endorses flexibility and experimentation rather than rigid requirements.

The general attractions of voluntary rather than coerced action are so obvious they do not need explication. No sane political actor would prefer to have policy changes forced on citizens rather than chosen by them. The general point, of course, holds for the particular case of desegregation; who denies that greater good arises from natural integration than from mandatory racial mixing? Thus, for example, the desegregation guidelines for the Los Angeles school board point out that "choice and voluntary behavior produces [*sic*] commitment and favorable attitudes. . . . Restricting choice and freedom can produce resistance and negative attitudes. . . . By allowing or inducing students and their families to voluntarily participate in a desegregation program, they will be more committed to making it work and feel greater personal responsibility toward it than those on whom it is forced."[102]

But voluntary desegregation plans work poorly. They seldom achieve the basic step of ending racial isolation. School desegregation from 1954 to 1968 relied on students' "freedom of choice" to attend any school in their district; virtually no whites transferred to black schools, and by 1968 only one-sixth of blacks attended white-dominated schools in the South. Only after *Green v. New Kent County* (1968) held choice "unacceptable" as a sole means of desegregation were other strategies, both voluntary and mandatory, developed and real change begun.

Today, voluntarism works admirably once in a while.* Every district that has made a serious effort can point to one or several successful magnet schools and dozens or hundreds of black students who have thrived after transferring to white schools. But a few success stories do not a good policy make. The story generally remains that of 1968: voluntary methods do not desegregate school districts.

Data on magnet schools show that, with a few exceptions, magnets have little effect on racial isolation unless they are part of a districtwide mandatory plan. Among eighteen large city districts with magnet schools, five of the six most desegregated use magnets as part of a broad mandatory program; five of the six least desegregated use magnets only. Four of the five districts that showed the greatest decline in racial isolation after desegregating use magnets as components; four of the five that showed no decline or even an

*This section deals with voluntarism at the level of individuals. Chapter 5 addresses voluntarism at the level of districts—whether and when a school system devises a desegregation plan at all. Note that the distinction between voluntary and mandatory transfers is not the same as the distinction between plans ordered by the courts or HEW on the one hand, and those ordered by state governments or local school boards on the other. Some judges order plans calling for voluntary transfers (e.g., Houston, Milwaukee, San Diego), and some school boards design plans with mandatory student movement (e.g., Seattle, Berkeley). See Rossell, "Applied Social Science Research," p. 70.

increase in racial isolation after desegregating rely on magnet schools only. Magnet schools are correlated with districtwide desegregation effectiveness when they are part of mandatory plans and when the percentage of minority students participating in them is relatively low. In fact, magnet school effectiveness is determined by the amount of desegregation in the district more than the reverse—magnet schools are best able to attract both black and white students *after* a district has already started a broad desegregation plan. Only one district, in which magnets were added to an existing desegregation plan, was judged to be high in both magnet school and districtwide desegregation effectiveness.[103] The only other systematic study of magnet schools is generally more sanguine about them: "our analysis shows that magnets do offer an extraordinarily flexible and powerful tool for use in desegregating public school systems." It continues, however, by pointing out that "their presence in a district does *not* signify that the tool has been used for this purpose." The study finds no correlation between districts' emphasis on magnets and overall desegregation; half of the extensively desegregated school districts rely heavily on magnets, as do half of the severely segregated districts. It too concludes that magnets can be an effective component of a systemwide mandatory plan, but only in particular circumstances (for example, few minority students, appropriately located magnets, very extensive and strongly supported magnet systems) do they have much independent impact.[104]

Reasons for magnet schools' minimal effect on racial isolation are not hard to find. The most important is simple arithmetic: they do not involve very many children. The first study found that magnets served 30 to 40 percent of the district's students in three cities, about 12 percent in three more cities, and 2 to 8 percent in the remaining twelve. The second study found that, for all magnet programs in 1981–82, the average (mean) number of students served was 5.2 percent of district enrollment.[105] Magnets are better characterized as a drop in a bucket than a cure for what ails us.

When we abstract from a few districts and specific programs, we find the same results: in the nation's forty-nine largest districts with desegregation plans, mandatory reassignment achieves, on average, 85 percent of possible racial balance for schools in that district, whereas voluntary plans achieve, on average, 60 percent. As one would by now expect, plans to desegregate entire districts or metropolitan regions achieve 93 percent of possible balance, whereas mandatory partial plans reach only 73 percent. The amount of change from before to after a desegregation plan is implemented is much greater for mandatory than for voluntary plans, and much greater for districtwide than for partial mandatory plans. On average, the proportion of totally isolated black students is reduced in mandatory districtwide plans by 97 percent but in voluntary plans by only 5 percent.[106] The more sophisticated methodology of regression analysis shows essentially the same results—mandatory student reassignment has a vastly greater effect on levels of school segregation than any of eleven other political, demographic, or economic variables.[107]

This conclusion has two caveats, one empirical and one speculative. Voluntary desegregation techniques do work well in districts with less than one-third minority students. The explanation is simple; "only a small proportion of whites needs to volunteer to completely desegregate a small minority student population."[108] As the proportion of minority students in the district declines, magnet schools are increasingly effective in helping to desegregate the district, and in maintaining enrollment and community support.[109] But in districts with more than one-third minority students (that is, virtually all large districts not yet desegregated), voluntary plans achieve barely more than half of their possible racial balance, on average.[110]

The second caveat is really a prediction. Mandatory plans desegregate more, but they also produce more white flight from the system than voluntary plans. White enrollment declines as much as three times more in the first years after mandatory plans than before them, but only one and one-half times more after voluntary plans.[111] Hence some argue that in the long run voluntary plans will increase interracial contact more than mandatory ones because they retain more whites.[112] Specific cases produce mixed evidence: San Francisco and Detroit are more segregated now than they were before their massive mandatory plans. Boston, Pontiac, and Nashville are more *de*segregated, despite vehement white resistance to their mandatory plans. San Diego and Houston remain as segregated as before their voluntary plans. In Los Angeles a voluntary plan produced less flight and hence more desegregation than the mandatory plan that succeeded it. But "enrollment in Los Angeles' magnet schools dropped by 50 percent when the district was freed from

court order and sought to desegregate through parental choice."[113] Overall, the prediction appears unfounded when one extrapolates from a decade of experience in a large number of districts. The key point is that white flight from mandatory plans levels off; cities with voluntary plans actually lost proportionally more whites from 1968 to 1980 than cities with mandatory plans. When the loss of whites is weighed against the increase in student transfers, mandatory plans come out ahead. Districts with such plans began and ended the period under study with the same high level of racial balance (83 to 84 on a scale of 1 to 100 over eight years), whereas districts with voluntary plans increased the level of balance as predicted, but never reached the level of mandatory plans (60 to 70, over five years). Plans involving part of a district do about as well as voluntary plans—as the discussion of spatial incrementalism would suggest.[114] Other studies using more complex methods of analysis show the same results: the more extensive the mandatory plan, the greater the interracial exposure even when white flight is at its greatest.[115]

Voluntary transfer plans have mixed but predominantly negative effects on quality as well as quantity of desegregation. Whites seldom transfer to black or Hispanic schools,[116] so minorities bear the full burden of busing and loss of neighborhood schools. The inequity here is obvious, and has not gone unnoticed.* One-way voluntary transfer plans generate a few "outsiders" who "invade" a neighborhood school that was content with the status quo ante and whose staff and students are overwhelmingly white. That is hardly a formula for egalitarian race relations and high minority morale. Such a situation reinforces whites' view of desegregation as blacks' problem, not their own obligation and opportunity. An additional problem is that most transfers are high school students, who on average gain less academically and socially from desegregation than grade-school students, as we saw in the first section of this chapter.  Transfers do nothing to end the racial isolation of the schools and students left behind. Inner-city schools lose state and federal revenue

*As one St. Louis mother of six school-aged children put it, "It's abusive to our children, who need to be in their own neighborhood. Why uproot our babies? The Caucasians stay in their own environment until they go to college. It's unfair. It's unsafe. It's a darn shame." E. R. Shipp, "2 Court Cases Watched as Barometers on Integrating Schools," *New York Times*, December 8, 1983.

when enrollments decline, while relatively wealthy suburbs gain, especially if states give them financial rewards for admitting black transfers. The rich schools get richer and the poor schools poorer. In all of these ways, voluntary plans at best meet educational and social goals for only a few and at worst are detrimental to districts' chances of achieving the outcomes that make desegregation worth the effort.

Finally, plans for voluntary transfers usually include a promise by the school system of free transportation to the receiving school. Without transportation, the inequities and disincentives are obvious; with it, a transfer plan can become extremely inefficient and expensive because buses (or taxicabs) have to transport each participant in a neighborhood to a different school. Seattle traded its voluntary plan for a mandatory one after one year because it found partial voluntary desegregation more than twice as expensive as total mandatory desegregation. The irony here, of course, is that the more successful the voluntary program, the greater the confusion and expense.*

Magnet schools pose even more disappointing ironies than voluntary transfer plans. Not only do they generate similar problems of racial imbalance and financial constraint for other schools; they also, paradoxically, have trouble balancing themselves. Seventeen of 216 magnets studied in 1977 had fewer than 20 percent minority students, and 74 had 60 to 100 percent minorities. A few of the remaining schools, moreover, met their goals for racial balance only by enrolling fewer students than their capacity permitted, and about one-fourth of secondary schools met less than 60 percent of their enrollment goals for at least one race. In 1981, "two-thirds of the systems [among 15 studied] take pains to see that their magnets are racially and ethnically balanced," but the proportion of blacks enrolled ranged from 1 to 80 percent.[117]

However, in the case of magnet schools as well as voluntary

*Ironically, this problem may not be too serious because the number of students involved has been so tiny. In St. Louis, for example, a voluntary plan overseen by the federal district court during 1981 moved 200 blacks from city schools to the suburbs, 39 whites in the opposite direction, and 280 whites within the city to magnet schools. "Predictably, this miniscule number has had almost no impact on the metropolitan system of 250,000 students, which is about 25 percent black, nor on the city system of 60,000 students, which is 80 percent black." Morgan, England, and Laverents, *Desegregating Public Schools*, pp. 137–38.

transfer plans, quality of education is of greater concern than simple racial balance. Really to improve the quality of education requires resources—excellent teachers, special equipment, innovative administrators. To convince parents that educational quality is improved may require even more resources—a new building, security guards, small classes. All these things cost money, which large urban school districts of the type remaining to be desegregated notably lack. In 1976, St. Louis spent roughly double the average per-pupil expenditure for regular schools on its magnet program.[118] In Boston the same year, magnets cost $844 per pupil for regular teachers, and $221 per pupil for special instruction, compared to $714 and $184, respectively, in regular schools. Pupil/teacher ratio, age of school buildings, and expenditures for supplies also favored magnets substantially.[119] More generally, "front-end costs for magnet schools may be phenomenally high, especially when a new facility is planned. . . . Fortunately, once front-end funding is established, magnet schools do not seem to require significantly higher budgets to operate than non-magnet schools."[120] Thus the 1981 magnet study (which is generally more enthusiastic about them than the 1977 study cited) found that "in terms of total cost per pupil, magnet schools cost about 8% more than non-magnets. . . . However, this difference narrows over time." Magnets cost about 27 percent more than nonmagnets for student transportation, however, and there is no reason to expect this cost to decline. (Indeed, if magnets succeed in meeting their enrollment goals, transportation costs will increase.)[121]

We need not be surprised or, in the abstract, displeased about the extra costs of magnet schools. After all, their whole justification is to provide better education than the district had been providing, and the best staff, newest equipment, most recently renovated facilities, and widest possible drawing power all obviously cost money. And the money works: "higher financial investments in magnet schools were associated with higher levels of integration and educational quality," although it is disquieting to see how shaky the relationship is.[122] The real problem of costs, however, lies not in the magnets but outside them—in their financial drain on the rest of the district. To obtain extra resources for magnets, school systems must expend great energy in seeking outside funding, reduce the resources of other schools or engage in the "magnet school hustle" of giving "glamorous new labels" to recycled programs.[123]

Magnet schools also siphon off commitment and morale from the rest of the system; what principal, teacher, or student is pleased to remain in the nonmagnetized, mediocre school of the bad old days? Magnets are difficult to set up and administer and take a disproportionate amount of staff time and energy. Resources and their disparities are not only financial. Case studies unanimously assert that successful magnets are given the most energetic, innovative, and powerful principals, who pick their own staff and teachers and who often have much more leeway in removing incompetent personnel than do other administrators. Since no district has an unlimited supply of top-notch teachers and principals (to put it mildly), other schools and their students disproportionately bear the burden of lazy or ineffective employees. Successful magnets are also given "special treatment" by the central district office, a dispensation that permits them to evade rules and standard operating procedures that many school personnel complain of. Again, it is reassuring to discover that strong leaders, excellent teachers, and reductions in red tape affect the quality of education and race relations, but such findings will hardly gratify the 60 to 95 percent of the school system not so benefited.[124]

Finally, magnets create serious political problems. Like programs for voluntary transfers, magnet plans can become a political fig leaf to demonstrate to courts, citizens, and OCR that the school system is working hard to desegregate its students, even if not much is changing. They create jealousy and resentment among citizens who are not involved, especially blacks living in the neighborhood of a magnet who are denied its use. Personnel at other schools may also resent them, whether because of their special treatment or because of their implicit criticism of the less-than-magnetic performance of other schools. Again, healthy competition can be valuable for an organization with assured funding and a captive audience, but resentment reduces the diffusion of innovation and exacerbates frustrations among staff already struggling against the odds to improve education in urban school systems.[125]

And magnets expend all of these financial, intellectual, and emotional resources so that "a limited number of middle-class families are . . . persuaded to keep their children in the public schools for a few more years."[126] Since most of those middle-class families are white, a new and more subtle dual system of schools threatens to emerge. In Detroit, Milwaukee, and Los Angeles,[127] magnet schools have "not aided desegregation but . . . served as an escape route for whites assigned to predominantly black schools; and the magnet concept itself set up a new type of dual structure with unequal educational opportunities."[128] If, as everyone agrees, "a dual system based on race is a violation of the Fourteenth Amendment's equal protection clause, it is not at all clear that a dual system based on educational quality is not also such a violation."[129]

A final problem of voluntary transfers is shared by both types of voluntary plan. Whether through self-selection or the actions of receiving schools, the best and most motivated minority students are likely to be involved. This selection process may benefit those students, but it hurts the already fragile community of the inner-city schools they leave. The only black state senator in Wisconsin criticized its new voluntary interdistrict transfer program as "providing an incentive to Shorewood and Whitehead Bay to come in and rip off the cream of the crop—and then the state provides a bounty for them to do it." He predicted that scholars and athletes would be recruited, and others rejected.[130] The aggregate data on skimming in magnets largely, although not entirely, justifies this fear. Some students who transfer into magnets are not the cream of the crop, but rather are academically or socially unsuccessful. Apparently some parents "used magnet schools as a means to give their children with learning or behavioral difficulties a last chance."[131] However, 90 percent of the forty-five magnet schools studied in 1981 were at least somewhat selective, and close to one-third were "highly" or "very" selective. Not surprisingly, selectivity is highly correlated with math and reading achievement scores.[132] School officials in Houston respond to the criticism that magnets create a new form of dual school system by suggesting that the vacuum created by the departure of student, faculty, and staff leaders may induce followers to step forward, thus generating a whole new crop of leaders.[133] The implausibility of this hypothesis may be the best indicator of the depth of the skimming problem.

The case against voluntary plans, however, has flaws that leave its ethical status ambiguous. The schools (and students) left behind are unquestionably hurt, but the students who transfer (and possibly the schools to which they go) are better off.[134] Minority transfers attend better schools, meet higher-status classmates, develop different perspectives and more connections, and acquire more education and better jobs than their peers back home. Whites in the receiving schools become less ignorant and fearful of blacks and desegregation (so one hopes—we have almost no systematic research on the subject).[135] The few white transfers develop (one hopes) empathy, perspective, and humility. Magnet school students probably receive a better education and certainly receive a type of education that they (or their parents) prefer to the one they left behind. Magnet schools reduce community conflict over desegregation and white flight, increase the enthusiasm of students, parents, teachers, and administrators for schooling, create innovative and excellent programs, and enhance educational diversity.[136]

How do we weigh the benefits for a few against the harms, absolute or relative, to many? I do not know. How do we evaluate giving benefits to whites as inducements to remain in urban magnets or accept suburban transfers? It seems unfair to provide scarce and finite resources to the best-off, but if that is the price of reducing racial isolation, it may be worth it. Finally, freely chosen action is obviously better than coerced action. Overall, mandatory plans can avoid most of the harms and provide more benefits than voluntary plans. But voluntary plans do have virtues that concerned citizens and responsible policy-makers should not ignore.

ORGANIZATIONAL INCREMENTALISM

Incrementalism is, by definition, remedial and serial. We normally distinguish remedial action, which focuses on solving a particular problem, from would-be synoptic action, which tries to "move toward a known and relatively stable goal, . . . chosen for its attractiveness without thought of its feasibility."[137] But remedial action has another connotation—"if it ain't broke, don't fix it." It implies focusing on those few problems that present themselves as urgent needs rather than on the many features of a system that could probably be improved but seem to function adequately at the moment. The serial nature of incrementalism embodies the same prescription: act in steps rather than all at once, presumably addressing the most serious or visible problems first and ignoring others until later on. Since many policy efforts will "turn out to have missed the mark or to have worsened the situation, . . . informed and thoughtful leaders and citizens . . . will prefer to see the political system act on the elements one at a time. Not that errors will be avoided, but each element will consequently receive greater attention and will be more carefully watched for feedback and correction."[138]

This feature of incrementalism implies that school systems should pursue only a few desegregation goals at a time and make progress on them before charging ahead with new goals. It stretches resources, tempers, and abilities too far to disrupt all standard operating procedures at once; after all, the logistics and politics merely of reassigning students are awesome. Changes should come not only serially but also remedially. Schools will face more than enough chaos and resistance in complying with the court order or OCR guidelines; it would be counterproductive to seek changes tangential to desegregation or less urgently demanded. Thus the desegregation guidelines for the Los Angeles school board point to complexity, ignorance, and the need for community acceptance in their conclusion that "plans should . . . initially be implemented on a small enough scale so that available resources can be concentrated and observable benefits will occur."[139]

But once again experience contradicts incremental logic. Making many simultaneous changes achieves more desegregation goals and avoids more problems than making few or serial changes. On this point, in fact, almost all observers (but few actors) agree.* Even the

*Some actors do. OCR, in cautious bureaucratic language, urged HEW Secretary Joseph Califano to insist on massive rather than incremental change:

> Following are nineteen basic components of a plan to desegregate a large Northern city that are grounded on research findings. In light of the difficulties in desegregating a complex metropolis with heavy concentrations of children from low-income and minority families, in our judgement the likelihood of success would be greatly increased by implementing all or most of the components rather than a weak, diluted effort.

Office for Civil Rights, "Secretary's Desegregation and Chicago Briefing," a briefing book for Secretary Joseph Califano, U.S. Department of Health, Education and Welfare, February, 1979. Quoted in Sarah Rosen, "School Desegregation in Chicago" (Unpublished manuscript, Princeton University, Woodrow Wilson School of Public and International Affairs, 1983), p. 31.

A few actors even deeper in the trenches are more direct. The headmaster and program director of South Boston High School have "completely restructured the school. . . . We did this because a single innovation—no matter how powerful—cannot effect lasting change." Geraldine Kozberg and Jerome Winegar, "The South Boston Story: Implications for Secondary Schools," *Phi Delta Kappan* 62, no. 8 (April 1981): 567.

author of the Los Angeles guidelines, who is generally skeptical about desegregation policy, quotes approvingly the words of one of desegregation's greatest cheerleaders:

> In the early 1960's many proponents of desegregation declared that overcoming segregation and deprivation required no more than attendance of black and white children in one school. *Today, the same contention is seen more properly as a prescription for failure.* . . . The relationship between education and integration bears far more explication than it has thus far received. A disjunction between the two is often assumed by both partisans of and antagonists to integration. *Nothing in the research evidence supports such a view.*[140]

Let us first examine magnet schools. They benefit participants but harm those students—usually the vast majority—left out. But the solution is not to eliminate them. We can retain their virtues and avoid their drawbacks through more, not less, change; if the whole system is educationally reorganized, then choice and quality can conceivably characterize all schools for all students. Such was Milwaukee's strategy—to embed desegregation in a radical restructuring of its entire educational offering. After a court finding of intentional segregation, most schools were simultaneously restructured as "specialty schools," and a majority have been desegregated by voluntary transfers of whites and (mostly) blacks.[141] Although blacks still bear excessive burdens and the plan has apparently destabilized some integrated neighborhoods, community support is high and achievement scores are rising.

A school system need not be magnetized in order to embed desegregation in other improvements. We have little systematic data, but case studies[142] show that a desegregation order can work as a catalyst for other reforms if the school system takes advantage of the opportunity. Districts have used the upheavals of desegregation as cover for other upheavals, such as closing schools, redistributing resources, reassigning faculty and staff, reorganizing curricular and teaching techniques, and creating middle schools. They have used an order to desegregate to pry money from state and federal coffers. They have used the imperatives of a court order or OCR agreement to begin collecting and analyzing data. Courts in Boston, Detroit, and Los Angeles, among others, have ordered pedagogical changes along with physical desegregation, sometimes with mandatory state financing and sometimes at the instigation of the school system itself.[143]*

As always, the effects of this activity are mixed, depending on additional factors. Although we should take testimonials from school personnel with a grain of salt, those that back up enthusiasm with specificity are encouraging. After noting that achievement test scores of both blacks and whites had risen in his district, the assistant school superintendent of Hillsborough County, Florida, went on to describe how the district had approached desegregation:

> The implementation of our desegregation plan provided us an opportunity to do a number of things that we either did not have the courage to do [beforehand], or did not sufficiently feel a need of doing, or did not feel it feasible to do. Some of these opportunities were: study and re-evaluate curriculum; re-study organizational patterns; institute special teacher training programs; implement training programs for administrators and support personnel; re-study our assessment instruments; and study our total educational delivery system. The opportunity to do the aforementioned things contributed to the academic progress of our students in an integrated setting.[144]

Conversely, administrators sometimes find desegregation a conven-

*It might be possible for desegregators to ride in on the coattails of the recent concern about educational quality. The spate of reports in 1983 and 1984 on the quality (or lack thereof) of American education has strengthened citizens' and policymakers' resolve to take steps to improve education, even if such steps require money and upheaval. School districts could desegregate their schools as part of that process. At this point, however, this possibility remains a fantasy. Those systems in which desegregation would be relatively easy to include in a package of educational reforms have already been desegregated; districts with the most remaining racial isolation will find it hardest to overcome. In addition, school politics at present usually portrays desegregation as a disruptive and expensive *alternative* to improving schools, not an integral part of it. If anything, the current concern about educational quality seems to be leading people away from rather than toward desegregation. For example, a conference planned by the House Education and Labor Committee for the winter of 1984 on "improving school excellence" will not raise the issue of "busing" because it is "divisive and distracting," according to a committee staffer. Two of the most widely cited reform proposals, both of which barely mention race and neither of which promotes desegregation, are National Committee on Excellence in Education, *A Nation at Risk* (Washington, D.C.: U.S. Government Printing Office, 1983), and Task Force on Education for Economic Growth, *Action for Excellence* (Denver: Education Commission of the States, 1983). Nevertheless, the analytic point remains: deseg-

ient scapegoat for other organizational and educational failings, and a resentful white public is all too easy to persuade. A chilling illustration of this phenomenon (and the most powerful argument I have seen against metropolitan desegregation) is the case of Wilmington. Administrators' confusion, incompetence, and timidity (to give them the benefit of the doubt) became blurred with problems of desegregation per se. The school system deteriorated so badly in the first years of implementation that parents stood in line for up to two hours for the chance to defeat a school tax increase that would have supported the hated "forced busing."[145] Obviously, massive change without reform is a formula for disaster—but so is minimal change that includes only student reassignment.

Successful desegregation requires change within schools and classrooms as well as in the school system in general. A standard and powerful criticism is that segregation recurs within schools, so all the effort is for naught. There are as many explanations of resegregation as there are observers, and it is fruitless to seek the "real" reason. What matters is that most possible reasons can be ameliorated by changing some features of the schools and that without such changes school-level racial balance may cause more harm than good. For example, the evidence is overwhelming that interracial and mixed-achievement work groups decrease racial prejudice, whereas typical classroom practices promoting individualistic or competitive relations among students may increase it. Seventy-two studies support, and one rejects, the hypothesis that cooperative work groups do more to improve race relations than interpersonal competition or complete individualism do.[146] Cooperation also increases academic achievement, help students give one another, cross-racial interactions outside the classroom, self-esteem, liking for teachers, ability to share the emotional perspective of others. Cooperation reduces stereotyping[147] and school crime: "schools where students strive to get good grades . . . [and engage in] intense competition for leadership . . . have more vandalism."[148] Educators have developed sophisticated and detailed packages to introduce cooperative learning techniques to classroom teachers and to enable them to overcome

---

regation must be part of a package of school reforms to succeed, and it is acceptable to whites if it is so perceived. It would be worth trying to push politics in the direction of analysis.

status differentials within heterogeneous groups.[149] The techniques are inexpensive and need not wait upon systemwide change; there is no good reason not to incorporate this pedagogical reform in a desegregation plan.

One reason besides inertia that most classrooms lack cooperative learning groups across races and achievement levels is that the students for these groups are not available within a single classroom. This is the result of tracking—separating students by ability, and inadvertently by race and class as well. Just as competition within classrooms exacerbates tension, so separation at the school door into high and low ability (and status) levels reinforces racial and class stereotypes:

> At Wexler [a "model" desegregated magnet school] whiteness became associated with success in the most fundamental role of children in the school situation—that of the student. White children accepted readily being part of a group that performed well in the student role. But the more whites worked at achieving academically and obeying school rules, the more they tended to appropriate for themselves success in the role of student and to leave blacks the choice of accepting that role but admitting failure in it or rejecting it and condemning themselves to conflict with the demands of the school.[150]

Teachers and administrators reinforce the connection between whiteness and brightness by their insistence on ignoring racial implications of their "pure" academic concerns. A white mathematics teacher speaks for most at Wexler when he describes his teaching philosophy:

> Being a teacher, I guess academics is more important [than personal or social development]. . . . I think we were told once that we shouldn't be concerned that much in sixth grade with the academics of the children who aren't too socialized yet, you know. . . . It was presented to us that socialization, them getting along with each other, black, white or from other areas, is the important skill development right now and the academic is secondary. . . . I think teachers say, "Yea, yea, right, sure," and then they go and teach, try to teach.

Even though they realize that "the kids who are the . . . poorest academic students are the same children that are always being suspended," they endorse the claim of a black principal: "I really don't address myself to group differences when I am dealing with youngsters. . . . I try to treat youngsters as youngsters and not as black, white, green, or yellow."[151] If academic achievement is all that matters, and if race should be dealt with by ignoring it, then blacks' disproportionate academic failure and associated social failure should not be taken into account in the design of schooling.

As experience at Wexler implies, quantitative evidence shows mixed but mainly good results for (predominantly white) students in upper tracks,[152] and mainly detrimental or no results for (largely black) lower-track students. Poorly achieving elementary students do better academically and psychologically in heterogeneous classrooms than in special compensatory "pull-out" classes.[153] It may be neither necessary nor desirable to eliminate distinct classes for exceptionally slow or gifted students,[154] but schools can be much more imaginative in finding ways both to meet special needs and to avoid resegregation. They can "structure intergroup contact around some aspect of the curriculum [such as social studies or science] that does not explicitly emphasize reading and mathematics, since these are the . . . dimensions on which the average performance levels of whites and minority students are likely to differ."[155] They can make it easy for students to move up a level as their skills improve. They can avoid sharp distinctions among college preparatory, vocational, and general tracks in secondary schools. They can guard against stereotypical placement of students by race, language ability, or economic status, and they may want to avoid standardized intelligence and norm-referenced tests altogether. The list could go on forever but the point should be clear; by changing standard practices of ability grouping that persist mainly because teachers are comfortable with them,[156] and parents of successful children like them,[157] schools can promote both achievement and interracial harmony.[158]

Many other changes, ranging from seating students at interracial tables rather than separate desks[159] to reorganizing large schools into smaller, more personal environments[160] reduce resegregation. Among those with the strongest empirical backing are the following:

- Desegregating faculty and staff, making sure to equalize power and status among ethnicities and to have at least some minority superiors and Anglo subordinates
- Fully incorporating multiethnic programs into all students' curriculum, with explicit treatment of racial issues
- Fairly designing, clearly articulating, and consistently applying

discipline codes, making sure that they do not punish minority students for stylistic differences from white middle-class culture
- Establishing extensive extracurricular activities and student organizations that draw equally on the talents and interests of both races
- Changing symbols and customs of the school to put "new" and "old" on equal footing
- Making sure that teachers and staff expect minorities to achieve as well as whites, and working as hard as necessary to realize these expectations
- Providing detailed, practical, timely, and empathetic in-service training for teachers to help them deal with their academically and socially more complex classes [161]

This list is not merely another call for better education; its purpose is more precise. Each item, when properly implemented, improves race relations and/or academic achievement. In the absence of each item, physical desegregation has fewer good and more bad effects. Each change reinforces the others.[162] Thus to make a few changes and wait for them to produce good results before undertaking more is exactly the *wrong* strategy. As many organizational changes as the schools can handle should be made at the same early point in order to benefit as much as possible from any. Obviously, schools should avoid unnecessary confusion, and they must "keep institutional insurance in being." But the considerable disruption attendant upon simultaneously changing many facets of interracial behavior is worthwhile and may even be essential if the initial disruption of reassigning students is to achieve any of its purposes.

Perhaps the most encouraging evidence that, in the right circumstances, good education and good race relations can go hand in hand is the high (0.53) correlation between those magnet schools that offer the highest quality education and those that have the greatest real integration. Integration has also been significantly correlated with math and reading achievement scores (although selectivity was not controlled for).[163]

The evidence from magnet schools bolsters the most attractive argument for simultaneous, broad educational and desegregative changes: they can avoid the trade-off so frequently encountered between benefits for minorities and white opposition. Here, for once, changes that improve minority achievement and student race relations also decrease Anglo resistance and flight. Everyone supports improving the quality of school offerings and climate, and whites are more willing to accept the costs of desegregation if they perceive educational benefits for their children. Busing opponents never tire of telling of white parents eager to send their children long distances to black schools of exceptional quality.[164] And the more parents perceive improvements in their children's learning and satisfaction with school, the more even those with the economic means to leave will choose to stay in the system—hence the more upper-status students, and the greater the improvement in educational achievement for all.* Cycles need not be vicious.

I see only two flies in this ointment. Many (although not all) substantial efforts to restructure schools are expensive, and school bond votes have not been notably successful in recent years. But they have rebounded to a 73 percent approval rate in 1982 from a low of 45 percent approval in 1979,[165] and the nation appears to be recognizing that school improvements are both essential and costly. Money can also come from other sources than hard-pressed urban parents: partnerships with businesses or cultural institutions (as in Boston and Washington, D.C.), state finance equalization measures (as in New Jersey), and federal funds can all mitigate the budgetary squeeze.[166] In addition, many reforms—notably but not only the "effective schools movement" that is the current favorite among reformers of big city schools—require energy and commitment more than money. Most generally, the issue of financing simply illustrates my main point—only if we have the political will to do it right can desegregation succeed.

The other fly is resistance by school personnel, especially teachers' unions, to disruptive changes. Many of the least expensive reforms, such as faculty desegregation and heterogeneous, cooperative classrooms, are those most likely to meet faculty or staff opposition. This problem can be eased through strong and effective leadership, which I discuss in chapter 5, and through demonstration that changes benefit everyone,[167] but the core issue remains. We can desegregate

*Some changes, in fact, may be beneficial more because they create the impression of educational improvement and thus deter white flight than because they actually affect student outcomes. For example, new or refurbished buildings and highly visible security measures reassure white middle-class parents about their children's environment. Obviously such changes by themselves will not delude people for long, but in conjunction with other changes, they can help establish a positive momentum.

our schools successfully if we choose to do so; conversely, failure to desegregate successfully is to be blamed not on the goal itself but on the means used. A few serial, remedial changes that merely reduce racial isolation among schools will do little good and considerable harm. But moving beyond incrementalism to broad simultaneous change in the whole educational structure and process can produce mutually reinforcing improvements. Cynical French proverbs are not always true: in the right circumstances, the more things change, the better off everyone is.

GOAL FLEXIBILITY

A final feature of incrementalism whose worth is belied by desegregation experience is its celebration of shifting goals. Incremental politics "is exploratory in that the goals of policy-making continue to change as new experience with policy throws new light on what is possible and desirable." In this sense, it does not move "toward a known and relatively stable goal" but instead "reveals . . . an unsettled, shifting compromise of conflicting values."[168]

In the context of desegregation, this argument calls for attention to local circumstance and idiosyncracy and rejection of strict a priori demands. Former civil rights lawyer Derrick Bell, for example, castigates Nathaniel Jones, former general counsel of the NAACP, for "rigid reliance . . . on racial balance and busing remedies":

> The busing issue has served to make concrete what many parents long have sensed and what new research has suggested: court orders mandating racial balance may be (depending on the circumstances) educationally advantageous, irrelevant, or even *disadvantageous*. Nevertheless, civil rights lawyers continue to argue that black children are entitled to integrated schools without regard to the educational effect of such assignments. . . . The time has come for civil rights lawyers to end their single-minded commitment to racial balance, a goal which, standing alone, is increasingly inaccessible and all too often educationally impotent.[169]

The issue of flexibility in goals raises two quite distinct concerns. Let us take the easier one first: *if* the primary goal—whether temporally, constitutionally, or morally primary—is to end segregation and discriminatory treatment, incremental wisdom leads to policy failure. As early as 1954, districts faced with a clear statement of the law were more willing to comply with new mandates than were districts given less clear instructions,[170] and history continues to teach that lesson. The South desegregated once judicial requirements became "unambiguous—immediate and complete merger of the separate black and white schools." The North, in contrast, has done less partly because "there has never been a clear and unambiguous set of principles of northern desegregation law."[171] Standards for Northern desegregation shift from district to district and year to year. This situation leaves each school district with the plausible argument that it cannot comply until it knows exactly what compliance means, and with the hope that by dragging out litigation, it may eventually be released from distasteful or disruptive changes.

Regulatory history resembles judicial history. A study of OCR's effectiveness found that by 1976, "the two areas in which implementation had been most successful are the ones in which the most precise regulations have been promulgated." They are Title VI (of the 1964 Civil Rights Act) guidelines that called for the abolition of racially identifiable schools in the South, and guidelines from the former ESAA program that established thresholds beyond which a school district was presumed to discriminate against minority students or faculty. The success of Title VI in the South is evident from table 1 (see chapter 2); ESAA's success is shown by the fact that "districts subject to these ESAA standards have less discrimination than other districts." Conversely, OCR has had vague and shifting standards (at best) for Northern districts with regard to blacks and for all districts with regard to Hispanics, and in both cases, segregation has increased.[172] OCR's major drive during the 1970s to desegregate the nation's five largest school systems achieved only two of its original thirteen goals in New York City and spent "the bulk of the time, effort, and controversy . . . [on] issues . . . which had not even been part of the original model." OCR fell "so short of the stated goals" mainly because of "Title VI's basic goal ambiguity" for the North. This case study of New York

> indicates that if a deliberate policy perspective is not engrafted into the statute by the Legislature, the administrative agency charged with its implementation tends in practice to emphasize the issues, priorities, and compliance approaches with which it is most familiar. In other words, the legislative decision to leave basic policy making to the enforcement agency

had, at least in this circumstance, the rather surprising effect of promoting a conservative ordering of issue priorities, rather than creating a viable open field for new policy concepts and initiatives.[173]

Within schools, the message is similar. Schools that set clear goals, systematically diagnose obstacles to their accomplishment, and "set time aside to evaluate the progress which has been made toward meeting their goals" have higher morale and less racial tension than schools that evade or set no goals.[174] In-service teacher training is most effective when it specifies in advance "specific goals for training and strategies for their achievement."[175] Additional support for this argument is scattered throughout this chapter (and will recur in the next). One virtue of metropolitan desegregation, for example, is that its very magnitude makes clear the permanence of a desegregation plan, whereas partial or short-term changes always leave open the possibility of returning to the *status quo ante*.

The second concern raised by the issue of shifting goals calls into question the first. Should, in fact, school desegregation seek to abolish the effects of segregation through racial balance? Or should it seek something else, such as improvements in educational outcomes regardless of whether the school setting is racially mixed or not? Derrick Bell as quoted above is a thoroughgoing incrementalist. He argues that since experience often shows racial balance to be impossible, even if desirable, we should learn from experience and seek some other way of eradicating the evils of racism.[176] The NAACP rejects Bell's incrementalism. It insists that the goal has always been, and remains, ending racial isolation. Thomas Atkins, general counsel of the NAACP, responds to the suggestion that the NAACP "abandon those school desegregation cases because 'they divide the community'" by insisting: "*We* didn't divide the community. We simply insisted that others not insist that we accept second class citizenship rights and that our children be willing to be relegated into inferior schooling . . . . To the extent that it's divisive for us to insist on our rights, you're damn right we're dividing the country. We're dividing it between right and wrong. That's always been our goal, for the past 70 years. To weaken now would be morally wrong, tactically unwise and I would think Constitutionally impermissible."[177] I will duck this critical issue until chapter 6, since here I am concerned only with the consequences of incremental change for school desegregation, defined as first ending racial isolation and then proceeding from there. Incrementalism's "virtue" of shifting or ambiguous goals ill serves that definition of school desegregation.

What, in sum, are the consequences of incremental policy-making? It works poorly in two ways to desegregate schools. It does less than full-scale, rapid, extensive—but unpopular—change to improve race relations, achievement, and community acceptance and to minimize white flight. Both minorities and Anglos would benefit more from greater than from lesser change. More controversial and more serious, incremental policy-making sometimes causes more harm than no desegregative change at all would cause. Both minorities and Anglos can end up worse-off in a halfhearted, restricted, timid—but more popular—"reform" than if nothing had been done. Race relations worsen, minority self-esteem declines, black achievement declines absolutely or relatively, white flight and citizen resentment increase.

The first assumption of the anomaly thesis is false. Myrdal and his ilk argue that racism can be weeded out of American society by conventional and normally desirable policy-making processes, specified here as incrementalism. They do not see such a change as popular, painless, or rapid—but they do see it as possible. Thirty years of school desegregation history, however, belie that hope. Incrementalism—policy-making as usual—does little to help either minorities or whites and does a lot to harm them. Half a loaf, in this case, may be worse than none at all.

FIVE

Popular Control vs. School Desegregation

"What this illustrates are the advantages of the . . . government . . . which provides the strength for the resolute implementation of necessary social reforms despite the opposing powers of political short-sightedness, heartless insensitivity, sluggish routine or economic recklessness."

As scholars and gentlemen, how "objective" do you regard these remarks to be?

—Peter Flora, reflecting on Flora and Arnold J. Heidenheimer, *Development of Welfare States in Europe and America*[1]

A leitmotif of chapter 4 was the frequent, although not ubiquitous, contradiction between effective, desirable policies and majority public opinion. Many whites and some minorities protest or flee from policies extensive enough to benefit almost everyone in the long run. This phenomenon points to the second assumption of the anomaly thesis—deep down, most Americans are ashamed of racism and would like to eradicate it. Myrdal represents the view that although it is unrealistic to expect whites to sacrifice racism's benefits of their own accord, they recognize it as a violation of their deepest ideals and will accept, even welcome, an authoritative command to put temptation behind them. Thus anomaly theorists do not imagine that many white communities will spontaneously desegregate their schools, but they do expect citizens to facilitate rather than hinder racial justice once desegregation begins. Furthermore, they expect that even if whites oppose the desegregation mandate within which they must act, the process of popular control will yield a more just and palatable specification of that mandate than authorities acting without the aid of citizens would.

Note that neither of these expectations that I attribute to anomaly theorists assumes that the more popular control there is, the *more* desegregation there will be. Only a participatory democrat with his head in the sand for the past twenty years would make that claim. But Myrdal and his fellows do believe that the more popular control there is, the *better* desegregation there will be. Let us examine this package of expectations, values, and hopes.[2]

CITIZEN PARTICIPATION IN PLANNING DESEGREGATION

A standard prescription for successful schooling is parental involvement. The literature is voluminous; one decade-old bibliography of "citizen participation in education" lists four hundred items that "represent only a small percentage of the material that might have been included even after the topic was narrowed and many potentially relevant areas excluded." Justifications range from normative claims that parents or the community in general have a right to shape their children's future, to pedagogical claims that parental involvement improves children's attendance and achievement, to policy analytic claims that people more willingly comply with rules that they have formulated. Thus the bibliographer points out that even though he sought out "a diversity of viewpoints, . . . most of the references included are favorable . . . to the concept of an increased role for parents and other citizens in educational decision making."[3]

Of course, not all educators, policy-makers, or parents promote citizen influence on school policy or administration. The trend in the twentieth century, in fact, has been to professionalize education—remove it from the political fray and insulate it from meddling amateurs. School boards have been made small, elite, nonpartisan, and relatively invisible; the office of superintendent was invented to centralize and depoliticize policy-making and administration; teachers, especially teachers' unions, resist parental "encroachment" on their rights and responsibilities.* Many citizens agree that parents'

*As one unusually candid statement of this view puts it, "Employee organizations have invested years of sweat and tears in planning and negotiating for various rights

role is mainly to stay out of the way of experts. But even the most adamantly professional educators and deferential parents call for some parental involvement. Parents should, at a minimum, monitor their children's progress, participate in the PTA, and vote for school bond issues. Thus no one denies the value of some citizen participation in schooling, and many assert that the more noneducators participate, the better off children and the whole community will be.

When analysts focus on school desegregation, calls for citizen participation become louder and stronger. "*Decentralized decision-making that includes the community will enhance acceptance of the desegregation plan*" is one heading in the Los Angeles school board's desegregation guidelines. It goes on to point out "the powerful effects of choice and voluntary action upon commitment to . . . the action," the role of "parental and community involvement in . . . prevent[ing] community polarization," and the fact that "educators universally acknowledge [that parents'] . . . involvement is educationally beneficial [and] . . . will enhance student interest."[4] In fact, the belief that citizen involvement will improve the outcome of a desegregation process is one of the few points of agreement between skeptics and enthusiasts. David Kirp, who holds that on racial matters the state can best "do good by doing little," asks whether "honoring constitutionally bounded local wants promote[s] good policy." He answers himself affirmatively: "the recent historical record is generally cheering. . . . Political actions taken in numerous school districts . . . [in response to "the emergence of the race and schooling question"] confirm a remarkable capacity for change at the community level. . . . The willingness of long-quiescent individual citizens and interest groups to speak out in order to influence policy, . . . strengthens the political order . . . [and], the grandest hope, is . . . a means of redesigning the schools in order to better the lives of children."[5] The director of the Community Relations Service of the Justice Department agrees: "Your [community coalitions'] authority derives from an old American tradition of citizen respon-

---

and benefits. They cannot sit back stoically and watch a local school and its advisory group tinker with issues which are hard won and close to the hearts of their clients." C. C. Carpenter, "Principal Leadership and Parent Advisory Groups," *Phi Delta Kappan* 56, no. 6 (1975): 426–27.

sibility and initiative. . . . Desegregation in today's climate is too important to be left alone to the school board, the police chief, the mayor and the council. They need your help whether they know it or not."[6]

But with a few exceptions, community involvement in designing desegregation plans does little to improve their substance or enhance their support. Even when sponsored by the schools, citizen groups are generally ignored. In Chicago, for example, the report of the Coordinating Council of Community Organizations in 1963, the Hauser Report in 1964, the Havighurst Report in 1964, Chicago Urban League reports in 1964, 1977, and 1979, the Redmond Report in 1966, a student–school board forum in 1969, City-wide Advisory Committee reports in 1978, citizen and community group advisory committees of 1981—none had an impact on what continues to be one of America's most segregated school systems. Chicago is typical; school boards pay precisely as much attention to citizen reports as they wish to, while giving them enthusiastic lip service. The consequences of such charades have typically been "the opposite of what the board hoped to achieve. The board was hoping for a feeling of participation on the part of the community; in fact, it alienated a segment of the community because its citizens' efforts were not recognized. They were simply a sham committee put together to delude the community with a false notion of involvement."[7]

Although that inference is easy to draw, it is too quick. School boards are not necessarily hypocritical when they set up citizen groups, urge them to produce detailed reports and recommendations, and then ignore the results. The group may not act quickly enough; it may generate "unrealistic" proposals; the board may perceive financial, political, or organizational exigencies that prevent it from following through on its democratic intentions. The school board of Ypsilanti, Michigan, for example, established a citizen's committee in 1975 to examine problems of racial and enrollment imbalances. As the story is reported by a sympathetic observer, "This Task Force . . . presented four plans for the Board's consideration. The Board then requested the administration to present its own recommendations. . . . The essence of the administration's plan . . . was accepted by the Board and implemented in Fall 1976."[8] My point is not to fault the board, which presumably found the administration's plan more feasible and attractive; the point is that the administration's plan *was* more feasible and attractive, so the committee's four plans were not useful.

The skimpy aggregate data do not contradict evidence from case studies that citizen participation in plan design has minimal impact on desegregation goals.* In fifty-two desegregated districts, there is no relationship between the presence of advisory committees and desegregation success,[9] and only weak and nonsignificant relationships between advisory committees and white flight in either the year of implementation or succeeding years.[10] Black civil rights activity was "not important in desegregating schools in Georgia," nor, "despite some exceptions," does it "appear that efforts by blacks have had a significant impact on the implementation of OCR's postdesegregation policy."[11] In fact, black pressure has a strong *negative* association with desegregation change; "blacks seemed to have become active when their district was slow to desegregate but their activities did not produce the desired change. . . . Segregation remained rather high in districts in which blacks were the most active."[12]† In ninety-one Northern districts between 1968 and 1972, civil rights activity directed at the schools had no effect on the degree of school segregation and very little on the amount of desegregative pupil reassignment.[13] An earlier study of the same districts found that civil rights activity focused the school board's attention on racial

*One must beware of placing too much weight on findings of "no relationship"; they may result from methodological flaws in the data analysis or perfectly balanced contradictory relationships, rather than from irrelevance. Several such findings, however, give us grounds for believing that evidence from case studies is not misleading.

†One interesting bit of evidence shows that "a black population that is visible . . . in the political and civic culture of the city" is negatively associated with white flight—the *more* blacks protest and gain power, the *less* whites leave the system in later years. The author suggests that "early public demonstration of the need for blacks to be taken seriously politically (early and varied black protests) combined with an early recognition of the political and social rights of the black population (blacks appointed or elected to the school board) may produce, after a while, a more institutionalized and less fear-provoking environment for race related political conflict resolution. Remaining whites—those not scared off by the sheer numbers involved—may become more accustomed to life (and public schooling) in a city whose political culture provides for a legitimate outlet for political grievances of a formerly segregated racial minority." Becker, *The Impact of Racial Composition*, p. 18, table 5. We have no other data on this point.

problems, but neither it nor white support for desegregation had any effect on board actions to desegregate.[14] Finally, in forty-nine of the fifty California school districts, organized complaints by blacks between 1966 and 1972 had no effect on ethnic balance.[15]

Citizens' actions against desegregation have no more impact than citizens' actions for it. Organized white opposition "had a negligible impact on desegregation" in Georgia.[16] Several studies, in fact, find a *positive* association between white resistance and the amount of desegregation, suggesting either that white resistance *increases* desegregation or—much more likely— that the more desegregation there is, the more whites resist it (albeit to no avail).[17] White resistance does, however, significantly increase white flight before or in the implementation year.[18] And it has obvious deleterious effects on community race relations and white support for the schools.

Citizen planning groups may not merely waste time; they may inadvertently cause harm. First, they help schools to stall and thereby defuse desegregation demands. The school board-created community task force in Kansas City, Missouri, took over a year to propose a plan that had essentially been formulated for it by the district's desegregation advisor at its inception; meanwhile, the district "decided to forego" even the partial desegregation and educational improvement plan it had already designed. "Creating the Task Force was a means of sidestepping the issue and postponing a decision by the Board."[19]

Second, by permitting delay they may unwittingly serve as a political tool for desegregation opponents. In Kansas City, "the Task Force also gave . . . anti-desegregation [board] members time to lobby their colleagues and to work through political channels against desegregation."[20] In Richmond (California), Englewood (New Jersey), and Berkeley (California), granting time and opportunity for citizens to share in designing the plan simply helped opposition to grow, coalesce, and eventually defeat or reduce the plans. One chronicler of this process concludes that "once an issue becomes salient to a significant sector of the public, the mechanisms with which political leaders generally palliate conflict and soothe discontent fail to work."[21] Others are more blunt: "One lesson of these eight cities is clear. The less the public is asked for its opinion during the period of policy-formation, the greater the likelihood that the public will accept the integration plan. . . . It is not the size of the step taken but the way it is presented that elicits widespread, active opposition. . . . Schoolmen who ask the public what decisions they should make—especially on such a hot issue as desegregation—risk the incapacitation of the school system."[22]

Third, citizen planning groups can become scapegoats for unpopular school board actions and thereby diminish rather than increase real popular control. Nine of a sample of thirty-six school boards responded to desegregation demands by instituting broad-based citizen groups that "look[ed] democratic" and representative but merely "took the heat off the board." These groups generally were induced to put forth plans that, even if formulated by the schools, became the property of the group—allowing the school board to seem moderate and responsive (to white opposition).[23] This process diverts citizens' wrath onto a group which has responsibility but no power, and which apparently makes crucial decisions but is not answerable to the public. Meanwhile, the board and administrators avoid attention and demands, and citizens can hold no one accountable. A clearer recipe for hostility and impotence would be hard to find.*

Fourth, citizen groups may reinforce existing inequalities between low status—often minority—members and the inevitable blue-ribbon—usually Anglo—participants. In Boston, for example, minority parents were less effective in citizen advisory groups than Anglos partly because they aroused mistrust in educators (and vice

*Just as stupid incrementalism cannot be blamed on proponents of incremental politics, so proponents of popular control cannot be held responsible for stupid "public participation." Nevertheless it occurs and can have disastrous effects. Boston provides one example of a poorly managed public forum for "citizen input" into planning:

> Parents who had come eager to speak about specific problems in the District IX schools tried to come forward to testify. Time and again their attempts to speak were interrupted by jeers and yells from the group of ROAR [Restore Our Alienated Rights, a white antibusing group supporters. When the meeting resumed [after a cooling-off period], the antics of some members of the crowd became more outlandish. Printed material that had been distributed was shredded with Afro combs and thrown around the auditorium. Signs protesting "Communist busing" were paraded in front of the ever-present TV cameras.

M. Van Arsdell, "District IX CCC Hearings" (Unpublished report, City-wide Educational Coalition, Boston, 1976).

versa), behaved differently from middle-class parents and school staffers, faced logistical problems of transportation and day care, had less prior information and fewer political skills, and in some cases spoke poor English.[24] More generally, consider the following psychological dynamic: whites unconsciously equate the problems that desegregation creates or reveals with problems of minorities rather than with the school system or the socioeconomic structure of the community.[25] In addition, the legal history of desegregation leads whites to view racial balance as their punishment for having been found guilty of the crime of segregation. Minorities encountering these views even among presumably sympathetic coparticipants in planning are likely to feel defensive or angry. Add to that psychology the fact that minorities both on and off citizens' committees are likely to be poorer, less politically "plugged in," and less organizationally sophisticated than the whites they are dealing with, and the situation looks grim. Thus, in a depressing and ironic twist, the very effort to make citizen groups widely representative may, at least in the short run, exacerbate the problems of racial hostility and inequality that such groups are intended to ameliorate.*

Finally and most important, even when citizen groups do influence the plan and enhance its support, minorities may have little to thank them for. The much-praised Dallas Alliance Plan,[26] which was received enthusiastically by the judge and peacefully by the citizenry, left out eight of thirteen grade levels and one-fifth of the schools, all black. Forty percent of the blacks in Dallas were to remain in segregated schools, and over one-third of the schools remained one-race. Dissidents from this "prime example"[27] of desegregation success concluded that "the Anglo majority [whose representatives dominated the planning] had to deal with both a minority school system and with their own . . . conservative, business-oriented views. . . . [They made] a few changes that would eliminate the more

*Some argue that it is precisely these mistaken assumptions about guilt, blame, and merit which mandate wide citizen participation—and the greater knowledge and understanding that go with it—in plan design. See Hawley et al., *Strategies for Effective Desegregation*, p. 79. If its implied hypothesis is true, the argument has great merit, but in my judgment only with extraordinary circumstances or individuals will the benefits of close contact among mistrustful, unequal people in a tense situation with deeply contested outcomes outweigh the problems.

obvious problems but . . . maintain the present power structure."[28] The Fifth Circuit Court of Appeals apparently agreed; it found the student assignment section of the plan unacceptable and remanded it to the district court for consideration of further steps toward racial balance.

Dallas is not unique. The Kansas City task force's structure and mandate "confined [black members] to a negative, passive role as far as boundaries were concerned: they could not make proposals for their sub-districts but could only argue for or against proposals by the white representatives. The person who proposes a solution always has an advantage over the person who just says 'no'; in this case, that advantage completely favored the white representatives."[29] The task force finally split along racial lines over two plans, one leaving an all-black corridor through the city, and the other equally desegregating all schools. The former plan (which had been proposed by the district's desegregation advisor) was the basis for the final design; the latter disappeared without a trace as soon as it was presented to the school board.

The only two aggregate studies to address the question whether citizen involvement is detrimental, not merely irrelevant, to desegregation planning disagree. One finds a strong negative association between civil rights activity directed at the schools and elite support for desegregation, which *is* strongly associated with schools' actions to desegregate. Apparently "high levels of civil rights activity cause elites to withhold their support; . . . the civic elite is unaccustomed to (and perhaps upset by) public conflict."[30] The other finds no white elite backlash in response to black civil rights activity.[31] I conclude that, overall, citizen participation in plan design is useless at best and harmful at worst.

This conclusion has an important caveat that goes far toward clarifying the general argument about the relation between popular control and desegregation success. Carefully structured citizen participation in plan design can augment white support for desegregation. Dallas is one example; the businessmen's plan that left out so many blacks also convinced hostile whites to accept busing of seventeen thousand students, one-third of them Anglos. That is no mean feat. Another is Milwaukee: the judge, the special master, and the school superintendent invited parents to exchange views and information in special forums, to submit plans for implementing the court order, and to shape the details of desegregation in their subdistricts. The result was a large number of people extensively participating and accepting, if not with great enthusiasm, desegregation.[32] White Floridians who feel efficacious—who believe that "people like you" have "influence . . . over school integration in this county"—are significantly less likely to flee desegregated schools than are whites who also dislike busing but do not feel influential.[33] Both whites and blacks who feel efficacious approve of the way desegregation was implemented.[34]* Magnet schools are more likely to attract white students, and thus to meet their goals for racial balance and enrollment if a "needs assessment"—a survey of parents' magnet preferences—shapes the choice of magnet programs.[35] Often, however, whites prefer programs for the gifted and talented or advanced college preparatory programs and once again blacks are relatively less benefited by citizen involvement in desegregation planning.

In short, to summarize an extensive literature, if citizens become involved early in the process, if their roles and responsibilities are clear, if their work is relevant and actually influences the process, they may improve the plan and increase white acceptance. But these conditions are seldom met, and—a big constraint—their outcomes usually come at the relative expense of minorities. Minorities seldom

*Another apparent caveat addresses the type of citizen participation rather than its outcome. All observers agree that increasing citizens' knowledge of the plan, once it has been designed and is on the verge of implementation, is essential to desegregation success. Citizens need to know, *in truthful detail,* the legal and moral reasons for change, the requirements of the court order if there is one, how changes in transportation and school organization affect their children, how the schools will deal with transition problems, who to turn to with grievances, how the schools plan to improve education, and so on. Individuals and citizen groups can be invaluable aids in disseminating this information, by staffing information and rumor-control "hot-lines," holding informational meetings in homes and neighborhood centers, working with teachers, distributing printed materials, operating a speakers bureau, and a myriad of other activities. Note, however, that none of this activity involves influence on or control over the plan, only after-the-fact learning and compliance so it is not precisely relevant to my argument. See Hawley et al., *Strategies for Effective Desegregation,* pp. 77–79; U.S. Department of Justice, Community Relations Service and National Center for Quality Integrated Education, *Desegregation without Turmoil: The Role of the Multi-Racial Community Coalition in Preparing for Smooth Transition* (Washington, D.C.: U.S. Government Printing Office, 1977).

end up worse off than they started when citizens design plans, but they always come out with more of the burden.*

How can we make sense of these apparently contradictory findings—that virtually everyone endorses citizen participation in the desegregation process, that citizen groups are usually irrelevant and sometimes harmful to desegregation success, that they do occasionally influence a plan and increase white acceptance, and that even in these circumstances minorities are often not well served?† We are dealing here with a vision that is normatively very powerful but empirically very seldom realized. Most citizen participation bears little resemblance to our ideal of democracy, but the ideal is strong, and we keep on trying. More particularly, citizen planning for desegregation usually fails for one of two reasons: almost all citizen advisory groups are ineffective, and citizen participation exacerbates existing inequalities between minorities and whites. Let us examine the specific arguments before returning to the general conclusion.

The literature on citizen advisory groups is vast; I can summarize it by saying simply that the inefficacy of desegregation planning is typical. Consider other school groups: "In 1978, with an estimated 1 million or more citizens sitting on thousands of advisory councils . . . even the most sanguine advocates of citizen participation feel that the movement has fallen appallingly short of its objectives."[36] One example should suffice to show how far even legally mandated

*On occasion, the harm is absolute as well as relative. The failure to include Hispanics in the citizen groups planning Milwaukee's educational and desegregation reforms meant that "notices to parents specifying options among schools and programs were sent out in English with no translation provided for limited-English-speaking families until after the deadline for submission of choices. As a result, many Hispanic parents exercised no choice for their schoolchildren" and were consequently left out of the new magnet school programs. "Some redress eventually occurred," but even in the best of circumstances, involving citizens in making school choices has deep and unanticipated pitfalls. Hawley et al., *Strategies for Effective Desegregation*, p. 77.

†One problem in defining success of citizen participation is the question, "Success for whom?" This problem is raised by findings that parental participation helps well-off children more than poor children, but it has ethnic as well as economic manifestations. For example, in California, organized political pressure from Hispanics is significantly associated with a *reduction* in racial and ethnic balance. Eldon L. Wegner and Jane R. Mercer, "Dynamics of the Desegregation Process," in *The Polity*

advice from citizens—never mind groups at the mercy of school boards—falls short. Parent Advisory Councils (PACs) were a required part of the former federal compensatory education program (Title I of the Elementary and Secondary Education Act).[37] The law stipulated that most members be elected parents of affected students, but over half of a sample of PACs had all appointed members. Appointees were usually chosen by school principals or staff; more than one-fifth *were* principals, teachers, or staff. The groups' independence from the school system was dubious, to say the least. Even if they were independent, however, PACs had few tools for making decisions (and no power to enforce them). One-third of PACs met less than once a month. When they did meet, no one was clear on their precise role. They were supposed to be involved in "planning, development, operation, and evaluation of programs under Title I," but at least half were not involved in the relevant district planning meetings. (Another quarter of the PAC chairpersons polled did not know whether their group was involved or not.) Almost all those who did participate described their role as "advisory." Title I administrative processes were "exceedingly complex," and many Title I parents have little education themselves; nevertheless, well over half of the school districts in this sample provided no training for PAC members (12 percent of the chairpersons did not know if their districts provided training.) Apparently only documents that were legally required to be distributed were given frequently to PAC members, and they were written in legal or technical language. PAC members were supposed to participate in Title I program evaluations; only two-thirds of the chairpersons even knew whether their district conducted such an evaluation, and only one-quarter knew whether their state did. Although they were supposed automatically to receive evaluation reports, only 55 percent of the chairpeople reported receiving them; 11 percent did not know if they had. The National Institute of Education modestly concluded from all of this that "exactly what is intended by the framers and supporters of the program requires considerable clarification."[38]

---

of the School, ed. Wirt, p. 134. For those seeking bilingual education within a monocultural setting, this finding may indicate success; for those seeking to reduce ethnic as well as racial isolation, it shows failure.

Citizen advisory groups in other arenas of local politics have an almost equally dismal record. Again, I will rely on one example. "Organized participation in Minneapolis appears to be generally reactive; groups tend to respond to policy initiatives generated elsewhere." As the median family income of the neighborhood represented by the group declines, conflict with local government and dissatisfaction with the results of participation increase. The complaints voiced in a survey of Minneapolis citizens involved in advisory groups are typical:

> few tangible results had been obtained because [the groups] . . . lacked real power. The advisory process is a "paper ideal"; participants have only the "illusion that they are making decisions." Indeed, one respondent argued that the current approach to structuring citizen participation "can dilute true citizen involvement by channeling too much energy into a process that is not very powerful." The process leads to "frustration" and "disillusionment"; the "double talk, red tape, and loopholes" and the fact that [the groups'] recommendations are "ignored" by "dependent, city funded staff" make the process "not worth the bother."

The more citizen groups' recommendations differed from the preferences of city council members, the less they were attended to.[39]

Reasons for the inefficacy of citizen groups are numerous. Entrenched officials are loath to relinquish power; citizens have few resources and short attention spans; goals are contradictory, and means are complicated; groups are poorly organized and weakly structured.[40] Most fundamentally, citizen groups may simply be a romantic remnant of a disappearing society. In our fast-moving world of highly organized professional institutions, efforts to increase citizen control do more to increase professionals' power than anything else, as experiments in community control and voucher systems show.[41] The story could continue, but its moral is clear: the citizen advisory group that has detectable impact on the recipient of its advice is rare indeed.

The second problem with citizen advisory groups is that, across all forms of citizen participation, whites act more, know and learn more, are more effective, and have more success than minorities. This point too can be demonstrated in issues both near and far from desegregation. In Takoma Park (Maryland), for example, a higher proportion of white than minority parents have heard of the district's magnet schools and have visited them, can describe their programs, are satisfied with them, have suggestions for their improvement, and had requested that their children be transferred to another school. Is it not likely that the school system will be more responsive to white than to minority concerns?[42] Or consider the 1972 recall vote on five school board members who supported desegregation in Lansing, Michigan: a higher percentage of white than black registered voters came to the polls, and a higher percentage of whites than blacks actually voted on the recall question once they came to the polls. As a consequence, 66 percent of the white but only 52 percent of the black registered voters voted on the recall issue. Is it any wonder that the five board members were recalled even though most black and one-third of white voters opposed the recall?[43]

In other arenas of citizen participation, we find the same phenomenon—whites disproportionately benefit from new opportunities for citizen influence. In Wichita, Kansas, more whites than minorities know of "policy innovations to increase citizen access to governments"; familiarity with these programs is associated with a greater increase in white than in minority voting; whites are more likely, but minorities *less* likely, to contact government officials after learning about their activities.[44] These results are confirmed in the most extensive study of participation in the United States. "Blacks tend to be overrepresented in the inactivist category, and they are especially disadvantaged when it comes to communal activity and particularized contacting." Translated from social scientese, this means that blacks are less politically active than whites, and the more political activity involves actions "aimed at the attainment of broad community goals" or actions "focused on the narrow problems of their own personal lives," the less active blacks are. These are, of course, the two forms of participation most engaged in by citizens attempting to influence a desegregation plan. The most active citizens (who are disproportionately white) support "government enforcement of school integration" less than the least active citizens (who are disproportionately black) and the population at large. Even if we look only at citizens with high levels of group consciousness and high socioeconomic status—presumably the most efficacious citizens—blacks are much less likely to contact government officials than are whites. Furthermore, white contacters are more likely than black contacters to seek government help on general problems, the solutions to which have broad (presumably favorable) impact on people with like concerns.[45] All of this adds up to the likelihood that policies responsive to citizen participation will gratify white more than black concerns where the two conflict.

Data on government responsiveness show just that result. Among high participators, the concurrence between the preferences of those high in socioeconomic status and government leaders is almost twice as great as the concurrence between low-status citizens and government leaders. Preferences of the lowest participators at all status levels least often concur with preferences of government leaders. That is, if one is both active and wealthy, the government strongly concurs with one's wishes; if one is active but poor, or inactive, the government does not.[46] And whites are much more likely to be active (as we saw above) and wealthy (as we saw in chapter 2) than blacks.

We have moved far from school desegregation and must return. But the point is worth reiterating: citizen planning and advisory groups are generally ineffective, and whites are generally more effective participants than blacks. Thus we should not be surprised to find that citizen planning for desegregation has few positive and many negative effects on desegregation goals. Nevertheless—and here we reach the broadest conclusion about direct participation—the promise of this form of popular control continues to tantalize us.

Policy-makers and analysts endorse incrementalism because it seems the most likely or most effective means of acting in a liberal democracy. Few endorse it for its own sake. Citizen participation, however, is in the eyes of many a constitutive value of liberal democracy. Regardless of whether it is the most effective or typical means of governance, it seems the *best*. The analytic implication of this difference is important. Unlike incrementalism, in which the problem is good implementation of an inappropriate idea, citizen planning demonstrates poor implementation of a good idea.* But the

*This line of reasoning suggests that we *could* improve outcomes for minorities through citizen participation, but only at the cost of lowering white support. That is, in most large cities a truly egalitarian and majoritarian participatory structure might produce good results for minorities, since there blacks and Hispanics equal or outnumber Anglos. Such a structure might, for example, generate a plan that shifts the

substantive implication is even more important. The link between good means and good ends is very tight for popular control and liberal democracy; the risks in trying to reject the means and retain the ends are correspondingly great. In short, the argument against citizen participation brings us more quickly to the new American dilemma of preferred modes of action for a liberal democratic society versus liberal democratic goals than does the argument against incrementalism.

CITIZEN PARTICIPATION IN IMPLEMENTING AND MONITORING DESEGREGATION

If popular control through direct participation does not work early, perhaps it does late, when the wheels have been set in motion and steering is more important than raw power. Calls for citizen involvement in implementation[47] and monitoring are loud and compelling. In the cautious clauses of social science:

> *If quality integrated education with a high degree of citizen involvement is a desired outcome of the desegregation process,* then . . . a broadly representative citizens monitoring group . . . should be at the heart of the activities. . . . Monitoring—especially citizen monitoring—can . . . help shift the locus of control of school systems . . . back toward the local community.[48]

In the expansive phrases of political exhortation:

> Monitoring commissions are helping to fulfill the nation's basic, constitutional obligations. . . . There is not a more noble contribution for citizens to make to their communities. The trial and error experiences with monitoring commissions are the beginnings of a knowledge base and a culture which can advance the citizen's capacity to find effective ways to cope with major social issues.[49]

However, Cassandra once again speaks; citizen participation in

---

racial and class burden of busing, brings parents into school decision-making processes, and restructures the form and content of teaching—all of which local elites, white parents, and school personnel would resist. These contentions are conditional because no such participatory structure exists. It is too radical a vision of popular control ever to have been implemented in the political system of American education. Once again, dramatic change might succeed where incrementalism fails (a connection I owe to David Braybrooke).

implementation and monitoring seldom has a powerful impact on school desegregation. The evidence is by no means unanimous, but it is strong. Consider first citizens' role in implementation. Parents' involvement in desegregated schools, classrooms, or grievance panels improves interracial behavior by minority students,[50] sometimes improves student achievement,[51] and enhances magnet schools' programs.[52]* But parents' programs are problematic. They "tend to fade away over time; . . . teachers and administrators . . . receive very little training in how to relate to parents and involve them more effectively in school affairs; [and] . . . obtaining and sustaining the participation of low-income and minority parents is often difficult since many must travel greater distance and may have employment obligations. . . . In-school parent-teacher committees can and often do become all middle-income or all-white over time."[53] One study, for example, found that in a program to involve parents in their children's education, "the propensity to enter into such partnerships varies according to the socioeconomic status of the families involved." The difference was not related to parents' interest in their children's achievement, but rather to "social and cultural differences in family life and the ways in which schools respond to these differences."[54] Teachers who involve parents of all education levels find them equally effective; teachers who do not, expect that poorly educated parents would not be willing or able to help their children, but that well-educated parents would.[55]

So it is not surprising that citizen involvement often does little good and even a bit of harm. There is virtually no association between the influence of black or white parents on the schools and

*An examination of second-generation discrimination may provide indirect evidence on citizens' positive effect on policy implementation. In Georgia districts with few blacks, black students are disproportionately enrolled in EMR classes, punished, and retained in their grades, and black faculty are underrepresented. "An explanation would be that, in districts with more blacks, their actual or potential influence on local decision making suffices to restrain discrimination in the schools." However, the data also accord with a completely different explanation. "In the most heavily black districts, . . . private, segregated academies have siphoned off the children of . . . the communities' most influential whites." Those who remain in the public schools may be no less racist, but "the ranks of the potential leaders of an antiblack pressure group may be seriously depleted," so the schools feel less pressure to discriminate after the first round of racial balancing has occurred. Whether blacks or "important whites" are influential, the evidence here for citizen control is hardly compelling. Rodgers and Bullock, *Coercion to Compliance*, pp. 117–18.

elementary students' racial attitudes and achievement, except that white students sometimes slightly prefer schools in which white parents dominate, and black students prefer the reverse—hardly an impressive finding. For high school students, the picture is a little more complex. Black students have worse racial attitudes, less racial contact, and less favorable views of their school's racial attitudes as black and (especially) white parents become more influential. Blacks' achievement scores rise slightly, however, when black parents become involved. White high school students are unaffected by parents' involvement.[56] Case studies of "effective schools" find "less overall parent involvement in improving" than in declining schools.[57] The most systematic study of citizen organizations reports mixed but overall unimpressive results. Of 130 groups in forty school districts, only 24 percent had a significant impact of any sort on their systems and 21 percent had no impact (using generous definitions of impact). The rest produced partial changes or plans for them, or simply a heightened awareness among decision-makers of the group's concern. A more rigorous measure of group impact found that among all groups, 42 percent had none, about one-quarter helped to remedy the ill effects of minority isolation, and about one-third affected desegregation success. A majority of the groups in fact made no effort systematically to affect the desegregation plan or its implementation. Only 28 percent of all group activities (only one-third of which addressed desegregation, remember) produced change beyond heightened awareness of problems, or transitory or partial changes in school practices.[58] Sifting through all the figures, one finds that a majority of the groups have some impact on the schools, about one-third facilitate desegregation, and about 10 percent of all activity has permanent consequences for desegregation implementation. Does this represent a surprising rate of success or a discouraging rate of failure? The answer to that question is philosophical or psychological, not statistical.

My research on fifteen court-ordered citizen monitoring groups generates the same frustrating impression of a good idea poorly implemented. I conclude:

- These groups reinforce social and economic inequalities both internally and between the group and the general public. Most members are white, middle- or upper-middle-class, professional, male, well-educated, without children in the city public schools, and already leaders of civic organizations. Minority and lower-status participants sometimes feel at a disadvantage (as in Los Angeles) and the group itself may seem a bastion of upper-class or professional domination (as in Boston and Cleveland, respectively). Thus these groups mainly grant more knowledge and power to elites, although they do provide a chance for a few nonelites to act.

- Being politically representative makes the body ineffectual. For example, the original forty-two members of Boston's Citywide Coordinating Council (CCC) represented all viewpoints on desegregation and consequently spent most of their service "retrying the case." After one year, Judge Garrity effusively thanked them and dismissed all but one member.
- Assuming that their mandate suits their means, monitoring groups of local elites (as in Dayton) or social scientists and lawyers (as in Cleveland) are most successful in reassuring the community, informing the judge, and improving schools' racial practices. These groups define ordinary citizens' role as receiving information or at most identifying problems, not as shaping the nature or direction of their city's desegregation.
- No matter how prestigious or professional, monitors are impotent without strong and consistent backing from the judge. They need court backing to extract information from recalcitrant or inept schools, court insistence on latitude for in-school monitors, and knowledge that their findings significantly contribute to the court's oversight activities. If the court will not impose its authority when needed (as in Dallas), the monitors simply cannot do their job, and they become a detriment to everyone, not least themselves.[59]

But "even Cassandra occasionally nods."[60] Citizen monitoring can inform the court, satisfy some grievances, increase the court's range of remedies and penalties, provide a sounding board for judge, parents, and school personnel, and publicize schools' successes and failings. It provides an entree for civic leaders into the schools; it can make schools physically and informationally more open to parents; it can explicate and justify often mysterious court orders; it can take political heat off the court and draw resisters into solving—not merely pointing out—desegregation problems. Thus citizen participation in monitoring need not be a waste of time, especially when the group has elite members and authoritative backing. The more participatory and grass-roots the group is, however, the less effective it is.

Perhaps the problem here, as with citizen participation in designing plans, is too little popular control rather than too much. We can speculate that citizens have had so little impact on implementation because they have had so little real control. If parents really had power to shape implementation they would, by definition, affect its course. However, that situation is not only conceptually tautologous but also empirically nonexistent, to my knowledge.

The closest that any group has come to extensive citizen control of desegregation implementation is Boston's uniquely ambitious monitoring system. Judge Garrity set up a four-tiered system, with a racially and ethnically balanced parent council in each school, nine subdistrict groups, and two districtwide bodies. The system is generally described as a failure. Battles among the groups over boundaries and agenda too often preclude any focus on the schools or the desegregation plan, and most parents and school personnel ignore the monitors when they are not berating them. School-level elections often lack candidates and attract a tiny fraction of potential voters. For example, in October 1975, "although letters announcing the election [of school council members] were sent to 80,000 parents, less than 3,000 parents turned out to vote. Only 1,326 of the 2,000 council seats were filled."[61] Robert Wood, the sole member of the original CCC to be retained in its second incarnation, was named its chairperson and subsequently served as school superintendent in Boston; he describes the parent groups as "training grounds for local politicos—they are simply an alternative to coming up through the ranks of ward organizations."[62] Some school councils include members of the antibusing organization and so are embroiled in retrying the case.

The picture is not entirely gloomy; some school- and subdistrict-level groups have had notable success in involving parents, publicizing problems, providing information, and promoting changes in their schools. So if Boston is a generalizable example, it is not utopian to seek widespread participation among previously powerless citizens of all races. But it is extraordinarily difficult for them to accomplish anything worthwhile.* As Robert Wood puts it, "Some specific projects proved successful. . . . Still it is fair to say that the role of comprehensive oversight eluded us. . . . Good intentions abounded; and, as predicted, so did randomized behavior."[63]

To summarize, citizen participation in implementation resembles citizen planning. Most desegregation experts recommend it, many districts have tried it, and a few have benefited therefrom. The evidence does not show, as it did for incrementalism, that the idea is inherently flawed when applied to desegregation, but it does show that, except in unusual circumstances, the game is not worth the candle.[64]

LEADERSHIP

What about the reverse side of the coin, leadership? If grass-roots popular control does not work, does control by an elite? This question is crucial for both theory and practice. Theoretically, if neither popular control nor authoritative leadership work well to desegregate schools, then I can draw no conclusions about popular control per se. Practically, if neither works well, policy-makers are at a loss; if one works well (or better), we have policy levers to manipulate.[65]

The answer to this crucial question, unfortunately, is "maybe." Few observers disagree with the oft-quoted dictum of the U.S. Commission on Civil Rights:

> Perhaps the most important ingredient in successful school desegregation is leadership, both at the community level and in the schools. . . . The record shows that where such leadership exists, desegregation is more likely to be achieved with minimal difficulty. Where it is lacking, on the other hand,

*One feature of citizen monitoring—the role of in-school monitors—does foster a sense of popular control despite minimal effect on legal compliance or policy implementation. In Cleveland and Denver, for example, several hundred residents have been trained and deployed by the monitoring body to go into the schools and report back in systematic, verifiable form. The monitoring bodies, not to speak of the court and local elites, sometimes do not take this grass-roots action very seriously, but schools and participants do. Anecdotes and the scanty data available indicate that parent monitors often become deeply involved in school affairs and that their presence makes school personnel more aware of citizens' concerns.

desegregation may be accompanied by confusion, anxiety, and . . . disruption.[66]

The analytic problem, however, is that whereas case studies and qualitative evidence powerfully support this pronouncement, aggregate and survey data show weak, conflicting results. There are good reasons for rejecting, or accepting, either type of evidence; I come down firmly in the middle and remain agnostic.

Let us first examine the evidence that leadership *can* promote desegregation goals. Chapter 4 makes the case for one form—clear, explicit statements by a court or other authority of exactly what is reqired of a school system. "If there is anything that the desegregation experience demonstrates, it is that hierarchically imposed rules can work. In the ten-year period of 1964–1974, the country did move closer to desegregation even if the world was far from perfect. The amassing of federal resources and the clarification of goals and strategies did have an enormous impact."[67] Not surprisingly, backing up these requirements with threats, whether of bringing in federal troops, withdrawing federal funds, citing school boards for contempt of court, putting the school system under receivership of the court, or something else, has the greatest effect.[68] We must remember that hundreds of school systems *have* desegregated, almost none through grass-roots initiative. Thus at the most basic level, it is almost trivial to assert that authoritative leadership reduces racial isolation, given that nothing else does and that considerable physical desegregation has taken place.

Within judicial and regulatory systems, we find the same result—leadership matters. "So long as the Secretary of HEW supported these efforts [to implement the 1968 guidelines for racial balance], OCR was able to apply sufficient pressure to secure desegregation agreements from most Southern school districts. . . . [When] the Nixon Administration began throwing sand into the gears of the desegregation machinery . . . the vigilance and aggressiveness directed toward achieving desegregation" declined.[69] Table 1 (see chapter 2) tells the story (once a lag factor is built in): Southern schools desegregated when pressured by OCR, which was being pressured or at least supported by its boss, Lyndon Johnson. Under a new president, OCR policy and activity changed, pressure let up, and the South stopped desegregating.

In broad outline, the story is similar in the judiciary. District courts became more stringent in the South after the Supreme Court spoke in *Green v. New Kent County* and *Swann v. Charlotte-Mecklenburg*; courts are less definitive in the North because the Court has been silent, inconsistent, or ambiguous in Northern cases.[70]

But an analysis of the role of leaders must go deeper. Federal agencies and judges determine *whether* and *how* a school system will end racial isolation; local leaders affect *how well* it does so. And as we saw in chapter 4, how well racial balance is achieved, and whether the schools move beyond it to other desegregation goals, distinguishes desegregation success from failure.

Case studies almost unanimously assert that actions by local officials and elites may prevent racial violence, enhance community support, smooth implementation, and bolster beleaguered school personnel.[71] In Wilmington for example, eleven school districts and eighty thousand students were peacefully reorganized, largely through the efforts of an informal association of community elites and the leader of a coalition of religious organizations. The religious coalition, the Delaware Equal Educational Process Committee (DEEP), was the "chief counterweight" to the antibusing organization, which was twenty-five times its size. DEEP's driving force was its chairman, the Reverend F. David Weber, who "cajoled, advised, argued, and helped others to work for desegregation." DEEP's unwavering support of desegregation, including busing if necessary, led it to be "eventually shunned by most other groups." Nevertheless, before that point,

> its very extremism gave those other groups more room in which to maneuver. Without DEEP the choice might have been between compliance never and compliance when hell froze over. With DEEP far out ahead, a group like DCSD (The Delaware Committee on the School Decision) [a group of leaders appointed by the governor] that was reluctantly willing to consider making the best of an unpopular judgment could appear neutral rather than dangerously out of touch with the public. . . . [DEEP's] boldness spurred neutral or hesitant groups to work more actively for peaceful implementation; and it also offered practical help with [implementation-related] activities.

The informal association of community leaders, the Breakfast Group, "was acknowledged by many to have been a significant factor in the desegregation process, for it established a . . . sorely needed . . . structure in which key leaders could reach agreement on implementation issues."[72]

Conversely, leaders' refusal to facilitate desegregation can make it almost comically disastrous. The Keystone Cops have nothing on the antics of officials competing to see who can be most recalcitrant, as the study of one city showed:

> Mayoral candidates often emerge from the school board. Mayors, therefore, have some stake in making the school board "look bad." . . . The school board, for its part, has little interest in making mayors "look good."
>
> Desegregation became entwined in these conflicts . . . when school officials refused to comply with federal and state regulations and substantial funds were forfeited. This had a greater impact on the city than the schools. . . . [Conversely,] the mayor, fearing that the school board was "using the desegregation process . . . to its own advantage by planning imprudent spending and claiming a relationship to desegregation," . . . proposed cuts. . . . The judge approved some . . . [but] refused to approve the teacher layoffs. . . .
>
> At this time, the mayor recommended a school department supplementary appropriation that was substantially less than the board's request. The board then ordered a halt in all desegregation related spending that exceeded the mayor's proposed cuts necessitating court authorization of desegregation related expenditures. Less than two weeks before the scheduled opening of school, the school board received a letter from the deputy mayor which reasserted the cuts. Claiming that this prevented them from making the necessary implementation preparations the board again ordered a spending halt. The judge, however, was "not impressed" and ordered school officials to make the necessary appropriations.
>
> Eleven days before the opening of school, the deputy mayor's assistant sent another letter to the school department's chief of personnel which voided the hiring of the additional temporary teachers. In court, the city called for a full evidentiary hearing on the number of teachers actually needed. The judge responded that with only days before the opening of school there was hardly time for such a hearing, and ordered the mayoral assistant to appear in court the next day. That day though, the deputy mayor sent another letter to the school board indicating that the city would pay for the teachers.[73]

Is it any wonder that this city (anonymous in the study) has had one of the nation's most tumultuous, bitter, educationally and socially harmful experiences with desegregation?

But despite convincing anecdotes, aggregate data show little effect of local elites on citizens' response to a desegregation order, or on the nature of the order itself. In fifty large districts across the country, the support of local elites for desegregation has a weak, nonsignificant effect on the amount of elementary school desegregation, no effect on the amount of secondary school desegregation, and no effect on white flight at either level, during or after implementation.[74] Florida parents' perceptions of national leaders' support is unrelated to whether they support, consider avoiding, or actually flee desegregated schools.[75] Community elites' preferences are unrelated to the amount of coercion needed to desegregate Georgia school districts.[76] In ten Northern districts, local elites' pronouncements on desegregation in the year before court- or HEW-ordered implementation had little effect on community protest. In fact, citizen protest seems to generate leaders' statements (usually opposing mandatory desegregation) more than leaders influence (supposed) followers. Furthermore, leaders' statements had no effect on white flight, once the extent of desegregation and white protest were controlled for.[77]

A few studies do show leaders' actions to have effects. In ninety-one Northern cities with desegregation controversies before 1972, the mayor's support for desegregation, the local elite's support, and general elite activity in the city were all significantly related to the schools' likelihood of taking desegregative action.[78] Mayors who actively work for civil rights have a strong impact on school systems' actions to desegregate, and mayors with liberal attitudes (regardless of their activity level) have a weak but noticeable impact. The attitudes of civic elites have a strong impact and their actions a weak one on schools. They also affect citizens. Inactive, conservative mayors are associated with greater white opposition; active, liberal elites are associated with greater support and less opposition.[79] ESAA-funded groups are more likely to act as advocates (and thus to have an impact on their school district's desegregation activities) if the groups are highly visible in the community, are covered extensively by local media, and have a leader with personal influence independent of his or her role as the organization's leader. These characteristics of an elite group, however, have no direct effect on the group's impact. In other words, organized elites do not directly influence desegregation success, but they may do so indirectly by making their group more willing to confront the school system than groups which lack such an independent base.[80] If we consider the media to be one form of community elite, we find further evidence of leadership influence—albeit negative. That is, the more the media emphasize problems in school desegregation, the more white flight and parental opposition the district encounters.[81]* Finally, although data from the U.S. Commission on Civil Rights are suspect because they are so saturated in politics, a commission survey of a national sample of school superintendents is worth noting. It shows a clear, strong association between local leaders' supportive or neutral positions on desegregation and the absence of serious disruptions in these districts.[82]

So far, I have been discussing local leaders who are not part of the school system. But how about school officials; do they have an impact? The guidelines for the Los Angeles school board assert, "*Public commitment to school desegregation by school authorities . . . will facilitate community acceptance* . . . [and] discourage organized community resistance."[83] Again, case studies support this claim. In Mobile, Alabama, to cite only one example, school board resistance throughout the 1960s ranged from prohibiting school personnel to participate in prodesegregation groups to refusals to obey court orders to develop a desegregation plan and expand bus service. The board's actions encouraged violence by the White Citizens' Council, defiance by white parents, and boycotts of judicially-desegregated schools by white students. By 1971, the Supreme Court had issued a final ruling, and a new school board chairperson had been elected and a new superintendent appointed. The new chairperson "decided to fulfill his responsibilities," and the board began immediately to devise a real desegregation plan. The school system and NAACP signed a consent decree, and the superintendent

*Some case studies show a different picture of the media. In Denver, Cleveland, and Charlotte-Mecklenburg, for example, the press has been persuaded to report positive consequences of desegregation and to point out problems of the school system that have been falsely attributed to desegregation. Observers and actors in these cities credit positive (and increasingly knowledgeable) media coverage with lessening white fears and promoting community support for school changes. See, for example, Lisa Meyer, *An Analysis of the Media Activities of the Cleveland Public Schools, Phase II* (Cleveland, Ohio: Office on School Monitoring and Community Relations, 1980).

launched a concerted public relations campaign to generate white support. Schools opened in September 1971 with more desegregation, less violence, and more concern for educational quality than at any time during the previous fifteen years.[84] Obviously many things happened during this period, and the precise influence of school authorities cannot be parceled out. But their role—in both resistance and compliance—seems indisputable.

Analysts of aggregate data do try to parcel out the influence of school authorities; their results sometimes show positive, sometimes no, and never negative effects. In Georgia, school boards' evaluations of the legitimacy of the Supreme Court's desegregation order and their support for law-abidingness in general are not related to the degree of coercion required to desegregate the schools. School authorities' preferences regarding desegregation are, however, associated with coercion, although not in a simple linear fashion. Hiring a new superintendent increases the amount of desegregation change the next year.[85] Similar results obtain for fifty large districts nationwide; superintendent and school board support is strongly related to desegregation change (especially at the secondary school level and in the South), and hiring a new superintendent is weakly related.[86] In ninety-one Northern cities, racial liberalism of school boards increased desegregative pupil reassignments but had no effect on actual levels of school segregation in 1972.[87] Superintendents who take a strong leadership role have a powerful impact on their school systems' actions to desegregate.[88] Only 6 percent of school districts in which the school board endorsed an imminent desegregation plan report serious disruptions, compared with 28 percent of districts in which the board opposed the plan.[89] White Floridians' perceptions of school officials' attitudes toward desegregation are weakly but significantly related to their evaluation of "the way desegregation has been handled around here." Perceptions of school officials' views have more effect on blacks' approval of desegregation implementation than any other variable measured.[90] However, white flight is not related to perceptions of school authorities' attitudes.[91] Nor is it affected by the actual attitudes of school officials or by hiring a new superintendent.[92] Abstracting from their particular features, these data all support one conclusion: school officials have more observable impact on desegregation success than civic elites do, but the findings are hardly robust and compelling.

Local elites, then, can affect the nature of, response to, and consequences of a desegregation plan—but support beyond descriptive case studies for this "obvious" statement is surprisingly thin. Why are the data so ambiguous?

Consider, first, substantive explanations. There are at least three powerful reasons to expect local elites to influence desegregation success. The first is affective:

> The civic elite has power simply because it is an elite; it has the respect of large segments of the community and the ability to influence them. They [*sic*] are living examples of the local community's value system. . . . Almost by definition you [*sic*] are above partisanship. This position prevents elites from advancing extremist views. Therefore, when they endorse school integration it becomes accepted as a non-extremist program; it is legitimate.[93]

This argument should hold, if it does at all, even more forcefully for school authorities than for other local notables, since they combine the prestige of elite status with the prestige of professional expertise and institutional authority. So if they endorse and facilitate school desegregation, parents might be expected to go along. Such apparently is the case—or at least was in the less-alienated early 1960s. In eight cities from 1960 to 1966, where school authorities presented the idea of desegregation as "a proper goal of the educational system" and the fact of desegregation as accomplished government policy, whites accepted it. Once a board promulgated a plan, "from that point on, any response had to be to a governmental decision. Government decisions are legitimate; for many people this is enough to settle the issue." Conversely, where they ignored, rejected, or polled the citizenry on desegregation—thus denying it the mantle of educational or legal authority—"the issue becomes a matter of competing demonstrations, . . . a show of hands on integration. . . . The conflict that emerges from such confrontations frightens most people away, and many whites say no to the whole disturbance, including the idea of integration, which 'caused' it."[94] In this view, then, community leaders can influence the path of a desegregation plan simply by virtue of being leaders.

The second reason to expect elite influence is cognitive. Citizens not swayed by deference and emulation may act on rational calculation. The point is made most forcefully through one of the "negative goals" of desegregation: "the violence occurring with desegregation so far has been surprisingly 'rational.' That is, violence has generally resulted in localities where at least some of the authorities give hints beforehand that they would gladly return to segregation if disturbances occurred; peaceful integration has generally followed firm and forceful leadership."[95] Furthermore, if citizens are led to believe, as many apparently were in Boston, that political action can overturn court orders, then it makes perfect sense for them to resist. After all, we are all taught that public opinion does and should shape our laws; it takes careful education to teach frightened and angry parents that the unfamiliar form of a court order is not subject to the same rules as an unpopular law.[96]

Finally, political leaders may be the only actors with the personal skills and institutional resources to induce compliance when neither emotion nor cognition moves citizens to acceptance. Crudely speaking, mayors control police forces, which have obvious effects on rioters. More subtly, "the large working class cities of the Northeast and Midwest . . . require the skills of a political leader or 'entrepreneur' . . . to peacefully implement the plan and bridge the gulf between the fiercely independent, working class, ethnic enclaves and the black community. In most of these cities, the only person with the resources and the skills to do this is the mayor." Thus as desegregation is increasingly a matter for large Northern cities, its success increasingly depends on political brokerage.[97] The same analysis holds for leadership by school authorities. Desegregation success depends as much on smooth implementation as on intelligent design. School boards and superintendents are the only actors with the resources and authority to make administrators, principals, and teachers play their parts. If they lack the skills or will to induce compliance and promote good outcomes within the schools, and to convince parents and community leaders that the education process is good and improving, acceptance outside the schools will be materially diminished.[98] Here, too, the more desegregation comes to center on large urban systems, the more leadership skills will affect success.

Conversely, there are two equally powerful reasons to expect local leaders to be irrelevant to desegregation success, or even to follow rather than lead the citizenry. First, it is plausible that people are more affected by their own circumstances, neighborhood environment, and very local opinion leaders than by pious emanations from districtwide, never mind national, elites.[99] But neighborhood opinion leaders in white communities are more likely to oppose than support mandatory desegregation. Thus, ironically, the paucity of findings about the positive effect of local elites may be due to the more powerful negative effect of less visible, even more local, leaders.

Second, even if citizens listen to local leaders they find little to hear, and not much of that supports desegregation. Elite endorsement varies inversely with white reassignment to black schools; the less burden on white students, the more white leaders support the plan. Thus "studies that find leadership support of school desegregation to facilitate peaceful implementation may be confusing the effect of leadership support with the effect of a token plan."[100] Even more important, local elites make "few leadership statements one way or the other. Most leaders avoided the issue, and the only positive statements about social [*sic*] desegregation made by city leaders were in response to negative statements by other leaders."[101]

Leaders in various positions have different reasons for the same silence. Elected officials fear defeat in the next election, and it is small comfort to them to know that after a few years antibusing candidates no longer win elections even in cities as resistant to mandatory desegregation as Boston and Louisville. School boards with high social and occupational status—arguably the most influential and racially liberal boards—generate less desegregation even than low-status boards; apparently high status produces political conservatism and responsiveness to the business community's desire to avoid "disruptive" change and the "degradation" of white schools.[102] School superintendents see desegregation as a political, not an educational, issue whose main effect is to disrupt their (relatively) smoothly functioning systems and to threaten their authority and even their jobs.[103]

Findings of a paucity of leadership have both methodological and substantive implications. Methodologically, few data points and little variation among them makes statistical analysis unlikely to detect even as much influence as exists. In addition, aggregating all cases of leadership across cities may obscure the importance of infrequent but powerful acts by leaders. It is possible, then, that even when leaders *do* speak out and *are* influential, the nature of quantitative social science enquiry does not fully show their effect. But the leadership vacuum has consequences much more significant than making life difficult for researchers. It refutes a key element of the anomaly thesis: even the (presumably) best and brightest Americans are reluctant to take the personally and systemically risky steps necessary to eradicate racism through school desegregation. Local elites can have effects, and the more who will speak out in a community, the greater their effect and the less their personal penalties. But high-profile support for a program that is anathema to one's primary constituency and that might fail is hardly a strategy favored by politicians. And if they will not provide the push that Myrdal and Allport described as essential to get the rest of society moving, then a key element of the anomaly thesis is lacking.

We have not only substantive but also analytic reasons for the ambiguity of findings about the effect of local leadership. Case studies can pick up subtleties of influence and control that aggregate and survey data miss, and their unanimity on the importance of leadership is impressive. But surveys and aggregate data are less subject to observers' political and theoretical preconceptions, and their findings of weak or nonexistent influence by leaders is cautionary.

What, then, are we to make of these conflicting data? What role leaders play is probably the greatest gap in our understanding of desegregation.[104] We have few data and fewer theories to explain when, how, on what points, and with what impact leaders speak out. Are the nature and consequences of authorities' actions influenced by their personal skills and commitment, the nature of the plan, the demography of their school district, their place in the local power hierarchy (to name only a few possibilities)? Let me emphasize once more the importance of this issue; the policy implications of finding that *neither* leadership *nor* citizen participation affects desegregation success differ profoundly from the implications of finding that leadership works and participation does not.

I can offer with certainty, then, only a fairly weak conclusion. Local leaders are less authoritative than they could be, but nevertheless "community leaders and elites . . . have more impact on the school desegregation decision than do the masses."[105] My judgment is that leaders *can* effectively promote desegregation goals, *if* they choose to do so. We are back to the new American dilemma. The desirable method of policy choice—citizen participation—does little good and some harm; the less desirable method—authoritative leadership—is efficacious if leaders choose to lead. The problem is one of willing the means needed to reach our goals, not of inability to achieve them.

The discussion of leadership is not complete until we consider one final forum—the role of educators in reaching desegregation goals *within* schools, once the races are no longer isolated. I treat this topic separately for two reasons. It is less central than other forms of leadership to my theoretical focus, the role of popular control in racial justice, and its lesson is clearer: what educators do in schools makes a difference. School authorities can sway outcomes for students, despite the profound importance of socioeconomic status, family environment, and other nonschool factors affecting children's achievement and attitudes. Every study of effective schools shows principals' and teachers' roles to be pivotal. Prescriptions for just how to exercise that role vary with the study, school, and personal style of the actors, but authorities who provide high expectations, strong guidance, a focus on the tasks of achievement and interracial understanding, repeated evaluations, and a powerful presence are always part of the formula for success.[106] Improvements in students' achievement are always desirable and especially important in placating and even gratifying parents reluctant to desegregate children. For once, common sense, case studies, and aggregate analyses concur: leadership in schools has good effects on the results of schooling.

Evidence on leadership for specific desegregation goals is as unequivocal as evidence on leadership for effective schools in general. I need not rehearse individual studies; they sum to the following findings (from highest to lowest levels of school authority):

- "Relatively more influence in the [desegregated] elementary school of the school board and/or the superintendent of schools is associated with [black and white] student achievement."[107]

- "All students of desegregation agree that principals play a key role in the effectiveness of desegregated schools."[108]

- "The one single variable which seems to have the largest impact on students' racial attitudes is teachers' racial attitudes."[109]

Prescriptions abound for making educators even more effective; they include a high-level office responsible for desegregation implementation, in-service training for principals and teachers, new curriculum and instructional materials, improved evaluation techniques, new disciplinary and counseling practices, release from bureaucratic routines, better systems for involving parents in the restructured schools, and so on. If this list sounds familiar, it is because I am reaching the same conclusion I reached in chapter 4 from another direction: more change (of the right kinds) is much better than less.[110]

Until now, I have addressed one form of popular control—direct citizen participation in planning and implementing desegregation—and its converse, authoritative leadership. The former works poorly at best, and sometimes causes harm; the latter works well at best, and sometimes has no effect. In both cases, the problem is one of poor implementation rather than inappropriate methods. Egalitarian, democratic, potent community participation might generate better outcomes for minorities and a sense of efficacy for everyone. But such participation seldom, if ever, occurs. Authoritative, committed leadership might generate compliance among reluctant whites and better outcomes for everyone. But such leadership is risky, so it, too, seldom occurs. We are left with an unsatisfying conclusion: leadership benefits desegregation more than citizen participation does, when leaders are willing to lead. We can choose either safe processes or good results, but not both; we face a new American dilemma.

DECISION-MAKING BY LOCAL OFFICIALS

Perhaps defining popular control as direct citizen participation in policy choice and enactment is too stringent. After all, participatory democracy is a dream, almost never a reality (and it is a nightmare, not a dream, to many). The more conventional, less stringent conception of popular control focuses on its indirect forms—routinely held, freely contested elections among competing elites, with both winners and losers appealing to the electorate for victory in the next round. A standard corollary of this view is that the smaller the scale of an election, the more democratic it is. Local elections have few voters, so each person counts more heavily; they have candidates who know and are known to many voters; they can frame issues and tailor solutions to local circumstances; and they make it possible for citizens to gain knowledge, urge proposals, evaluate outcomes, appeal decisions—and throw the rascals out. From left to right, from Tom Hayden to Ronald Reagan, Americans see local electoral decision-making as the answer to a bloated, arrogant, unresponsive federal government.

Thoughtful observers of the travails of desegregation present specific versions of this general case:

> If integration is to be something other than Justice White's "system of pains and penalties," it will necessarily depend upon the educational dynamics of the particular community. . . . Distribute money and establish minimum standards. . . . Beyond that, Washington can only encourage state and local educators, working within their own political frameworks, to . . . resolv[e] questions of race and schooling . . . [by] adopting a course . . . precisely tailored to local needs. These alternatives are sufficiently different to warrant leaving the specific choices in the hands of state and local institutions, whose grasp of nuance is necessarily better than Washington's.[111]

The argument here, note once again, is not that local control will lead to the *most* desegregation, but that (when bounded by constitutional mandates) it will produce the *best* desegregation.

The only problem with this argument is that what it advocates does not work. With a few exceptions, states and communities simply do not take action to end racial isolation and promote positive goals of desegregation. As we have seen, school desegregation in the South proceeded with the speed of a meandering snail until all three branches of the federal government interceded in the late 1960s. The North presents a more complex but similar picture. A few big cities (most notably Seattle) and university towns (Berkeley and Princeton) have mandated desegregation and reforms within their schools, but they are unusual. Large cities or small towns with significant proportions of minority students are hardly the vanguard of the racial revolution. (Neither, any longer, are OCR, the president, the Supreme Court, or Congress, but that only means that very little new desegregation is taking place at all except through district courts.)[112]

Systematic cross-sectional evidence confirms this reading of history. Consider first the basic goal of ending racial isolation. The punchline of a long story is that federal coercion is the most or one of the most important explanations of desegregation change in Georgia, the South, the North, and across the country.[113] Federal intervention can offset the delaying effects on districts of having a high proportion of minority students or of covering a broad area.[114] Even when local governments do impose desegregation, their plans reduce racial isolation only half as much as plans ordered by HEW or the courts.[115]

The Civil Rights Commission poll of one thousand school superintendents confirms these findings. Two-thirds report that desegregation resulted from HEW or federal court pressure rather than from state or local actors (many of whom acted under threat of federal intervention). The courts and HEW took on the hardest cases; over two-thirds of their cases were in districts with more than 20 percent black enrollment, compared to only one-third of the state and local cases. Over half of the state and local cases were in communities that already had low levels of segregation, compared to only one-tenth of the federal cases. Courts reassigned twice as many students as did local or state actors, and HEW reassigned one-and-one-half times as many. As these figures imply, state and local action yielded less change in segregation than did federal action. Locally initiated plans lowered segregation an average of 18 points (on a 100-point scale), whereas HEW and the courts lowered segregation an average of 47 and 59 points, respectively. Local and state initiatives reached only one-quarter of highly segregated public school students, whereas federal initiatives affected two-thirds of those students.

Local desegregation plans have some virtues; they are associated with fewer serious disruptions than HEW or court-ordered plans at all levels of black enrollment, all levels of change in the amount of segregation, and all degrees of school board support. Business leaders, white parents, teachers, and school boards all began and ended the desegregation process more supportive of local intervention than of federal intervention.[116] It is hard, however, to interpret these last two sets of results. We cannot say whether disruptions were fewer and support greater because the intervenors were local—a strong argument for local rather than federal action—or whether local and state officials acted only in those districts where they could expect relatively high support and low resistance. Given that ambiguity, we can conclude that the poll data confirm aggregate analyses and case studies—local plans generally reduce racial isolation less than federal plans, and local action occurs mainly in the "easiest" districts. The power of Washington is necessary to offset the power of custom and prejudice.

But the case for local control rests less on the amount of desegregation than on its quality. Here too, however, evidence shows that federal intervention produces better results than leaving reforms up to local initiative (or lack thereof). Although local groups funded by ESAA usually had less impact than non-ESAA-funded (and more assertive) groups, nonetheless almost one-third facilitated desegregation and another third helped to remedy the effects of remaining minority isolation.[117] ESAA-funded human relations projects had at least slight effects on minority students' interracial attitudes and behavior, and where the programs were run well, the effects were considerable.[118] Where ESAA funds were available for three years, and where they were substantial enough to differentiate ESAA-funded schools from others, elementary students had significantly higher achievement scores.[119] Southern districts with ESAA funding showed less racial disproportionality in EMR placement, suspensions and expulsions, and black teacher dismissals or demotions than districts without ESAA funds.[120] More generally, Southern districts whose budgets include a relatively high proportion of federal funds have relatively low rates of disproportionate punishment or dismissal for black students and discrimination against black faculty.[121] By the mid-1970s, OCR learned also to use Northern districts' desire for ESAA funding to compensate for its lack of credible threats against noncompliant districts. By threatening to deny their eligibility for ESAA funds (also CETA funds, on occasion), OCR induced Los Angeles, Philadelphia, Chicago, and New York to desegregate teachers and curtail tracking.[122] It was federal funding, through the ESAA magnet school program, that was mainly responsible for whatever voluntary desegregation has taken place in large cities.

To summarize, we are assured of neither the positive effects of federal intervention on desegregation nor its very existence (as the abolition of ESAA funding in large cities demonstrates). But the basic finding is clear: desegregation is much more likely and "second-generation" problems less likely to occur if the federal government acts rather than permitting local governments to make policy decisions. Increasing popular control by decentralizing decision-making can come only at a high cost to desegregation success. Once again, the anomaly thesis is called into serious question.

Why do local officials not desegregate their schools? Many do not want to. The Georgia desegregation study found that variation among white school authorities' desegregation preferences had little effect on the amount of coercion needed to desegregate because the variation was so small. Few endorsed the change, and none sought it out. Furthermore, only one out of 116 white school officials perceived any support in his community for desegregation.[123] This finding suggests a corollary to the observation about officials' own preferences. Mayors and school boards win elections presumably because a majority of the voters endorse their views on controversial, highly visible issues. Most whites and some minorities oppose mandatory desegregation; whites are more likely to vote than blacks and Hispanics. It would indeed be surprising to find elected officials publicly supporting a change that most of their politically active constituents oppose. (If they do support such a change, they may cease being elected officials—another reason why local authorities seldom desegregate on their own initiative. Those who do work for desegregation risk recall or defeat in the next election; the category of "elected officials who support desegregation" has a built-in self-destruct mechanism, so to speak.)

These dynamics of the local electoral process augment the role of the federal government; officials who are unwilling to risk political suicide sometimes seek out a "federal requirement" to get them off the hook. In the words of a Justice Department attorney:

> If a board of education member says "OK, we'll desegregate," how long is he going to be on the board? Board members really are representatives of their communities and you can't expect them to be much more than that. . . . I'm sure many of the school boards we sued would just as soon have filed [a desegregation plan] and gotten on about their business rather than waste the school district's money, but they had no choice. They would have been kicked off the board and someone worse would have been put on.[124]

Some local officials do not want to desegregate; others want to and as a consequence either stop being officials or increase the likelihood of federal intervention; still others have no strong opinion but nevertheless also do not engage in very much desegregation. Members of this third set are, above all else, politicians. A successful politician brokers competing demands. The most likely outcome of a little pressure to desegregate and a lot of pressure not to is a little but not a lot of desegregation. And that is exactly what we find in almost all districts that initiate any desegregative steps—partial plans that are completely voluntary and that end up placing more burdens on minorities than on Anglos.[125]

In short, local officials do not desegregate precisely because popular control is, in fact, effectively exercised. The populace (or at least a majority of voters) does not want mandatory desegregation, and accountable local officials act accordingly. So why do federal officials, some of whom are also elected, work to desegregate schools? This is a harder question, and one I can only begin to answer.

Some national politicians (like some local officials) act out of simple moral commitment. President Johnson was one; Senator Lowell Weicker (R-Conn.) is another. They are not as likely to lose their offices as are local politicians who behave the same way, because their election does not hinge on one (or at least this) volatile issue. President Johnson's civil rights stance paled beside the issue of Vietnam; Senator Weicker's civil rights stance is acceptable in a state with no city facing a mandatory desegregation plan. Others who share the same moral commitment gravitate toward nonelective positions precisely so that they will not be subject to popular control. Observers describe OCR officials as, "in essence, prosecutors who felt a moral duty to enforce vigorously the civil rights law. . . . Especially after the agency's experience in the Southern school desegregation battles, many OCR leaders . . . became . . . committed 'ideologues.' . . . [They] have a commitment to basic ideological goals which are not easily modified or compromised."[126] Local governments may also contain committed idealists in relatively safe administrative roles, but there are simply fewer positions with both independence and leverage in local school districts, and many more school districts than civil rights ideologues. Finally, some of the federal officials who produce the results I have been describing are judges. They operate in a rather different fashion from elected politicians and civil servants, and I will address them in the next section. In sum, not all federal officials endorse desegregation, and those who do cannot act with impunity. Nevertheless, federal officials are relatively less vulnerable to short-term public opinion on this issue than local officials are, so if desegregation is going to come from anywhere in the United States, it is more likely to come from the top than the bottom.

I have implied so far that action by local governments is preferable to, because more democratic than, action by the federal government. The inefficacy of local government therefore seems unfortunate. But perhaps that implication is not warranted. Ever since *Brown*, equal educational opportunity has taken on the coloration of a constitutional mandate. The famous paragraph in *Brown* is:

> Today, education is perhaps the most important function of state and local governments. Compulsory school attendance laws and the great expenditures for education both demonstrate our recognition of the importance of education to our democratic society. It is required in the performance of our most basic public responsibilities, even service in the armed forces. It is the very foundation of good citizenship. Today it is a principal instrument in awakening the child to cultural values, in preparing him for later professional training, and in helping him to adjust normally to his environment. In these days, it is doubtful that any child may reasonably be expected to succeed in life if he is denied the opportunity of an education. Such an opportunity, where the state has undertaken to provide it, is a right which must be made available to all on equal terms.

The Supreme Court set limits to that mandate when it stated in *San Antonio v. Rodriguez* (1973)[127] that "at least where wealth is involved the Equal Protection Clause does not require absolute equality or precisely equal advantages " across school districts and that "education, of course, is not among the rights afforded explicit protection under our federal Constitution. Nor do we find any basis for saying it is implicitly so protected." Nevertheless, American policy-makers and citizens increasingly treat elimination of gross disparities in education as an issue appropriate for federal and state intervention. Not only desegregation but also aid for handicapped, non-English-speaking, poor, female, and college students have become national concerns during the past few decades. In state capitals as well as the federal Capitol, courts and legislatures have acted to reduce disparities in school financing across districts. One can, then, view historical precedent and similar policies as support for endorsing, not merely reluctantly accepting, federal rather than local action to desegregate.

Normative arguments for federal intervention are, however, more compelling than empirical ones. Quality education and perhaps equality of its provision are public goods, "inherently communal, . . . a fundamental right of the individual and duty of the collectivity. . . . [Education is] fundamental . . . in the processes of allocating opportunity, status, fulfillment, and respect. . . . we do now have something very close to a national right to education, enforceable by a deprived citizen against the local school authority, based on federal statute."[128] Furthermore, if anything can eliminate the arbitrary unfairness of some school districts and some whites being forced to desegregate and others not, it is federal laws universally enforced. The problems caused by the occasional poor fit of a universal standard to particular circumstance are surely preferable, politically and ethically, to the problems of a controversial standard applied at random or with a class bias. Popular control defined as local action is not only ineffective; it is also not entirely desirable.

DECISION-MAKING BY ELECTED OFFICIALS

Popular control defined as citizens' choice of accountable decision-makers has a dimension other than locus of control. Elected officials are more responsive to the populace than are appointed ones, especially those with lifetime tenure. That is, policy-making by legislators and executives can be described as more democratic than policy-making by bureaucrats and judges. Applied to the case of school desegregation, this line of reasoning becomes a claim that presidents, Congress, mayors, and elected school boards should plan and implement desegregation. Senator John East speaks for many when he says,

> Certainly one of the basic premises of representative government, which is the basic symbol or concept of the American democratic tradition, is that major and sweeping and pervasive policy decisions ought to be made by the legislative branch through the deliberative process. It has the merit of being able to have all points of view brought in to build consensus and to be able to measure an infinite variety of perspectives. . . . Those areas where we have had the greatest public alienation and antagonism have come where issues

have been determined in this very difficult and sensitive area by court edict or bureaucratic edict. I think this is true in the area of busing. . . .

In a democratic society, what is the point beyond which you can[not] force people to do something that by their own judgment is uncalled for, unwarranted, indefensible, and has nothing to do with what they feel is an honorable, fair, and legitimate understanding of the Constitution? There have got to be limits to how far one can go in a democratic society in imposing a solution that publicly is very distasteful.[129]

How to fit judges into a liberal democracy is an ancient and honorable debate, extending back at least as far as Alexander Hamilton's *Federalist Paper* number 78 and the Anti-Federalists' response. But I will limit myself here to the role of the judiciary in school desegregation. Opponents of judicial activism argue that the Supreme Court, and therefore district and circuit courts, have so exaggerated the original mandate of *Brown* as to blow it far from its original and philosophically justified moorings. In this view, courts have taken a clear and correct constitutional mandate—"The equal protection clause requires laws to be color-blind"—and twisted it to mean its opposite—"The equal protection clause requires laws to be color-conscious, so long as the race being benefited is black." This shift, in the eyes of some constitutional scholars, is bad logic and worse philosophy.[130] It is also self-defeating policy; the courts' exaggeration of their mandate has destroyed the consensus on civil rights that made the early 1960s so impressive,[131] increases rather than decreases racial separatism,[132] and threatens the prestige and independence of the judiciary.[133] In short, "federal courts . . . who sit at the center . . . and run other people's lives so casually"[134] have turned the unquestionable constitutional mandate of *Brown* into demands that meet the standards of neither liberalism nor democracy—a strong critique indeed.

But critics of judicial activism in desegregation cases do not stop there. They argue that courts exceed their capacity as well as their legitimacy: "the courts are being asked to solve problems for which they are not institutionally equipped or not as well equipped as other available institutions."[135] Judges are ill-suited for making social policy because, among other things:

- They are generalists, not educational experts. In desegregation cases, either they are excessively legalistic, thereby ignoring crucial issues of educational quality, or they make naive or arbitrary educational judgments, thereby inhibiting educators from using their expertise.

- They are not politicians or administrators. They lack both the theoretical knowledge and the practical experience needed to run a large organization and juggle interest group demands. They therefore set unrealistic or counterproductive requirements for organizational change which inhibit the desegregation process.
- They are geared more toward determining guilt or specifying rights than fashioning remedies. In most civil cases, remedies are single acts that flow almost automatically from the finding of guilt. But in desegregation cases, remedies are complex, on-going, and unobvious; they have unintended consequences; they are not always complied with; and one often cannot even determine whether they are being complied with or not. Judges and traditional legal procedures are not equipped to deal with such messy situations.
- The kind of information that judges are used to is often not helpful in these cases. Most cases focus on specific individuals, flagrant abuses of rights, particular historical (and usually untypical) facts. But desegregation cases need to deal in social facts, that is, "recurrent patterns of behavior," or consequential facts, "those that relate to the impact of a decision on [future] behavior."[136] Thus the judge's well-honed ability to draw conclusions from a single circumstance serves him or her poorly in evaluating trends, probabilities, and institutional contexts.
- Courts have inherent rigidities. They cannot choose their cases; once in a case, they must move slowly, with all due process; their procedures encourage adversarial rather than negotiating stances; they have only a few blunderbuss enforcement capabilities; they are poor at drawing lessons from each other's experiences; and they cannot backtrack or change their minds.
- Public law litigation and class action suits create ambiguities. Who do the plaintiffs and defendants speak for? Who do the lawyers speak for? Where, if at all, can affected third parties or members of the affected class with differing views enter the process? All actors in these cases purport to represent a broad segment of the population or broad and important interests, but they may not represent anyone beyond themselves.

• Finally, the explosion of litigation that overburdens judges from Manhattan's family courts to the Supreme Court is due at least partly to the new fad of public law litigation. School desegregation cases and similar cases on prisons, mental hospitals, and sex discrimination take an enormous amount of time, and each begets similar cases in other jurisdictions.[137]

The critique is powerful and sweeping, but each element can be answered. Constitutional lawyers argue that court orders mandating racial balance and other changes within a school system are logical successors and essential supplements to *Brown*. Simply abolishing obvious de jure segregation does nothing to remedy the evils of prior discrimination and obeys the Fourteenth Amendment in name only, not in fact. Even the cautious Burger Court notes that equitable principles require that a remedy "directly address and relate to the *condition* offending the Constitution" and that "pupil assignment alone does not automatically remedy the impact of previous, unlawful educational isolation."[138] Proponents claim that public law litigation, far from being chaotic and unwieldy, provides a deliberative forum for expressing a wide range of interests and concerns, for carefully sifting facts, and for tailoring remedies to wrongs—all under the direction of a judge who is both independent of and attuned to the political context.[139] The Supreme Court can control its workload, and in any case, the explosion of litigation has more to do with private grievances (and an excess of lawyers) than with social impact cases. Courts are the ultimate repository of liberal values and an essential constraint in a democratic society. And so on. Arguments and rebuttals multiply and do more to employ scholars and law review editors than to settle the issues they raise.

We can escape this endless debate by turning to the evidence. It is persuasive: were it not for courts, there would be little reduction in racial isolation, especially in big cities and the North. Simple arithmetic shows that if by desegregation we mean active remediation, not merely the passive abolition of segregative laws, we need courts. In one sample of 113 cities, courts ordered three-quarters of the plans that were more than token. Court-ordered plans on average reduced segregation more than board-ordered plans, and districts that reduced segregation most had acted under the mandate of courts, not HEW or school boards.[140] The overwhelming majority of documented desegregation efforts in large districts up to 1976 (81 percent) came about at least partly because of a suit or a court order.[141] The Civil Rights Commission poll of school superintendents shows courts more visible even than HEW (and much more so than state and local actors) in the hardest cases. "More than half of the court interventions took place in districts with enrollments above 40% black, compared to 23% of the HEW-pressured districts and 11% of the locally-initiated plans." Courts were six times as likely to be involved in urban districts as HEW was (although no more likely than state and local groups). They were twice as likely as HEW, and four times as likely as state and local actors, to be involved in districts with very high initial levels of segregation. Courts also generated the most change, mainly because they reassigned more students (although, contrary to popular belief, they did not bus more students) than did HEW or state and local actors. Segregation declined under court orders from an average of 74 in 1968 (on a scale of 1 to 100, with 100 being total segregation) to an average of 15 in 1972. Although the total remains slightly higher, the change was much greater than in HEW cases (from 56 to 9) or state and local cases (30 to 12). Courts reached half of all highly segregated students in 1968, compared to 16 percent for HEW and 24 percent for state and local actors.[142]* In short, by 1978, "the Justice Department could report that approximately 200 school districts with . . . more than 5 million students are presently operating under court-ordered desegregation plans,"[143] and these tend to be districts with the largest numbers and highest proportions of blacks, the highest levels of initial segregation, and low levels of remaining segregation. Not a bad record for an incompetent, ignorant, rigid institution.

*Court intervention is associated with higher levels of serious disruption then HEW or state and local plans. Business leaders, Anglo parents, teachers, and school boards are all less supportive of court-ordered desegregation both before and after it takes place than they are of HEW or state and local intervention. As I noted in the previous section, however, the data have not been analyzed in a way that permits us to determine whether it is court intervention per se, or the fact that courts intervene in the most difficult cases, that generates disruption. Similarly, we cannot tell if citizens oppose court intervention per se, or if courts intervene in districts with the greatest white opposition. For all of these groups, however, the reduction in opposition over several years is greater in districts where courts intervened than in districts where HEW or state and local authorities intervened. See U.S. Commission on Civil Rights, *Reviewing a Decade of School Desegregation, 1966–1975*, pp. 82–104.

In heavily minority or urban districts, courts generated less white flight than local or HEW plans (pp. 74–81).

The more sophisticated statistical technique of regression analysis reinforces these simple comparisons. Coercion by a federal court is a more powerful determinant of desegregation change than any other political, demographic, or geographic variable, especially in the South and in secondary schools.[144] It also significantly affects the amount of desegregation reassignment and the actual level of school segregation in the North even when other factors are controlled for.[145] Court-ordered plans may[146] or may not[147] increase the amount of white flight, probably depending on the amount and nature of mandatory busing (especially for whites), the proportion of blacks, and the availability of alternatives.

But this evidence only begins to resolve the controversy over the proper role of courts. No one doubts that courts *can* mandate racial balance. The issues are whether they ought to do so, and how well they do in designing both techniques for racial balance and the intraschool changes that must be part of a successful desegregation process. The first question—whether courts ought to mandate racial change—restates the basic question of this book: does our society will the means, even if they are relatively undesirable, necessary to eradicate racism through school desegregation? If the answer is yes, court intervention is legitimate because necessary; if no, then court intervention is illegitimate even if necessary. I will discuss this point further in the next chapter. Here I focus on the second issue: how well do courts design and oversee plans so that schools achieve desegregation goals beyond ending racial isolation?

The evidence is mixed and murky. I know of few systematic and no statistical analyses of how or how well courts design and oversee plans, so I must rely on case studies and qualitative judgments. Cases in which courts have done badly—demonstrating rigidity, shallowness, naiveté, or some other serious flaw—are easy to find.[148] These stories are cautionary, to say the least. But they may not be typical or even common. Many—most—of the several hundred districts that have desegregated under court order or prodding have done so without generating horror stories. Furthermore, "judicial arrogance" and intervention appear to emerge not through spontaneous generation but in response to school administrators' recalcitrance or incompetence. Judges, at least by their own telling, are not eager to rush in where angels fear to tread. They are reluctant to take on desegregation cases—one has maintained that he would rather handle any other sort of case—and hesitant about issuing orders once they have taken on a case. The California Supreme Court's unanimous opinion in *Crawford v. Los Angeles* is quite clear:

In light of the realities of the remedial problem, we believe that once . . . a school board has implemented a program which promises to achieve meaningful progress towards eliminating the segregation in the district, the court should defer to the school board's program . . . [and] stay its hand even if it believes that alternative techniques might lead to more rapid desegregation of the schools. . . . *In the absence of an easy, uniform solution to the desegregation problem, plans developed and implemented by local school boards, working with community leaders and affected citizens, hold the most promising hope for the attainment of integrated public schools.* . . . In those instances, however, in which . . . a local school board has not embarked upon a course of action designed to eliminate segregation . . . , [when] school authorities default in their constitutional obligations to minority children, a court has no alternative but to intervene.[149]*

A classic case in which a court "has no alternative but to intervene" is Boston. The Boston School Committee refused to submit desegregation plans, refused to implement plans imposed on it, and refused to solve problems caused at least partly by its earlier refusals. Once Judge Garrity had taken the first step of ordering mandatory desegregation, he was drawn inexorably, even if unsuccessfully, into taking further steps to try to make his initial orders succeed. It is

*More personal testimony by Federal District Judge James B. McMillan about the Charlotte-Mecklenburg case (over which he presided) tells the same story:

I grew up . . . accepting the segregated life which was the way of America for its first 300 years. . . . I hoped that we would be forever saved from the folly of transporting children from one school to another for the purpose of maintaining a racial balance of students in each school. . . . I first said, "What's wrong in Charlotte?" . . . I set the case for hearing reluctantly. I heard it reluctantly, at first unbelievingly. After . . . I began to deal in terms of facts and information instead of in terms of my natural-born raising, I began to realize . . . that something should be done. . . . I have had to spend some thousands of hours studying the subject . . . and have been brought by pressure of information to a different conclusion. . . . Charlotte—and I suspect that is true of most cities—is segregated by Government action. We need to be reminded, also, as I did remind myself in 1969, that the issue is one of constitutional law, not politics; and constitutional rights should not be swept away by temporary majorities.

Hon. James B. McMillan, Statement to Senate Judiciary Committee, Subcommittee on Separation of Powers, *Hearings on Court-Ordered School Busing*, 97th Cong. 1st Sess., 1981: 511–17.

simply disingenuous to blame him for judicial imperialism or for the problems of the Boston schools in "isolation . . . from the more fundamental social and political problems of which they [courts' actions] are at best symptoms."[150]

If we lack systematic data to decide either that courts usually make a bad situation worse or that they usually do the best job anyone could in the circumstances, we can at least draw two conclusions. First, judges are getting much better at handling institutional reform litigation. They are learning to evaluate and use (or ignore and work around) social science data.[151] They are reshaping old forms of assistance, such as special masters, magistrates, and court experts.[152] They are inventing and refining new institutions, such as monitoring bodies and desegregation administrators.[153] They are becoming more activist—searching out intervenors or *amici curiae*, proposing compromises to the parties, questioning facts and the representativeness of litigants, negotiating settlements.[154] They engage litigants in designing remedies that they can live with. They are inventing modulated punishments (such as awarding attorney's fees or removing a particular official) and rewards (reducing monitoring or reporting requirements, lessening their own involvement) for defendant school districts. They are developing techniques to allow them or their agents to evaluate compliance and consequences of previous orders; they are changing orders where necessary.[155]

These new or newly refined institutions, processes, and skills go a long way toward solving the problems of courts' incompetence. Court experts gather and interpret "social facts." Special masters design and oversee complex remedies. Desegregation administrators penetrate the political and bureaucratic activities of school systems. Monitoring groups permit oversight, compliance reviews, and even incremental change where desirable. Conferences and seminars make judges familiar with these new forms of litigation and each other's actions and effects. Litigants' involvement in designing remedies permits negotiation, nuance, co-optation, and restructuring. None of these responses to the list of judicial flaws cited earlier works perfectly, but all make critiques of court competence sound faintly out of date.[156]

In the case of school desegregation, we find, in fact, that courts sometimes produce better policies than do other institutions. A systematic court-ordered plan may be more efficient than an ad hoc school board plan (as in Los Angeles). A court may order a state to finance educational improvements that the district cannot afford and legislators and mayors will not support (as in Detroit and Los Angeles).[157] A court can give school officials the power to make curriculum and organizational changes that they have wanted to make all along but could not, for political or bureaucratic reasons.

In fact, the only systematic comparison of educational policy-making by courts, legislatures, and bureaucrats gives surprisingly high marks to judges in education cases in general, although the authors do not address school desegregation:

- On the issue of principled versus political decision-making, courts do not overstep their bounds. In only three of sixty-five cases examined did plaintiffs base their requests for court intervention on policy arguments rather than on constitutional or statutory principles. They were denied relief in all three cases. Over half of the remaining cases based on principle also raised "subsidiary policy issues," but the courts tended to ignore or reject them. OCR, in contrast, is more ideological than principled, and state legislatures are mainly engaged in balancing interests.
- Concerned parties participate as much in judicial as in legislative proceedings, and more than in OCR proceedings: 57 percent of the cases had more than one plaintiff and defendant, and courts readily accepted intervenors and *amici*. On issues that came before both state legislatures and judges, the same parties appeared in both forums, and all of the views aired in one setting were also voiced in the other. OCR, however, permits virtually no intervention by interested parties in its compliance reviews and negotiations with school boards.
- After the judge has made a liability decision, parties negotiate remedies in legal cases concerning education. OCR also negotiates remedies with the school districts involved, and it has a "pragmatic, grass roots orientation that is lacking in the judicial process." The authors count this as a virtue of OCR (and the legislatures, which resemble OCR); my discussion of incrementalism suggests that here, too, the courts may come out ahead.
- The judicial discovery process, in which lawyers can subpoena or

request relevant documents, provides courts with enough "social facts" to make good decisions. "The evidentiary records accumulated in the court cases were more complete than the factual data obtained through hearings and other methods of the state legislatures." OCR gathers even more information than do the courts, at least where it makes a substantial commitment to do so.

- Most judges use "avoidance devices" that obviate the need for them actually to interpret and use all the data accumulated in the courtroom. Where they have used complex data, "courts appear to be better equipped than legislatures to evaluate social fact evidence systematically and to render analytically reasoned decisions." OCR is more prosecutorial in its initial use of data, but by the time it begins to negotiate, it is impressively "impartial and pragmatic" in its analyses and interpretations.
- Judges are not particularly intrusive. They entered remedial orders in forty-one of the sixty-five cases studied, but only fifteen required ongoing judicial supervision. Where extensive reform decrees "were issued, since the defendants or related public agencies substantially participated in their formulation, we concluded that the courts serve largely as catalysts and mediators for processes that are basically undertaken by the affected school officials themselves."
- Compliance levels are high. In the forty-one cases with court orders, there was "full compliance" in thirty-two, partial compliance in the remaining nine, and token or no compliance in none.
- Judges have a "wider range of coercive tools that can be fine-tuned to the needs of particular remedial situations" than OCR has. In addition, courts can be involved for a long period of time if need be, can retain jurisdiction to permit new hearings or changes in their decree, and can set up extensive reporting requirements. OCR has the same capacity in theory, but is subject to political upheaval; legislatures are much more volatile and have much shorter attention spans.[158]

I have cited this analysis so extensively because it is, to my knowledge, unique in its comparison of educational policy-making across the three branches of government. It demonstrates that many criticisms of judges' capacity to reform institutions are unsubstantiated, and that judges are no less capable and sometimes more adept than other actors. Courts are by no means ideal policy-makers, but it is a long and unwarranted step from that statement to the claim that they create worse desegregation outcomes than do the alternatives.

The second conclusion about courts' capacity is that courts often do more than any other political institution to remedy the ills of racism. The problem of courts' overwork is in large part the reverse side of the coin of other officials' underresponsibility; citizens turn to courts because they have found school boards, legislators, executives, and private actors unresponsive. Courts become "the agency of last resort . . . to guarantee actual receipt of the benefits or entitlements that have been promised by the system" but not delivered. They are also seen as a better source of "value clarification" than their alternatives—"the balancing of competing social interests in the legislative process or the bureaucratic inertia of the administrative process."[159] Even critics of "activist courts" sometimes agree that they are not to blame for their excessive involvement: "It is when the court is able to define the constitutional right to an education free of discriminatory school board action—and then confidently to expect the school board, the state commissioner of education, or other state or federal officials or agencies to formulate and implement the requisite changes to implement that right—that the role of courts can be reduced to more traditional dimensions. The failure of political leadership to play that proper role has led to the expansion of equity jurisdiction; only a reversal of that failure will lead to the contraction of equity jurisdiction."[160] In short, judges become intrusive to the degree that other actors become invisible.

Debates over how to fit bureaucrats into liberal democracy are not as ancient (or as honorable) as debates about judges, but they are just as heated. The core argument against bureaucratic decision-making is simple: to have popular control, public officials must be within reach of citizens (generally through elections), so that their actions can be rewarded or punished. Since bureaucrats are relatively insulated from the public, they can more easily go off on their own tangents. Thus, critics argue, by 1968 zealots in the Departments of Justice and HEW had moved far beyond what Congress, most citizens, and even the Supreme Court wanted, to illegitimately redefine the Civil Rights Act to require specific racial outcomes, not merely color-blind laws and programs.[161] For similar reasons, appointed officials in local communities are less responsive to the public and are more attentive to friends and their own wishes than are local elected officials. They are too quick to "move children around like pawns on a chessboard," as a frequently used metaphor puts it, and too slow to respond to citizens' grievances.

Once again, though, unimpeachable arguments run into contradictory evidence. If by desegregation we seek remediation beyond a passive end to discrimination, we need appointees. Elected officials by definition respond to constituents; when they stop being responsive, they stop being elected officials. Regardless of their own beliefs, representatives of mainly white constituencies cannot afford to be in the vanguard of civil rights.[162] Stated thus baldly, this claim is too strong, of course. Two presidents lobbied for, and several Congresses passed, tough civil rights laws. Senators occasionally defy public sentiment—witness Lowell Weicker's 1981 filibuster against antibusing and court-limiting bills. State legislatures sometimes seek to end racial isolation—witness Massachusetts's 1965 Racial Imbalance Act.[163] But Congress regularly proposes and sometimes passes legislation to deny federal funds, staff, and even court jurisdiction to pursue mandatory desegregation. No president has endorsed, and several have condemned, "forced busing." Their political calculations are clear; when a reporter asked John Ehrlichman for the "hard evidence" that led to President Nixon's opposition to busing, Ehrlichman answered, "This is the front burner issue in most local communities. . . . Now that is the evidence. It carries by such a preponderance that it cannot just be swept under the rug by some sort of statistical evasion."[164] Conversely, once OCR and the Justice Department began to desegregate the South in 1968, their staffers became increasingly committed and adept. It took firing the director of OCR for newly elected President Nixon to halt the bureaucrats' momentum.

Electoral incentives and their effects are as evident in local governments as in Washington. HEW plans reduce segregation twice as much as even districtwide school board-ordered plans.[165] Appointed school superintendents needed less coercion to desegregate Georgia schools and countenanced less second-generation discrimination than did elected ones.[166] In the North, governments run by a city manager have perhaps been associated with more student reassignments than governments of strong mayors, probably "because a reformed political structure [that is, one less dependent on election outcomes] is better able to cope with issues that are divisible."[167] Reform governments also affected the amount of desegregation in the South in 1968, although they did not influence desegregation change between 1968 and 1972. Cities in which the school system is included in the municipal budget and is therefore presumably subject to political pressure, showed little desegregation in the South in 1972 or in the North in 1968. They also showed less change between 1968 and 1972 than cities in which the school system is independent.[168] In general, elected school officials desegregate less than appointed ones, and cities where school policy-making is subject to popular control show less change than cities with relatively insulated policy-making processes.

The effect of elections on school board activity is mixed but tends toward the same conclusion. Appointed boards have more blacks than elected boards and are located in the least-segregated school systems.[169] Administrators who answer to appointed boards are more willing to act as trustees—to ignore public opinion in favor of their own judgment about policy choices—than administrators responsible to elected boards.[170] Appointed boards either do,[171] do not,[172] or do in the North but not in the South[173] desegregate more rapidly than elected boards. These mixed results may indicate a complex political process in which, in the right circumstances, popular wishes unite with board insulation to generate desegregative change. That is, there is some evidence that heavily black Northern districts run by the city and facing federal pressure respond to black demands if their boards are insulated from white electoral backlash.[174] Demands from some of the public may be met if policymakers are protected from counterdemands by the rest of the public—an odd, constrained notion of popular control at best.

Upon reflection, these findings should not be surprising. In fact, they should reassure those who value pure procedural democracy over particular outcomes. Roughly speaking, popular control works; elected executives and legislators do less to facilitate and more to impede desegregation success than do nonelected judges and bureaucrats. The catch, of course, is that success for popular control means little change in racial isolation and racial injustice. Blacks know this—why else have they relied on the courts (and, at times,

OCR) in their drive to desegregate schools? Judges and bureaucrats may be the least desirable agents for affecting desegregation success, except for legislators, mayors, presidents, and the general citizenry.

CONCLUSION

It is harder to draw conclusions about popular control of policy choice than about incremental methods of policy enactment. One reason is methodological: we have few rigorous studies of the effects of citizen participation on ending racial isolation, and very few indeed of its effects on goals beyond bean-counting. The influence of leaders, the impact of parents, the effectiveness of courts—all involve complex, subtle processes that are very difficult to measure and extremely difficult to disentangle from other processes. So we fall back on opinion surveys, case studies, or comparisons among a few cases—analytic methods even more prone to ideological bias or simple sampling error than are quantitative data analyses. The evidence is thin, and it is hard to tell whether contradictions among studies and findings of no relationship reveal methodological flaws or real phenomena.

A more interesting reason for my difficulty in drawing clear conclusions is that I really come to two opposite conclusions based on the two different types of popular control. Electoral accountability presents a problem structurally similar to that of incrementalism. It works all too well. There are more whites than minorities; whites register and vote more than minorities do; whites oppose mandatory school desegregation more than minorities do. Thus it is a rare school district indeed in which majoritarian elections yield policies requiring racial balance. The more perfect the means of popular control, the worse for racial equity.

However, the problem with direct citizen participation in policy choice may be different. If participants mirror the relevant population, we encounter the problem just described, writ small. In the more interesting (and typical) case, however, participants emerge because of their interest, expertise, visibility, personal connections, or some other nondemographic reason. Here the problem is too little democracy, not too much. That is, citizen groups seldom have any power, and when they do they usually act in the interests of the most powerful members of the group—who are more likely to be high-status whites than low-status blacks or Hispanics. *If* citizen participation were efficacious, and *if* all viewpoints were equally represented, popular control might produce excellent results. The problem here, then, is poor implementation of a good idea.

A third difficulty in drawing conclusions is that the solution to the problems of popular control are not as clear as they are for incrementalism. Political and educational leaders affect the design and success of a plan—probably, if they choose to. Courts effectively oversee ongoing remedies—probably, if they are lucky, skilled, and determined. Federal bureaucrats can successfully ignore local idiosyncracies and pressures—probably, if they retain sensitivity and common sense, and supportive bosses. Nothing is certain. But what is mainly at issue here is authorities' volition—whether they choose to solve the racial problem, not whether it has solutions.

That point leads us back to my basic question: do Americans will the means necessary to achieve our ends? Gunnar Myrdal and other subscribers to the anomaly thesis answer "yes." Ordinary American citizens will find it difficult and painful, but ultimately they will choose to follow their consciences and their greatest leaders in eradicating racism from their midst. Democracy, perhaps after a nudge from the Supreme Court or world opinion, will vindicate the American Creed. But the evidence in this chapter calls this belief into question. White Americans apparently do not choose to eradicate racism by mandating school desegregation, even after receiving considerably more than a nudge. The final and most important obstacle to my drawing conclusions in this chapter is that I with other Americans am reluctant to jettison popular control. Incrementalism makes good sense, but it is not the stuff of Fourth of July speeches. "Democracy" is. Nevertheless, if most citizens choose not to grant the rest of the citizens their full rights, then perhaps democracy must give way to liberalism. We turn now to that issue.

SIX

Where Do We Go from Here?

If we are serious about this business of public education, we know what to do. We know how children learn. We know how to teach. We know that the real issue is the reconstruction of an education system so that it addresses the needs of a pluralistic society. . . .
Dare the school build a new social order? . . . Probably not.

—Geraldine Kozberg and Jerome Winegar,
program director and headmaster,
South Boston High School.[1]

There is nothing new under the sun. After writing this book I discovered that, like so many social scientists, I had reinvented the wheel. In a 1956 reflection on New Guinea, Margaret Mead observed:

A . . . contribution of the Manus experience is the suggestion that rapid change is not only possible, but may actually be very desirable, that instead of advocating slow partial changes, we should advocate that a people who choose to . . . enter into drastically new kinds of . . . relationships will do this more easily if they . . . [have] the transforming experience of entering a world where everything [is] different. . . . Partial change . . . can be seen not as a bridge between old and new, something that permits men, slow to learn and fumbling at the unfamiliar, some respite from the unbearableness of change, but rather as the condition within which discordant and discrepant institutions and practices develop and proliferate—with corresponding discrepancies and discordancies in the lives of those who live within them.

Just as the survival of some parts of an old pattern tends to reinstate the rest, and so continually acts as a drag on the establishment of new habits, so also the establishment of part of a new pattern calls for other congruent elements, facilitates their establishment, and each element supports the

> other. . . . [Thus] some drastic alteration in a culture . . . —land ownership for sharecropping, *non-segregation among castes for a former rigid segregation*—may well work best if . . . accompanied by as many other congruent changes as possible.[2]

And even before the Supreme Court's 1954 *Brown* decision, Kenneth Clark reviewed all known cases of desegregation and derived principles uncannily like mine. First, his views on incrementalism (all in his words):

- Longer time periods for preparation may be accompanied by greater rather than lesser difficulties.
- Segmentalized "gradual" desegregation not only does not insure the "effectiveness" of desegregation, but . . . increase[s] the chances of resistance and resentment of those whites immediately involved.
- The larger the scale of the desegregation, the greater the likelihood of general acceptance or the lack of overt resistance.
- Effective desegregation in one area . . . of a community does not necessarily bring about a desegregated pattern in other areas . . . of that community.
- Active resistance, and sometimes violence, though rare, are associated with . . . ambiguous or inconsistent policy.

Next, on popular control:

- Court-determined desegregation is as effective, if not more so, than desegregation due to other causes. In fact, desegregation resulting from the decision of Federal Courts has more extensive effects than voluntary desegregation.
- Active resistance, and sometimes violence, though rare, are associated with . . . ineffective policy action, [and] conflict between competing governmental authority or officials.
- The accomplishment of efficient desegregation with a minimum of social disturbance depends upon:

  A clear and unequivocal statement of policy by leaders with prestige and other authorities;

  Firm enforcement . . . by authorities and persistence . . . in the face of initial resistance;

A willingness to deal with violations . . . by a resort to the law and strong enforcement action;

A refusal of the authorities to . . . tolerate . . . devices for evading the principles and the fact of desegregation;

An appeal to . . . religious principles of brotherhood and . . . acceptance of the American traditions of fair play and equal justice.

Clark concluded that "wherever desegregation has occurred under the above conditions, it has been consistently evaluated as socially beneficial or otherwise successful."[3]

With the exception of the clause about "religious principles of brotherhood and American traditions of fair play and equal justice" (which suggests the distance we have come from Myrdal-type optimism to contemporary cynicism), Mead or Clark could be writing an abstract for chapters 4 and 5. So I cannot claim originality. I can, however, claim what both of them could not: thirty years of experience and an overwhelming number of studies validate these propositions. It no longer suffices, as it might have in 1954, to counter one plausible proposition with an equally plausible but opposite one. We can now say with a fair degree of certainty that Clark and Mead were right and that the gradualists (such as the Supreme Court in *Brown II*) were wrong.

But there is little use crying over spilt milk. The important question is Martin Luther King's: "Where do we go from here?"[4] Three possible prescriptions emerge from this analysis: continue muddling along as we have since 1968, with some but not too much positive action to desegregate; stop trying to impose desegregation on unwilling whites and ambivalent minorities and do something else instead; or learn from the evidence and fully—in several senses of the word—desegregate. Let us examine each possibility.

Note first, however, one prescription that I do not consider worth careful discussion. It is a return to the era of benign neglect which mostly characterized school desegregation policy in the decade after *Brown*. One could (falsely) conclude from the evidence I have described that partial desegregation harms minorities and whites, that full desegregation is impossible in the United States today, that the condition of blacks has improved since 1950, and that therefore the government should withdraw from active intervention and let natural instincts toward racial integration take over. The first three clauses of that sentence are largely right; the last is completely wrong. The condition of blacks does not improve through natural processes in the United States. We talked about the gradual abolition of slavery for two hundred years; slavery spread and deepened. We talked about gradual betterment for emancipated slaves; Jim Crow laws spread and deepened. We talked about natural housing integration; old, large cities are now more residentially segregated than they were forty years ago.[5] Very few whites deliberately put themselves and their children in positions to discover whether their fear and dislike of blacks are warranted. Very few whites will voluntarily give up, even in the unlikely event that they recognize them, the political, economic, and emotional advantages that come from being the preferred race in a segregated society. School desegregation—and the general obliteration of racism and its effects—will not happen naturally. Rejecting mandated racial change will leave blacks stranded in ghettos and whites stranded in suburbs. Such an outcome is politically, morally, and psychologically unacceptable if we can do anything about it.

CONTINUE MUDDLING ALONG

So where *do* we go from here? Can we do anything about racism? Muddling along seems the most likely but least desirable future. We will probably continue to desegregate some students and schools in some places, with a few educational reforms and considerable white flight, through a mix of federal and local elective and nonelective leadership, for the same reasons that we have done so in the past. Our system of policy choice is, at best, one of popular control and our policies are therefore fundamentally incremental. By this I mean several things.

At the most basic level, popular control means just that—the preferences of a majority of citizens are transformed, *mutatis mutandis,* into government policy. Most Americans are white; most whites resist large-scale or mandatory school desegregation. It is a backhanded compliment to the viability of majoritarian democracy that school desegregation seldom occurs through channels of popular control and seldom takes the form of large, system-shaking changes.

At a slightly more subtle level of analysis, one can argue that the United States is not a majoritarian but a pluralist democracy. We modify majority rule to give most interested actors some voice in policy choices that affect them deeply. From the perspective of the political theorist, pluralism is a virtue of American government; "the existence of multiple centers of power, none of which is wholly sovereign, . . . may . . . be necessary to tame power, to secure the consent of all, and to settle conflicts peacefully."[6] From the perspective of the beleaguered educator, pluralism is an endless series of cross-pressures, as one handbook for "making desegregation work" inadvertently demonstrates (see figure 3). And from the perspective of this book, pluralism is important because it gives interested actors some influence over what will not happen as well as what will. This "dispersion of veto powers throughout the political system . . . makes even incremental moves difficult and insufficiently frequent. This same structure, moreover, makes drastic, less incremental moves even more difficult—ordinarily simply impossible."[7] Thus white opponents, teachers' unions, business and civic leaders, the NAACP, school boards—all induce some changes and prevent others. Mandatory transportation is ordered, but some parts of town or some children are exempted; faculty are desegregated, but seniority rules remain intact; resources shift among schools and from the city to the schools, but hierarchies are undisturbed, and so on. Pluralist politics lead, at most, to incremental changes.

But even this description of American politics is naive in its assumption that all interested parties have roughly equal influence. Some argue that influential participants do not in fact represent all interests and values in the population. Instead, they share dominant interests and values that conflict with those of subordinated people, and their mutual accommodation gives the lie to people who find in pluralism a healthy competition of ideas. "In the extreme form, critics allege that policy is set by a ruling class with trappings of pluralist diversity," says Lindblom; like him, I "find it hard to deny a large core of truth in that criticism."[8]

There are two points here: participants share values that contravene those of nonparticipants, and some participants have much more influence than others. Consider the second point first. I do not

Fig. 3. Educators' Relations with Various Groups in Improving Desegregation

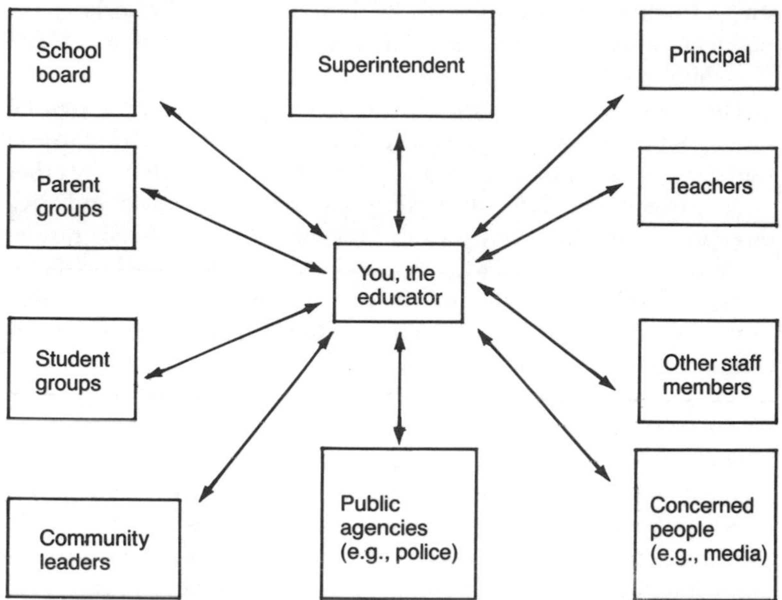

Source: Mark A. Chesler, Bunyan I. Bryant, and James E. Crowfoot, p. 10 in *Making Desegregation Work: A Professional's Guide to Effecting Change.* Copyright © 1981 by Sage Publications, Inc. Reprinted by permission of Sage Publications, Inc.

need to demonstrate a strictly hierarchical community power structure or a dictatorial ruling elite to establish it. All I need to assume is that time passes, that few issues are ever definitively resolved, and that policy actors have normal human impulses. Under these (hardly controversial) assumptions, policy outcomes disproportionately benefit those political actors with the greatest assets, access, and staying power. "Policies usually result . . . not from a few key decisions, but rather from a series of decisions. . . . Decisions at one stage may be negated by the absence of follow-through action. . . . Proposals rejected at one point may be revived, altered, or even replaced by substitute proposals that still enable objectives to be realized. Policy success, then, is rarely a matter of winning spectacular battles. Rather, it is more akin to prevailing in a war of attrition." In these circumstances, actors with the sophistication, resources, and ability to persist usually win; "those groups fare best which are able to acquire detailed information and to maintain an unrelenting pressure on behalf of their interests."[9] These are traits of middle-class, politically organized and practiced interest groups, not of poor black (or white) parents.[10]

The argument goes a step further when we consider the pivotal role of public officials. "No one is in a better position to develop and use the skills of conflict management. . . . They, more than any other group, can manipulate the timing and scope of issues and give direction to conflict" and policy implementation. Officials do not slavishly follow the wishes of local elites, but because they themselves are local elites they are likely to share "predispositions and preferences" with them. They are also likely, in the long run, to be responsive to community members who can consistently and persuasively communicate their views and invoke slight but steady pressure. Poor blacks, however, face the same disadvantages interpersonally as they do temporally;[11] they share less of the officials' world views and concerns and have less time, resources, and opportunity with which to communicate, than do officials' social peers. In short, issues that extend over a long period of time, that involve many interlocking decisions, that pit the more powerful against the less so, and that allow public officials a lot of discretion are likely to produce outcomes that maintain or exaggerate existing structures of inequality. One should not be optimistic about local officials promoting bold new steps toward school desegregation.*

The second element of Lindblom's comment about "the trappings of pluralist democracy" is that powerful and weak actors do not share values about schooling. If they did, disproportionate influence would not matter (except to a pure procedural democrat). At one level, values concur: everyone agrees that children should learn as much as they can in a safe and pleasant environment, get along with peers and teachers, expand their mental and social horizons, and graduate ready for employment and adulthood. But beyond these glittering generalities, values probably differ. Elites seek mainly to preserve the status quo; poor blacks seek to change it, at least enough to gain access to the benefits enjoyed by elites, and at most to restructure the whole system. James Madison said it most elegantly:

*This analysis goes a long way toward explaining why even a court-ordered racial balance plan, which is usually necessary to interrupt these temporal and interpersonal

"From the protection of different and unequal faculties of acquiring property, . . . [which] is the first object of Government, . . . the possession of different degrees and kinds of property immediately results: and from the influence of these on the sentiments and views of the respective proprietors ensues a division of the society into different interests and parties. The latent causes of faction are thus sown in the nature of man; and we see them everywhere brought into . . . activity."[12]

The roles of schools and desegregation are intimately tied up in this classic tug-of-war between the propertied and the propertyless. Desegregation, in fact, may be partial and halting precisely because it is constrained to remain within the boundaries of elite property-holders' values and interests. The most careful formulation of this thesis is Derrick Bell's:

> *The interest of blacks in achieving racial equality will be accommodated only when it converges with the interests of whites; however, the Fourteenth Amendment, standing alone, will not authorize a judicial remedy providing effective racial equality for blacks where the remedy sought threatens the superior societal status of middle- and upper-class whites.*
>
> It follows that the availability of Fourteenth Amendment protection in racial cases may not actually be determined by the character of harm suffered by blacks or the quantum of liability proved against whites. Racial remedies may instead be the outward manifestations of unspoken and perhaps subconscious judicial conclusions that the remedies, if granted, will secure, advance, or at least not harm societal interests deemed important by middle- and upper-class whites. Racial justice—or its appearance—may, from time to time, be counted among the interests deemed important by the courts and by society's policymakers.[13]

When completely spelled out, this argument is as complex as it is controversial, but its main elements are as follows. The United States has, if not a rigid class structure, at least a system of self-perpetuating stratification that largely determines one's life chances at birth. Pub-

---

dynamics, produces less change than first appears likely. Interest groups become involved in designing the plan; school officials implement it; later, smaller, less visible decisions resegregate within the purportedly desegregated school. In these and other ways, even a dramatic and authoritative break from the usual mobilization of bias slides back into politics as usual unless the judge maintains strong monitoring of even "trivial" details.

lic education anchors this system by providing the poorest children with virtually no skills, by training working-class children to be skilled and obedient workers, and by teaching middle- and upper-class children to be managers, owners, and creators. Segregated and/or inferior schooling also keeps most blacks subordinate to most whites.

However, this argument continues, Americans cherish the belief that we have, not a class structure, but an aggregation of individuals with opportunities to rise (or fall) as far as merit and ambition take them. Public education, we believe, is the lynchpin of equality of opportunity because it is both the great leveler—everyone shares it equally—and the great divider—a person can use success in school to rise far above his or her starting point. For blacks, we believe, schooling is the road away from the sharecropper's farm and out of the ghetto.

The fact of class structure and the belief in individual mobility are apparently contradictory but actually reinforcing. That is, our faith that people rise and fall on their own merits allows us to deny the existence of systemic rigidities. Our belief that public education is free, equal, and open to all legitimates the failure of some and the success of others, and it hides the class socialization that schools engage in. Black subordination is a key element in joining belief to fact; keeping blacks poorly and separately schooled reduces job and wage competition, enhances even poor whites' sense of success, and otherwise bolsters our faith in individual (white) advancement. In short, schools both glorify the myth of equal opportunity and prevent too much of it from occurring, and racial segregation sustains the hidden class structure.[14]

Up to a point, school desegregation does not jeopardize, and may even bolster, this happy conjunction of myth and reality. After all, some white elites believe deeply in liberal values and support equality of opportunity across races. They are among our society's most principled members, and the moral health of a society requires that its best exemplars help to shape and be able to endorse its actions. Desegregation also has pragmatic value for the United States. The *Brown* decision was needed, NAACP and government lawyers argued, to "provide immediate credibility to America's struggle with

Communist countries to win the hearts and minds of emerging third-world peoples."[15] *Brown* and subsequent decisions also "offered much needed reassurance to American blacks that the precepts of equality and freedom so heralded during World War II might yet be given meaning at home." Finally, some whites "realized that the South could make the transition from a rural, plantation society to the sunbelt with all its potential and profit only when it ended its state-sponsored segregation."[16] So up to a point, desegregation benefited all of American society and obtained elite white as well as mass black support.

But only up to a point. Pushed too far, desegregation undermines the hidden but pervasive class structure, indirectly by revealing its existence, and directly by attacking the precarious position of poor whites and the privileged position of rich whites.

The direct attacks are the easiest to describe. The simple increase in people with academic and work skills competing for the same number of jobs threatens the opportunity structure for poor whites. And what is true for employment is true more generally; "a remedy that requires change in practical conditions must have some dislocative impact. And a regime of formal equality will insure that the dislocative impact is disproportionately borne by lower-class whites."[17] Formal equality means that everyone has the same formal rights—to send their children to whatever school they wish, to compete for and work in whatever job they deem appropriate, to live in whatever neighborhood they choose. But formally equal rights set on top of actually unequal positions generates different outcomes for different people. Rich and poor alike have an equal right to pay private school tuition or suburban housing costs, but only the rich can do so. Rich and poor alike have an equal right to compete in the marketplace of job openings, but only the poor will be threatened by a sudden influx of newly trained and educated black youths. Too much desegregation harms poor whites' psychological, social, and economic status and jeopardizes their willingness to settle for the meager benefits they receive from a class society.[18]

If it were carried further, desegregation would also directly attack the privileges of the well-off by undermining "the legitimacy of vested rights."[19] Full and complete desegregation would call into question parents' rights to send their children to private schools, teachers' seniority rights, the sanctity of city/suburb school district lines, and local financing and control of schools, to mention only a few sacred cows. Not only poor but also rich whites would have to give up precious components of their class position for desegregation to be complete.

Desegregation's indirect attack on the class structure—its revelation of the hollowness of the equal opportunity ideal—is most dangerous of all. A demand for full and complete desegregation, and the responses to such a demand, unmask the role of schools in perpetuating rather than mitigating the class structure and the structure itself. Desegregation demands expose unwarranted tracking within schools, disparities in resources, expectations, and curriculum between schools, and the strong connections among family background, academic achievement, race, and occupational success.[20] The more blacks focus on results rather than opportunities and on institutional biases rather than individual acts, the more the liberal values of opportunity and individualism appear fraudulent or at best weak.[21] Once these values are questioned, the whole social structure is called into question; once that occurs, the class structure becomes visible and therefore a subject of contention.

A truly liberal society could—must—have desegregated schools and the equal opportunity they permit. But an apparently liberal, actually stratified society cannot pursue full desegregation without revealing its feet of clay. So elites will endorse some desegregation but not too much—which is what we have and are likely to continue having. From this perspective, the American dilemma is neither the one Myrdal described nor the one I am proposing, but rather a third—a conflict between what whites want and what they are told they must do:

> The tragedy of race relations in the United States is that there is no American dilemma. White Americans are not torn and tortured by the conflict between their devotion to the American creed and their actual behavior. They are upset by the current state of race relations, to be sure. But what troubles them is not that justice is being denied but that their peace is being shattered and their business interrupted.[22]

While this analysis of the relation between stratification and school desegregation policy is compelling, the reader need not accept it in order to accept my general argument in this section. I can identify several more mundane reasons to expect the United States to continue muddling along with a little but not very much school desegregation. Our policy-making system is profoundly fragmented. Even those who endorse school desegregation seldom make connections among schooling, housing, and employment; "the extent of mutual ignorance among officials is astonishing. . . . Actual coordination is virtually nonexistent."[23] And this comment refers to only two issues; no one even tries to address the ties among "school change [and] municipal finance, jobs, housing, social services, transportation, human rights, and all the other factors which determine the quality of life in local communities."[24]* In ignoring such ties, we continue to rely on single-dimensional busing plans to paper over racial discrepancies in wealth, physical location, prospects for the future, and so on. We now know that busing plans by themselves cannot even paper over, never mind reduce, these discrepancies, but fragmented incremental politics leads us to continue to do battle over broad problems in separate, narrow arenas—with the result that none are really resolved.

Even if a visionary and self-sacrificing elite or a powerful citizens' group did draw the connections among schools, housing, and jobs and were willing to promote broader changes, it could not. Our structure for enacting policies is too fragmented to change simultaneously many facets of "the quality of life in local communities." Boundaries impede. The Senate Judiciary Committee, which writes court-limiting legislation, lacks jurisdiction over aid to public education, which is the domain of the Labor and Human Resources Committee, and neither can deal with urban blight, which is the domain of the Banking, Housing, and Urban Affairs Committee. City governments often have no control over the school system's

*When in 1979 OCR found the Chicago school system ineligible for ESAA funds because of its continued segregation, David Tatel, OCR's director, proposed a task force to coordinate the flow of federal funds to Chicago. He hoped to use this mechanism to get various federal programs, such as HUD housing subsidies, Community Development Block Grants, and Department of Labor vocational education aid, to reinforce desegregation efforts. He was heeded in neither Chicago nor Washington. For similar recommendations, similarly ignored, see National Project and Task Force on Desegregation Strategies, *State Leadership toward Desegregating Education* (Denver: Education Commission of the States, 1980).

budget, employment policies, or tracking practices. Schools have no control over housing, employment, or urban services. Courts have jurisdiction only in specific localities; unless a suit is filed in a community, no judicial action will take place there. And, of course, the all-important boundary between urban and suburban school districts constitutionally can be breached only under specific and unusual circumstances.

Next, consider the particular nature of school systems. They are loosely coupled,[25] which means that an administrator cannot give a directive and expect it to be implemented in all classrooms. They are full of street-level bureaucrats,[26] which means that their captive clients are profoundly affected by discretionary decisions made by employees under severe resource constraints and conflicting mandates. They are organizationally rigid, which means that they inhibit effective teaching, successful learning, and creative innovation.[27] They provide a public good, which means that everyone must pay for them and be affected by their actions whether they wish to or not. They are political as well as educational bodies, which means that incumbents from the school board on down have no desire to rock the boat and jeopardize their own position and relations.[28] Finally, they educate our children—and few tasks are more important and emotion-laden than that one. Thus many people care fervently what happens in schools, yet no one can really determine what happens even within a single classroom. This is a recipe for small and cautious changes influenced by large numbers of participants with different desires.

Finally, consider the nature of policy innovation. Any new policy passes through a myriad of checkpoints that delay and distort it.[29] Subordinates have different goals and perspectives from superiors, so even (perhaps especially) those with the best of intentions will modify a policy directive to accord with their views.[30] The more reforms that are implemented, the less time and resources an administrator can devote to any one, so the more they elude his or her grasp.[31] New policies require new resources, but time devoted to seeking new resources takes time away from implementing new policies.[32] There is many a slip between cup and lip, especially if the drinkers are not eager to complete the transition.

Even if one rejects the most controversial argument of this section—that schools reify a racist class structure—one can expect the United States to make no more than incremental, relatively less unpopular desegregative changes in the foreseeable future. A majoritarian society gratifies the majority; a pluralist society gives all interested parties a little of what they want; an elitist society gratifies those with extensive resources and powerful positions; a class society maintains systemic inequalities; a fragmented society does very little at all; the polity of the school is uncoordinated and defensive; and any new policy starts out with two strikes against it. Given all of this, we should not be surprised to find that democracy usually dominates liberalism in the realm of school desegregation.

Thus the best predictor of the future is the past. We know roughly the consequences—slight decreases in racial isolation, slight improvements in minority achievement, both improvement and worsening of race relations, continued white and black middle-class movement to the suburbs, and little change in our deeply conflicted race, status, and power relations. Whether this outcome is tolerable depends partly on its alternatives, to which I now turn.

DO SOMETHING ELSE INSTEAD

Muddling along is one of three possible responses to the new American dilemma—the fact that our preferred and routine means for policy choice and implementation cannot successfully desegregate our schools. Muddling along means continuing to use those means and continuing, therefore, not to achieve our ends. One path out of the dilemma is to change our goal. We could keep the basic goal of eradicating racism and its consequences, but decide that school desegregation is not the way to achieve it. We could pursue other school reforms—community control, enrichment of ghetto schools, voucher plans—or concentrate on policies that ignore schools in favor of some other arena—housing desegregation, jobs, welfare reform, or electoral politics. Let us examine arguments for and against this path away from our dilemma.

One reason not to impose mandatory school desegregation is that people do not want it. If what they wanted were clearly racist, we could dismiss preferences as morally unacceptable, but that is not the case. Whites deeply and increasingly endorse racial equality and abjure discrimination,[33] but they also abhor "forced busing." White support for "strict segregation" declined from 25 percent in 1964 to 5 percent in 1978, and white endorsement of desegregation increased from 27 to 34 percent in that period. Nevertheless, white agreement that "the government in Washington should see to it that White and Black children are allowed to go to the same schools" declined from 38 percent in 1964 to 24 percent in 1978.[34] More pointed questions generate similar but stronger responses. For example, 51 percent of whites in 1981 thought black children would do better in integrated schools, 72 percent did not think white children would be harmed in integrated schools, and 52 percent expected that most children would be in desegregated schools within five years. This is not a profile of racial separatists. Yet 79 percent thought busing for desegregative purposes "would be too hard on their children."[35] More data would be superfluous; every study finds the same results.[36] Whites endorse desegregation in general and school desegregation in particular; they expect it to occur; but they object to being required to participate in it. For some believers in liberal democracy, these findings suffice for rejection of mandatory desegregation. If most people consistently and vehemently express a clear policy preference that violates no one's basic rights,they ought to have their way. That, after all, is what popular control means.

This claim is bolstered by evidence that minorities themselves are ambivalent about mandatory school desegregation. Black support for desegregation has *declined* in the past two decades—from 78 percent in 1964 to 55 percent in 1978. Fewer blacks now seek the federal government's assurance of school desegregation; 75 percent did in 1964, but only 60 percent in 1978.[37] In the 1981 Harris poll, blacks agreed with whites that desegregated schooling helps black children (67 percent), does not harm white children (92 percent), and is the wave of the near future (53 percent).[38] But they too have mixed feelings about busing; 61 percent of this sample endorsed it. And even that support may be unusually high; 53 percent of blacks endorsed busing for desegregation in a 1977 National Opinion Research Center(NORC) poll;[39] 56 percent were strongly or mildly supportive in a 1980 Survey Research Center poll.[40] Hispanics are apparently more strongly opposed—only 36 percent supported busing in the 1977 NORC poll.[41]

Qualitative evidence reinforces the survey's depiction of an intraracial split. Blacks are increasingly willing to speak out in congressional hearings,[42] newspaper columns,[43] scholarly journals,[44] public forums,[45] and court testimony,[46] against mandatory desegregation, at least as it has been implemented. Blacks have organized in Boston, Norfolk (Virginia), St. Louis, and other cities to press for neighborhood schools or freedom-of-choice plans. Local NAACP chapters in Atlanta and Norfolk have questioned mandatory busing. In four of thirty-eight cities in one survey, black protests increased after implementation while white protests declined, and in another seven cities blacks were at best ambivalent about the plan.[47] The few blacks who can afford to do so are joining whites in their flight to the suburbs or private schools.*

These findings carry more weight than those showing white opposition to mandatory desegregation. Politically, as they see minority demands diffuse, "many white people have grown hesitant to pursue desegregation efforts. Their rationale is clear: if the victims no longer believe remedies are feasible and, indeed, their victimization can be

*In 1979, 7.3 percent of blacks living in central cities attended private schools (compared to 20.4 percent of whites). Nationwide, 5 percent of blacks and 11 percent of whites attended nonpublic schools. National Center for Education Statistics, *The Condition of Education, 1981*, p. 64; *Statistical Abstract, 1982–83*, p. 149. "For the first time, the rate of black suburbanization exceeds that of white suburbanization" and is accelerating. Twenty-five percent of the black metropolitan population lives in the suburbs; the rate of growth for black public school students is greater in the suburbs than in central cities. Black enrollment in private schools is increasing, while white enrollment is stable or declining. Nevertheless, blacks still represent only 6 percent of the suburban population, and many "suburbs" are simply extensions across city boundaries of inner-city ghettos. See John Herbers, "Census Finds More Blacks Living in Suburbs of Nation's Large Cities," *New York Times*, May 31, 1981: 1, 48; Martin T. Katzman and Harold Childs, "Black Flight: The Middle Class Black Reaction to School Integration and Metropolitan Change" (Unpublished report, University of Texas at Dallas, Southwest Center for Economic and Community Development, 1979); Martin T. Katzman, "The Flight of Blacks from Central-City Public Schools," *Urban Education* 18, no. 3 (October 1983): 259–83; and W. Norton Grubb, "The Flight to the Suburbs of Population and Employment, 1960–1970," *Journal of Urban Economics* 11 (1982): 348–67.

turned to their own benefit through the control of segregated institutions, then why seek desegregation?"[48] Morally, in a liberal society people whose rights are denied should count for more than those who deny them. If large numbers of both have the same policy preference, and if that preference arguably respects individual rights, then liberalism and democracy unite in a call to satisfy it.

Before drawing this conclusion, however, we need to know why so many people, and especially why some blacks, oppose mandatory desegregation even while they affirm nondiscrimination. Setting aside simple racism, the reasons are legion. Consider first the harms to whites and to school systems in general. Despite all the ruckus about amounts of and motives for white flight, "the *fact* that White loss is associated with desegregation in some instances is not in dispute." Furthermore, "the effect appears strongest for central-city districts surrounded by accessible white suburbs, . . . when there is a significant shift in the racial balance of schools, . . . [and a] substantial proportion of Blacks (or minority) students[49]—exactly the condition of the large Northern cities where most desegregation will have to occur in the future if significant numbers of blacks are to be reached. Those who flee, those left behind, and society in general all suffer from this phenomenon. Family plans are disrupted; cities lose middle-class taxpayers; schools lose students and supporters; feelings of community, efficacy, and trust are all eroded.

A second problem is that mandatory desegregation involves new expenses at a time when school budgets are increasingly shaky. Schools must spend scarce resources on new buses, drivers, gasoline, security guards, and other "noneducational" functions. Even though these added expenses are generally orders of magnitude lower than school boards estimate or parents perceive, and even though voluntary plans sometimes cost as much as or more than a mandatory plan would, any new expense for increasingly unpopular schools in increasingly poor cities is questionable at best. And if whites blame higher taxes or larger classes on black demands, race relations as well as school finances suffer.

For other reasons also, poorly implemented (that is, typical) desegregation plans harm race relations. Testimony abounds of both black and white students and parents becoming more racist after hostile and inegalitarian classroom encounters; some systematic data[50] and psychological theory[51] reinforce the horror stories.

The most serious harms from desegregation, however, fall on those already worst-off—blacks, especially poor blacks. One painful irony lies in the effect of desegregation on minorities' self-esteem. A basic argument in *Brown* was that segregated schooling "generates a feeling of inferiority as to their [black children's] status in the community that may affect their hearts and minds in a way unlikely ever to be undone." But evidence seldom shows that racially isolated blacks have impaired self-esteem, and it all too often shows that blacks in desegregated schools do. The most thorough examination of "minority self-evaluation" concludes "that there is no need to assume that blacks suffer from low self-esteem or low aspirations, whether they attend segregated or desegregated schools."[52] Others, however, "find that school desegregation, if it has any effect, lowers rather than raises the self-esteem of black children."[53] In a segregated setting, "those persons who matter most to him [the black child]—parents, teachers, and peers—tend to be black and to evaluate him as highly as white parents, teachers, and peers evaluate the white child. . . . Comparing himself to other economically disprivileged blacks . . .in his immediate context, . . . the black child does not feel less worthy as a person on account of race or economic background. In fact, encapsulated in a segregated environment as are most urban black children, they may be less aware of societal prejudice than is assumed."[54] In contrast, desegregation too often entails removing ghetto blacks from their local schools, transporting them long distances, and depositing them in overwhelmingly white schools. Students and teachers in receiving schools share personal styles and patterns of interaction, expectations that whites will do well and blacks poorly, a history of student (and teacher) success not matched in the schools left behind, and thinly veiled racial and class antagonism. Is it any wonder that such "social disasters" make blacks feel "bitter rejection, isolation, and intellectual incompetence"?[55]

Even schools that struggle to avoid racial stereotyping by holding all students to the same standards usually use middle-class, white standards that unintentionally denigrate blacks (and lower-class whites).[56] This fact may explain the rather startling finding that parents of white participants in one mandatory desegregation plan were somewhat happier with it after implementation than white nonparticipants, whereas parents of black participants were less satisfied than black nonparticipants.[57] The most plausible reason for such a switch in viewpoints is that the plan satisfied the desires of white but not of black participants. Other studies find that whites in dominantly non-Anglo schools may actually benefit from their new minority status. Schools deeply want to retain their "good students," and whites of average ability and status may suddenly be treated as stars. Thus blacks, on average, lose status in the eyes of their peers and teachers and are less likely to obtain positions of leadership and responsibility in the schools.[58] The effects on black self-esteem should not be hard to infer.

These problems help to explain blacks' ambivalence about mandatory desegregation. Black professionals, for example, unfavorably contrast their children's experiences, even in "good" integrated schools, with their own memories of segregated schools. They remember that their teachers "had made very strong demands" and "strongly supported" their aspirations, while they see their own children "facing lower expectations on the part of the teachers," having "reduced confidence in their ability because of the racism they were experiencing," and finding that their own "strong drive for educational achievement was not being reinforced."[59]

We have no systematic evidence on how widespread such subtle or unintentional racism is or how much, alternatively, black parents' perceptions are a function of rosy-hued nostalgia. But two facts should give us pause. First, many blacks *believe* that their children are harmed by required desegregation, and some are acting politically on that belief. Second, the best analysts are only now producing demonstrations of how extraordinarily difficult it is for even the best-intentioned schools to avoid racial put-downs. Most teachers are white and/or middle-class; most desegregated schools are very anxious to retain their middle-class and/or white students; many white Americans expect blacks to be poor, uneducated, and unmotivated; and most Americans assume that (white) middle-class standards of behavior and accomplishment are "correct." Thus blacks as well as whites adopt white, middle-class values, and desegregated schools may especially do so. At least initially, ghetto blacks almost inevitably fall short. We may decide, as parents and as a society, that these *are* the values to which all children should conform and which schools should inculcate, but getting from here to there through desegregated schools has left many more bruises on blacks than on whites.

More easily quantified variables also show harm to blacks from poorly implemented desegregation. Black teachers and staff have been disproportionately fired or demoted when schools were closed or reorganized. A 1971 observer of Mississippi, for example, reported:

> Visible control of the schools is still white; during the past two years, more than half of all black administrators were fired, demoted, or placed in tangential positions. . . . The State Department of Education reports a 5% decrease in black teachers, while independent surveys show the number to be 10–12% . . . [and] predict a 5 1/2% loss of regular teachers (over 1,000 teachers) in the coming year with a disproportionate number in majority black districts. . . . Teacher recruitment from Mississippi colleges also changed. Black colleges placed 38% fewer certified graduates last year according to State Department figures, while white colleges increased placement 52%.[60]

Hundreds of black faculty reportedly lost their jobs when Georgia schools desegregated, and black principals were typically demoted to lower-level schools or to being assistants to white principals at salaries lower than those of white assistants.[61] As many as six thousand Southern black teachers lost their jobs by 1970, and over one thousand black high school principals—more than half the total—were demoted or fired, while at the same time a few states hired white principals.[62] The losses were not only personal but collective: "The Negro principal was a big man. Frequently, he was the only channel of communication between the black and white communities. He shouldered the mantle of leadership in the black community, sometimes by default and not always effectively, but he was the only one with whom the white power structure would deal. . . . Perhaps the greatest impact of the black principal was upon the kids who observed and aped him day after day, and dreamed of standing in his shoes. . . . It was a training ground for leadership which, for a black, was seldom available anywhere. These leadership qualities are invaluable for the black community and the nation, and their loss must be regarded as catastrophic."[63] Litigation and favorable court rulings, especially *Singleton v. Jackson* (1969),[64] have slowed and perhaps halted the removal and demotion of black educators,[65] but as late as 1973 at least 63 percent of Southern school districts (and up to 98 percent in one state) had few enough black teachers to warrant OCR suspicion of faculty discrimination.[66]*

Black students as well as staff are displaced when schools are desegregated. I have presented data on second-generation discrimination; let me underline it with a few more facts. Racial isolation through EMR assignments increases as racial isolation at the school level declines; black EMR assignments vary from 15 percent more than the proportion of blacks in the district would suggest (in districts with fewer than 15 percent or more than 80 percent blacks) to 290 percent overrepresentation (in districts with 15 to 80 percent black students).[67] Punishment of black students also increases as racial isolation declines, at least at the district level: of the fifty largest districts in the country, the only ones that do not disproportionately suspend black students are either predominantly minority or almost all white.[68] The punishment rate soars in a few districts; one study found expulsion of minorities to be three to five times more frequent than that of nonminorities in 42 districts (out of 1200 studied), five to ten times greater in 49 districts, and over ten times greater in 25 districts.[69] A few districts, however, suspend proportionally fewer blacks than whites.[70] Disproportionate punishment may reflect white racism, administrators' fear of racial violence, a first-strike strategy resulting from students' anxiety and tension, black students' different styles of interaction, or black students' poorer self-

*An ironic twist here is that many blacks continue to be fired or demoted, not for racist reasons but in response to mandates to upgrade education for all students. Blacks often—although not universally—have poorer educations or less certification than comparable white faculty and staff; thus black educators may be harmed by attempts to better black education. For example, Florida's new minimum competency test for students entering teacher education programs reduced the number of new students by 25 percent and the number of minority candidates by 90 percent. C. Emily Feistritzer, *The Condition of Teaching: A State by State Analysis* (Princeton: Carnegie Foundation for the Advancement of Teaching, 1983), p. 94.

One cannot oppose a preference for better over worse teachers, of course, but choosing only by test scores does not weigh the value of empathy and expectations (which may be greater among black staff) against the value of credentials in determining that "better" education for black students entails.

discipline and greater propensity for violence. Presumably all of these causes come into play on occasion, but whatever the reason, longer and more frequent disciplinary action hardly benefits the students subjected to it. Furthermore, the evidence that racial differentiation in treatment of students is greatest in districts with the least racial isolation in schools, and that such differentiation varies so much across districts, suggests (although it does not prove) that resegregation depends more on authorities' choice than on students' behavior.

Second-generation discrimination is not only harder to discern than racial isolation, it is also harder to eliminate. OCR and (especially) the Justice Department have never been good at pinpointing and punishing resegregation, and we have no reason to think that they will become more motivated or adept at those tasks in the forseeable future.

A further reason for black ambivalence is not that black children suffer from entrance into a predominantly white school, but that they do not enter such a school. In heavily minority districts, black or Hispanic children are sometimes bused from a minority-dominated neighborhood school to a slightly less minority-dominated school across the city. Such a move may improve racial balance, but from the children's (and parents') perspective, it merely adds the disadvantages of busing to the disadvantages of attending a racially isolated school. Resistance in this case is hardly surprising.[71]

And the deleterious results do not end here. Black schools have been closed[72] or fumigated before admitting white students.[73] Formerly black schools are given new names, songs, mascots, dress codes, and anything else that can be done to erase their history and image. Black students are left out of cheerleading and band (although not basketball).[74] Businesses[75] and colleges[76] are endangered by the *Brown*-inspired belief that white institutions are superior to black ones. Small wonder, then, that a former civil rights lawyer describes school desegregation as "wasteful, dangerous, and demeaning,"[77] or that black scholars conclude that "to accept this principle [racial balance] is to accept an approach which might prove disastrous for Black children and their communities."[78]

One can deem these dismal findings irrelevant if active remediation of past segregation through racial balance (or at least through an end to racial isolation within school districts) is an incontrovertible constitutional mandate. After all, we inhabit, not a majoritarian democracy, but a liberal democracy—which means that preferences or consequences cannot override basic rights. Nathaniel Jones responds to poll data and black antibusers by pointing out that "constitutional issues are, under our form of government, not resolved by public opinion polls or plebiscites." He responds to evidence that desegregation harms blacks by asserting that "segregation is itself the deepest educational harm because it is the result of institutional racism and a condition of state-imposed racial caste." He argues that proposals to ignore racial balance in favor of improving black schools "could have the effect of trading off constitutional rights in favor of expedient, short-term objectives that would result in perpetuating the evil proscribed by law. This constitutes a form of plea bargaining by school systems caught with their hands in the constitutional cookie jar of black children."[79]

But this argument is not as definitive as its proponents believe. Constitutional conservatives can make a respectable case for the claim that the Fourteenth Amendment, *Brown*, and the 1964 Civil Rights Act require only the end of de jure segregation, not official restitution that causes new harm.[80] The Supreme Court hedges its own demand for desegregation "root and branch" with concerns over health and safety of bused students, de facto rather than de jure isolation, and—above all—historical boundaries between school districts. One can make an equally respectable (although not conservative) claim that *Brown*'s mandate was for equal educational opportunity, which may or may not entail desegregated schools, depending on circumstances and alternatives. Judge Robert Carter, a leading attorney in the *Brown* litigation and former NAACP general counsel, argues that in 1954 the plaintiffs and the Supreme Court saw "equal education and integrated education . . . [as] synonymous," but that that view was mistaken. Experience has proven the possibility of having desegregated schools without equal education or integration; perhaps there can also be equal education without desegregation. Carter is not sure of that point, but he warns against "allow[ing] ourselves to become the prisoners of dogma" and insisting on desegregation regardless of its consequences.[81]

In light of all this, I see two powerful reasons for taking the next step, to examine whether we can find alternatives to desegregation that fulfill liberalism's promises. The first reason involves the interaction of race and class. Wealthy whites (and blacks) generally exempt themselves from burden; poor and middle-class blacks, Hispanics, and whites must redeem our unkept promises. But why should the poor—or the doubly shackled minority poor— suffer so that the privileged can retain their immunity? Even if mandatory desegregation benefits participants in the long run, it causes problems and pain in the short run; if it did not, it would not have to be mandated. Until the best-off must live under the policies they make, it is hard to see why the worst-off must do so.

The second reason for seeking alternatives is that the power of minority arguments has made opposition to desegregation no longer synonymous with racism or capitulation to it. An observer of 1974 Boston pointed out that "whites who intuitively support the black community have been faced with a bitter dilemma. No expression of that support seems to make much sense in the current political situation. To argue *for* busing means to condemn black pupils to the role of cannon fodder in a school system that at best brings 'death at an early age.' . . . To argue *against* busing is to go on the line with the most reactionary elements of society; and even if the reasons are different, the common position is uncomfortable, to say the least."[82]

But the political climate has changed in a decade. Some blacks and Hispanics now insist that equal educational opportunity means improved educational quality—with or without Anglos in the same classroom. Some minorities now define "equal protection of the laws" as provision of a setting like whites have, in which they can run their lives and raise their children free from interference by another race. To some, desegregation itself seems a statement of inferiority, a statement that brown or black students cannot learn unless seated beside white ones. Surely the many rich, sophisticated, and considered arguments of this nature ought to matter. After all, liberal democracy can take the form of people creating and controlling their own institutions and rules within the bounds set by basic rights; it need not entail majorities creating and controlling a single community in which all must live.

Let us briefly consider, then, candidates for politically, educationally, and normatively viable alternatives to mandatory desegregation. Begin with the views mentioned in the previous paragraph. From calls for black power in the 1960s to ethnic studies programs in the 1980s, minority groups have kept up a steady stream of demands that they be allowed to design, run, and control their own schooling as they see fit. Sometimes the argument has a political cast: desegregation disperses black or Hispanic electoral and interest group strength, permitting whites to dominate and use minorities for their own purposes. Local schools under minority control, however, would concentrate power, train leaders, and assure that the educational system would act in the interests of the appropriate group. Thus the Atlanta NAACP gave up its fight for mandatory desegregation in favor of black control of the city's public school system.[83] Sometimes the argument is couched in material terms: desegregation means firing or demoting minority staff, closing ghetto or barrio schools, transferring contracts for school materials and services from black to white businesses. But local, minority-run schools would provide jobs, contracts, and employment training to blacks, thereby reinforcing the economic base of the community. The argument may be psychological: minority students are traumatized, and their parents intimidated, by injecting them into a hostile and strange white environment; a local, minority-run school could provide support, high standards, role models, family reinforcement, and fair discipline. There are cultural versions of the argument: desegregated schools celebrate "Black History Week" or teach a few Spanish courses, whereas local, minority-run schools can thoroughly and unselfconsciously teach pride in and knowledge of one's history, culture, and language.

Most important are educational arguments. More frequently and urgently than ever before, black parents and spokespersons are demanding good schools. The presence of white students seems irrelevant, a diversion from the main purpose of learning. W. E. B. DuBois made the point first and best:

> [T]he Negro needs neither segregated schools nor mixed schools. What he needs is Education. What he must remember is that there is no magic, either in mixed schools or in segregated schools. A mixed school with poor and unsympathetic teachers, with hostile public opinion, and no teaching of

truth concerning black folk, is bad. A segregated school with ignorant placeholders, inadequate equipment, poor salaries, and wretched housing, is equally bad. Other things being equal, the mixed school is the broader, more natural basis for the education of all youth. It gives wider contacts; it inspires greater self-confidence; and suppresses the inferiority complex. But other things seldom are equal, and in that case, Sympathy, Knowledge, and the Truth, outweigh all that the mixed school can offer.[84]

Modern black advocates of quality schools emphasize above all else the need for education in order to get ahead. The causal chain here is important (albeit painful to liberal arts professors). One's main goal in life is social and economic mobility—a good steady job, a house in the suburbs.[85] A crucial step to middle-class status is getting and keeping a good first job; necessary to that step is a high school diploma and the skills it presumably implies. Thus to many poor blacks (and whites), education's purpose is in the short run to provide a job and in the long run to further upward mobility. The ideal school might be desegregated, but if one must choose between white classmates and a good education that will generate employment, the choice is clear. That is the crux of the matter; black parents and leaders increasingly believe that they must make such a choice, and that the choice of desegregation in the past three decades has not worked. They are turning now to the road not taken—improving the quality of education in whatever school their child attends. Integration is a luxury that may be postponed till adulthood or the next generation; good schools are needed now.

Thus we hear praise of ghetto schools that exceed national test norms and nominations of Marva Collins to be secretary of education. Blacks echo whites' demands to divert money for gas and bus drivers on teachers' salaries and textbooks. Blacks urge that magnet schools be allowed to become racially imbalanced so that more blacks can benefit from their resources and morale. The Harvard University Center for Law and Education reportedly no longer can find any plaintiffs in the Boston desegregation case. The poor black plaintiffs and poor white antibusers in St. Louis have joined forces in an extraordinarily close emotional and political tie to demand better schools in both ghetto and slum. The Washington, D.C., school board is neither surprised nor upset at reports that Washington is the most segregated district in the country: "Our responsibility," says the board's vice president, "is to provide the best education we can for the students we have."[86]

It is easy to point out logical, philosophical, or political flaws in these arguments. The most powerful critique is that failing a miracle, race relations will not improve in segregated schools. Isolated whites cannot escape adopting the racial prejudice that permeates white society and will not learn how to live in the multiracial society the United States is rapidly becoming. Isolated blacks and Hispanics cannot learn to defend against or overcome white prejudice and will be unprepared to live in a society in which they will remain exceptions to the norm.

A second powerful reason to reject the argument for quality segregated schools is that "green follows white." Without an investment of white-owned resources, blacks and Hispanics will control bad schools in poor communities. And history shows that white communities invest substantially in local black schools only when blacks might otherwise try to leave or when whites must enter. Minority schools in central cities will find it extremely difficult to attain enough resources elsewhere (from the state or federal governments, for example) significantly to improve their quality and their students' chances for success.* In short, the search for excellent ghetto schools might simply recapitulate *Plessy*: once separation is certain, any chance for equality disappears.[87]

Volumes have been, and will be, written on this question. Advocates of community control, compensatory education, voucher plans, or fiscal equalization through the courts all battle each other as fiercely as they contend with the NAACP. I will not join these battles; my purpose here is only to point out that there are plausible educational alternatives to school desegregation. The idea of

*Although educational quality and outcomes are not simply or directly related to resources, money can help. Evidence on the economic returns to schooling from the late 1960s shows clearly that improvements in the quality of high school education through "increased expenditures per student have a large and statistically significant direct impact on the earnings of blacks. The total influence of a one percent increase in expenditures causes a .53 percent increase in annual earnings of blacks" (and a .16 percent increase for whites). Increasing the number of years of schooling without changing quality yields "negligible returns." See Charles Link and Edward Ratledge, "Social Returns to Quantity and Quality of Education," *Journal of Human Resources* 10, no. 1 (Winter 1975): 78–89.

minority-controlled, high quality, predominantly one-race schools is supported by strong arguments and successful examples,[88] and it satisfies at least some interpretations of liberal democracy. The new American dilemma can perhaps be so resolved.

Further down the first path away from our dilemma is the possibility of moderating our heavy reliance on education to solve our racial problems. After all, the ostensible job of schools is schooling, not social transformation. Democratic Senator Joseph Biden of Delaware, in a rambling but extraordinary confession of liberal bafflement, touches upon several reasons to shift our focus from the schools:

> We are asking the education system to solve a societal problem that the education system is not big enough to solve, even if it were constitutionally warranted, which it is not. . . . We would have to be fools to not suggest that something has to be done to make this society more integrated . . . , but I just think that what we do is undermine the willingness to . . . take that kind of initiative, whether it be housing, employment, or any place else, by taking the most vulnerable part of the system—the one that goes to the heart of people's . . . concerns. . . . And we say to that component of the system, "You are going to solve our problem." I do not know how it can do that. . . . There are a lot of people . . . who have very strong credentials in all other areas of civil liberties, . . . who are saying, "Busing is counterproductive, if for no other reason than it diminishes our constituency for the kinds of change we have to make in order to deal with the problem." . . . Just talking about the raw politics of it, . . . that constituency is leaving us, leaving guys like me who say, "We have got to spend more money on Title I, . . . we have got to pass the fair housing bill, we have got to do these things." But there is no constituency out there. People are fed up.[89]

Biden's point is that everything is connected. Busing is tied in the public mind to education in general, and federal policies in one arena are tied to federal policies in another. So if constituents reject busing, they reject education, and if they reject school desegregation, they reject civil rights policies in all fields. The educational system is not strong enough singlehandedly to reshape racial attitudes and behaviors in all other arenas of life; it has tried to do so but has only gotten sucked back into the general morass of American skepticism about government intervention and social upheaval. We should, Biden seems to be arguing, either treat policy arenas separately or keep them roped together but use a stronger handle than the public schools to tug the whole system in the direction we want to go.[90]

Biden would probably not accept the next step, but his reasoning points toward a stronger argument about pervasive institutional racism. Segregation in this view is an organic, self-perpetuating system of racial domination that pervades all facets of our society. Ending segregation for some students does not abolish the harm done them by the continued existence of a system of segregated schooling; even desegregating all schools does nothing to remedy systemic economic, political, and social discrimination.[91] And without changing those forms of discrimination, we cannot reshape the American landscape. If this argument sounds familiar, it is because we have once again returned to the debate between the anomaly and symbiosis theses. In policy terms, if racism is symbiotic with American society as we know it, then we must change many features of that society simultaneously in order to uproot it.

Perhaps, then, we should turn to other policy domains in concert with (in the strong version) or instead of (in the weak version) the schools. The discussion beyond this point becomes impossibly broad for this book; let me simply suggest ways to redirect our desegregative activities.

One branch of this path is housing. Sifting through the complex debate about race and residence, I draw two simple but important conclusions: housing is still much more segregated than blacks' incomes and preferences would suggest, and government at all levels has been derelict in its efforts to end housing discrimination or promote housing integration. The Fair Housing Act is hopelessly cumbersome and provides no enforcement capabilities. Federal rent and mortgage subsidy programs and public housing programs at all levels have done more to segregate than to desegregate. State activity is virtually nonexistent. Local planners and housing officials have shown no incentive and developed no capacity to maintain stably integrated neighborhoods.

And yet the advantages of residential integration are considerable. Busing for racial balance could end; neighborhood schools could flourish; parents and children could get to know each other by their own choice and at their own pace. Public opinion polls show whites increasingly willing to live near blacks.[92] It would not be difficult to promote residential integration; ideas abound for local officials and federal policy-makers.[93] Once again, the missing ingredient seems to be will, not way.

Housing integration is not without problems, however, both normative and pragmatic. More than school or job integration, housing integration undermines cultural differences that the country and its citizens may want to retain. Blacks may not want to assimilate into white society, just as Hispanics, Italians, Jews, or Asians often prefer to live in ethnic communities. Pragmatically, the housing choice (or its foreclosure) is diffuse, private, subtle. It is very hard for government to catch and punish offenders without intolerable intrusions in the housing market. But the government can set guidelines and offer incentives, and people should be able to choose freely between cultural diversity and homogeneity. Housing integration is clearly one possible lever for eradicating racism.

So are jobs. Here too, my suggestions are not new. Affirmative action policies for poor blacks (and whites) help to fulfill liberalism's promise of equal opportunity for all. Government and community support for minority enterprises would permit more blacks to become small-scale entrepreneurs. Businesses and cultural institutions can cooperate with schools, providing information, training, and job openings for disadvantaged (black or white) students.[94] Job training and placement programs, a revitalized Civilian Conservation Corps, urban enterprise zones— the list of economic possibilities for eradicating the material effects of racism (if not racial separation) is vast. Obviously, each has pitfalls, and each needs careful examination. But my point is not to detail policy proposals; my point is to show that we do have viable alternatives to consider if we are not willing to do what is necessary fully and successfully to desegregate our schools.

A final branch of this path away from the new American dilemma is politics. Blacks and Hispanics increasingly vote and increasingly hold elective and appointive office. The numbers are still small, and the translation between minority officials and constituents' satisfaction is by no means direct. But black officials do, on average, design and implement policies and practices that benefit black job-seekers, businesses, and others who interact with public officials.[95] Most important, seeing minorities take control of city halls, police departments, school boards, and party machines could eventually accustom citizens to the idea of black or Hispanic leaders with Anglo followers, and could thereby open up economic, social, and political opportunities hitherto closed off.

None of these policies—improved education, housing integration, jobs, or political control—need be alternatives to school desegregation. All would enhance it, and it could make all of them easier and more successful. But in one sense they are alternatives; they make it conceivable not to pursue desegregated schools in the 1980s in Northern cities and still to fulfill the promises of liberal democracy for all Americans.

Such, at any rate, is one possible, optimistic conclusion to this section. We have seen that the anomaly thesis does not hold up in the case of school desegregation; our conventional, preferred methods of action (incremental change through popular control) do not reach our goal (eradicating racism through school desegregation). That is the new American dilemma. But perhaps we can escape it by changing our goal, by seeking to eradicate racism some other way. In the perfect vision of hindsight, school desegregation does not look like the ideal vehicle for such a sweeping change, for several reasons. Children invoke too much emotion for parents to be able to take short-term risks in the hope of long-term benefits. Racial mixing  among children is too indirect a path to racial equity among adults. Schools are too weak an institution to be able to force their environments to meet their needs. Another method of eradicating racism might, however, get at the roots of the American racial landscape more fully. All parents seek high-quality education for their children, so they may not resist changes in school policy that promote it. Quality education, jobs, and housing integration are all closely and directly tied to overall racial equity. Political office provides the power needed to control one's environment. All of these policies seem, on the face of it, to be amenable to incremental changes and to be acceptable to significant numbers of citizens. Thus we can perhaps escape our dilemma by maintaining our preferred methods of action and using them to pursue different goals.

But this section also suggests another, more pessimistic conclusion. If the anomaly thesis is wrong for school desegregation, it may also be wrong for other policy changes. If there really is a powerful symbiotic relationship between racism and American liberal democracy, then quality education or jobs or housing or political office will meet the same fate as school desegregation. We may find, that is, that our preferred methods of action work no better in other arenas, that the dilemma remains even though its locus has changed. If this is the case, we must do more. We must change all facets of American society simultaneously—desegregate schools *and* improve education *and* provide jobs *and* integrate neighborhoods *and* promote minority political power—for the symbiotic relationship to be severed. But before I consider that possibility, let me try once more to outline an easier path away from our dilemma: changing our means but retaining our original goal of school desegregation.

DESEGREGATION, FULL SPEED AHEAD

Why might we decide to retain our goal of eradicating racism through school desegregation and will the means necessary to that end? Most of the answers to that question are implicit in chapters 4 and 5. *When fully and carefully carried out,* mandatory desegregation reduces racial isolation, enhances minority achievement, improves race relations, promotes educational quality, opens new opportunities, and maintains citizen support. *When fully and carefully carried out*, mandatory desegregation does not harm (and may improve) white achievement. It need not increase (and may decrease) violence and vandalism in the schools. It promotes reforms in educational structure and processes, and it may expand educational options. It can bring an influx of federal, state, or local money and talent into the schools. It seldom significantly increases (and may decrease) the cost or distance of bus rides. When properly implemented, busing itself causes no educational, physical, or psychological damage. Desegregation can teach students to respect, understand, and even like people different from themselves, and it prepares them for life in an increasingly multiracial nation. It can give parents more knowledge of and influence over their children's schools. Even the new harms to minorities—faculty displacement, resegregation through tracking, excessive punishment, denigration—do not occur *when the school district fully and carefully desegregates.* Despite evidence of black ambivalence, every poll with responsibly worded questions finds that more than half of blacks endorse busing where necessary to desegregate; virtually all blacks support busing when it is the route to better schools. Thus none of the prudential arguments against desegregation need be considered definitive.*

Note once more that I am not describing a Potemkin village. The evidence shows good results in districts varying in size, wealth, urbanization, region, black population, and racial history. No district has done everything right, but every right action has been taken somewhere. "Ordinary" school systems can desegregate fully and carefully and can thereby achieve the goals of desegregation, to the benefit of all.

Three additional sets of findings suggest that the trauma of desegregation is worth undertaking. The first set addresses long-term consequences for blacks. The evidence is thin, but it suggests that even when not ideally implemented, desegregation improves black students' educational and occupational opportunities. Controlling for socioeconomic status, blacks who attended desegregated schools during the 1950s were more likely to attend college and to attend desegregated colleges, and are now more likely to be in desegregated work groups and to hold nontraditional jobs than blacks from segregated schools. Adults of both races who attended desegregated schools before 1960 more frequently live in desegregated neighborhoods, have children in desegregated schools, and have close interracial friendships than adults from segregated schools.[96]

We have hints of how desegregation affects blacks' job prospects. First, it raises some students' occupational expectations; the more years of desegregated high school they experience, the more black graduates expect to enter a profession.[97] Second, desegregation improves at least some blacks' college attendance and performance.

*Some philosophical arguments against desegregation do hold up, no matter how the plan is designed and implemented. The benefits that blacks, Hispanics, or white ethnic groups derive from cultural and political separation are, by definition, harmed by mandatory desegregation. So is "freedom of choice" (which does not, however, exist anyway in public school systems).

Controlling for socioeconomic status and grades, blacks graduating from mostly white high schools in 1972 were slightly more likely to attend college and remain there, and much more likely to attend desegregated colleges. High school desegregation is associated with higher college grades for Northern blacks.[98] Desegregation may also facilitate the process of obtaining a job and being promoted. Young blacks find a first job through public employment agencies and welfare organizations more frequently than do whites, who rely more on relatives, personal ties to employers, and recommendations from people known to employers. The explanation for this difference is probably straightforward; white networks of employers and employees are broader (for reasons of simple arithmetic), and black unemployment is higher. Personal connections apparently do better than public agencies at generating first jobs, good jobs, and promotions.[99] Thus if desegregation increases young blacks' acquaintance with (comparatively well-off) whites, which it will do if the school does not resegregate, it should reduce the high rate of unemployment among young blacks. Furthermore, some research suggests that the best job-producing contacts are a far-flung set of casual acquaintances, not a close-knit group of good friends. If "weak ties" suffice to give young blacks employment, then desegregation need not generate intimate interracial friendships, but only acquaintance and mutual respect, to increase opportunity.[100]

Another reason for moving full speed ahead is that whites sometimes find desegregation much more palatable after implementation than before. Psychologists debate whether behavioral changes induced by laws can change attitudes;[101] the history of school desegregation suggests that they can.

Consider first the evidence from national surveys. I have already noted that white support for integration has risen considerably in the past twenty years while white support for segregation has declined, despite riots, "forced busing," and increasing cynicism and mistrust of the federal government and the schools. Whites also expect desegregation to persist and expand, whether they like it or not. By 1978, 53 percent of whites thought that "right around here most black and white children will be going to school together," and another 26 percent thought "some" would be. More people in the South (66 percent) and West (60 percent) expected that "most" would be than

Easterners (48 percent) or Midwesterners (43 percent)—exactly what one would predict, given the evidence in table 1 (see chapter 2). A further ray of hope for policy-makers facing desegregation in the 1980s is that people in cities and towns hold greater expectation of desegregation than people in suburbs and rural districts (59 and 64 percent, compared with 44 and 52 percent, respectively).[102]*

Most important, as table 2 shows, whites are increasingly comfortable with the thought of many or even most of their children's schoolmates being black. Clearly, as school desegregation has spread, its acceptance has also spread among the general public.

Table 2. Percentage of White Parents Who Object to Sending Their Children to School with Various Proportions of Black Students, by Region, 1959–1981

Region	If Proportion of Black Enrollment Were	Percentage of White Parents Objecting				
		1959	1965	1969	1975	1981
South	Few	72	37	21	15	5
	Half	83	68	46	38	27
	Majority	86	78	64	61	66
Outside the South	Few	7	7	7	3	5
	Half	34	28	28	24	22
	Majority	58	52	54	47	51

NOTE: only parents who said they would not object to sending their children to school with a few (half) blacks were asked the next question about half (majority) black schoolmates.

SOURCES: *The Gallup Poll, 1959–1971* (vol. 3), pp. 1598, 1940–41, and 2211; *Gallup Opinion Index*, February 1976, no. 127 p. 9; *The Gallup Poll*, February 5, 1981, "Whites, Blacks in Disagreement on Busing," p. 4.

*The fact that white parents increasingly expect school desegregation to continue and are learning to live with the idea (at least in the abstract), makes the Reagan administration's efforts to rescind existing or intended desegregation plans all the more pernicious. People learn to accept and even support what they cannot change; if they see hope for avoiding an undesirable future, they will struggle to do so. This mundane observation of a normally praiseworthy feature of human psychology has a depressing twist if one assumes that active efforts to end racial isolation are required

But we can disaggregate "the general public," and as we do so we find a "strange but true" phenomenon: "the most dramatic increase in support for integrated education has come from the public of the very region [the South] that fought it most fiercely. Perhaps this happened because it is the only region that has had much experience with integrated schools in recent years."[103] Table 2 shows that result; in absolute terms white Northerners object less to desegregated schools at all levels of minority enrollment, but in relative terms white Southerners' attitudes changed much more in twenty years. The claim that "exposure to integration fosters pro-integrationist attitudes" was first documented in a 1963 survey. A majority of Southern whites approved of school integration "in those few places where there had been (as of 1963) considerable integration." In communities with token desegregation, over one-third approved, and "in the hard-core segregationist communities," only one-fourth approved. The direction of causation was from policy change to attitude change:

A close analysis of the data indicates that official action to desegregate Southern schools did not wait for majority opinion to demand it, but rather preceded a change in community attitudes. In the 1956 surveys, only 31 percent of Southern whites in those few areas which had begun at least token desegregation expressed approval of integrated schools. Clearly there was no public demand for integration in those areas then. Furthermore, by 1963 the integrated areas included . . . many additional communities where anti-integration sentiment had in 1956 been even stronger. Yet by 1963 the majority of Southern whites in such communities had accepted the integration of their schools. . . . [By 1965,] of Southern whites whose children had attended school with Negroes, 74 percent said Negroes and whites should

---

by *Brown* and its successors. As soon as the Justice Department challenges the inevitability or permanence of a court order or school district plan mandating transportation (as it did in Nashville, East Baton Rouge [Louisiana], and Seattle in 1983), white opposition will skyrocket, even in cities where the plan is working fairly smoothly. This effect is probably unintentional, but nevertheless such actions are almost perfectly suited to making desegregation as difficult and unsuccessful as it can be. (They are matched only by the elimination of ESAA funds for already desegregated schools and for magnet programs, which has stopped many desegregation plans in their tracks. See note 128, this chapter.

attend the same schools; of Southern whites whose children had not attended school with Negroes, only 48 percent held that view.[104]

Attitudes continued to follow behavior even after the racial turmoil of the 1960s. Between 1963 and 1970, and between 1972 and 1976, support for integration in both the South and the North increased 5 percent or a little more a year. But from 1970 to 1972, Northerners became 13 percent more supportive of integration each year, and Southerners became fully 35 percent a year more supportive. This dramatic increase in support coincided with the most dramatic period of mandated desegregation in the South, from 1969 to 1971.[105]

Another type of disaggregation also yields results pleasing to proponents of desegregation. Parents of children in public schools are generally more supportive of school desegregation than are adults with no children or with children in private or parochial schools. Data cited below for specific school districts show this result, as do national surveys. For example, in 1971, 48 percent of public school parents but only 39 percent of childless adults agreed that "school integration has improved the quality of education received by black students." The absolute figures were lower, but the ratios the same, for a question on quality of education for white students—26 percent of public school parents and 21 percent of childless adults saw good results. The same pattern held for race relations; 44 percent of public school parents felt they had improved, compared to 36 percent of childless adults.[106]

Even more striking because more focused are survey results from people directly involved in desegregation. Table 3 shows how parents react to the mandatory busing of their children. The findings are robust and surprising. The great majority of parents of bused children find busing partly or very satisfactory. Whites continue to oppose busing in theory (79 percent objected to the *idea* of busing for desegregation in the 1981 survey) but are content to live with it in practice. Both the races give essentially the same reasons for their evaluation. Whites endorse busing because they find "no problems, no complaints from children" (39 percent) and because "children learn to live with each other" (16 percent). Blacks agree (28 percent cite the first reason, 16 percent the second) and add a third claim: "children learn more, [attend a] better school" (19 percent). The races also agree on their objections: "distance [is] too far" (12 percent

Table 3. Reaction of Parents Whose Children Have Been Bused for Racial Reasons, 1978–1983

Question: How did the busing of children in your family to go to school with children of other races work out?*		Percentage Responding		
		1978	1981	1983
Blacks	Very satisfactory	63	74	66
	Partly satisfactory	25	21	28
	Not satisfactory	8	5	6
Whites	Very satisfactory	56	48	64
	Partly satisfactory	23	37	24
	Not satisfactory	16	13	11

*Respondents were first asked, "Have any of the children in your family been picked up by bus to go to a school with children of other races, or hasn't that happened?" In 1978, 35 percent of blacks and 10 percent of whites answered affirmatively. In 1981, 43 percent of blacks and 19 percent of whites with schoolchildren answered yes; in 1983, the figures were 36 percent of blacks and 25 percent of whites with children in school. The question about busing experience was asked only of these respondents.

SOURCES: Louis Harris and Associates, Inc., *A Study of Attitudes toward Racial and Religious Minorities and toward Women* (New York: Louis Harris and Associates, Inc., 1978), pp. 38–40; Louis Harris, "Majority of Parents Report School Busing Has Been Satisfactory Experience," *The Harris Survey*, no. 25, March 26, 1981; Louis Harris, "Black Voting the Key to Outcome in 1984," *The Harris Survey*, no. 58, July 21, 1983.

of whites, 8 percent of blacks); and there has "been trouble, fighting" (9 percent of whites, 8 percent of blacks). Even the pollster is moved  to observe that "rarely has there been a case where so many have been opposed to an idea which appears not to work badly at all when put into practice."[107]

Surveys of desegregated communities show a similar, though more complex, picture. Many whites apparently agree with the Charlotte, North Carolina, mother who reports that "it hasn't upset my child like I expected. And though I'm surprised to hear myself saying this, I think in years to come, we'll see that it's something that had to be done."[108] In Mississippi, white parents who had opposed their children's desegregation supported more integration after one year of implementation than they had beforehand, while whites who withdrew their children from public schools endorsed less integration than they had a year earlier.[109] In one Southern countywide suburban district, white parents whose children were directly involved in a mandatory plan were consistently more supportive of the idea of desegregation, mandated techniques, the outcome of their new plan, and their children's education than were parents of unaffected white children.[110] In Louisville, whites with children in public schools supported desegregation more after one year than white parents of pre-school children.[111] Although white residents of Milwaukee generally became less enthusiastic about broad-gauged civil rights issues, whites with children in public schools approved more of school desegregation and busing after the court ruling than before it, whereas whites with children in parochial schools approved much less.[112] Among white Akron parents contemplating the possibility of a mandatory plan, those with children already attending schools with 30 percent or more black students were significantly less opposed to busing for further racial balance than those with children in white schools.[113]

The most extensive survey of postdesegregation attitudes was recently conducted in New Castle County (Wilmington, Delaware). Praise for the school system among parents of public school children declined drastically when desegregation was implemented, but three years later had returned two-thirds of the way to predesegregation levels. All of the decline in approval and most of the subsequent rise took place among suburban (roughly speaking, white) parents; central-city (roughly speaking, black) parents show a consistent rise in their approval ratings. Citizens without children are much less supportive of the schools than public school parents are.[114] Over two-thirds of public school parents are satisfied with the school atmosphere, discipline, and bus safety their children encounter, whereas roughly half of the parents were satisfied in 1978 (the year desegregation was implemented). Even one-third to one-half of those who oppose busing for desegregation purposes gave the school district a grade of "A" or "B." The more knowledgeable citizens are about school activities, personnel, and achievement test scores (which have risen since desegregation was implemented), the more supportive they are. Public school parents' ratings are predicted better by information about the schools than by attitudes toward busing.

Wilmington parents' views on the effects of desegregation are mixed. "Whether a child rode a bus to school was not related to school district evaluation," and "there is some evidence that feelings of whites about blacks have become more positive or understanding [since desegregation]." Furthermore, 70 percent of black parents and 90 percent of white parents now believe that blacks have equal education opportunity, compared with about 60 percent of both groups in 1977. In 1979, 56 percent of public school parents thought desegregation had worsened school quality; by 1983, one-third thought so. (Citizens were not asked, apparently, whether desegregation had improved school quality.) Nevertheless, opposition to busing has increased (nonsignificantly) from 74 to 79 percent of the citizenry. In short, schools have improved; public school parents, especially the most knowledgeable, perceive improvements; opposition to desegregation has been almost halved; but opposition to busing remains overwhelming.[115]

As the Wilmington survey implies, not all findings are positive. I have already noted that in some cases blacks are less pleased with the results of desegregation than whites are, or than they had expected to be. This suggests that some desegregation plans maximize benefits to whites rather than to minorities—a result hardly in keeping with the spirit of *Brown*. Furthermore, whites are by no means always pleased. White parents in Pontiac, Michigan, remained consistently opposed to, and black parents consistently supportive of, court-ordered busing four years after the plan began.[116] White Louisville parents opposed desegregation more after one violent year of experience with it than beforehand.[117] Thirty percent of Wilmington's public school parents still described desegregation as their district's biggest problem after four years (second only to discipline, which 35 percent are most concerned about). And 36 percent still claim that desegregation has lowered the overall quality of education in their district. Suburban New Castle County schools still rank more than twice as high as Wilmington schools in public school parents' eyes.[118] Nevertheless, that even poorly implemented desegregation generates as much after-the-fact support as it does from resistant whites is rather surprising.

People in the direct line of fire—students and school staff—generally find desegregation better in reality than in anticipation. A principal in Charlotte, North Carolina, reflects, "It's hard to remember the pain and agony of those first few years because we've now replaced it with something else. . . . We don't have a perfect society here. But we've come a long way."[119] A white high school student in Columbus, Ohio, says, "When you first go into school you're easily influenced by what you're told about black people, but after you get to know some of them, you're influenced by their niceness." A black in the same school echoes her: "When I was younger and would see integrated couples, I used to wonder, 'How can they associate with each other like that?' Then I realized [after moving from a segregated grade school to a desegregated junior high school] that . . . an integrated situation, it wouldn't have to seem bad, that the relationship could really be nice. It really was for me."[120] We saw in chapter 4 that the longer a school is desegregated, the better are staff's and students' racial attitudes. Although in a 1978 poll of parents across the country, a combination of integration and busing tied for second place as the "biggest problem in the public schools in this community," only 18 percent of the students in a North Carolina poll identified student race relations as a problem, and it ranked dead last in a list of fifteen problems presented to them.[121] High school students are more enthusiastic than adults (with or without children) about the effects of integration. A majority see it as improving race relations and black achievement, and one-third agree that it has improved the quality of education for whites.[122] In 1983, over 50 percent of college freshmen endorsed busing for desegregative purposes, up from 37 percent in 1976.[123] More white (but fewer black) Georgia students found desegregation "serving a useful purpose" after it was implemented than had supported it before implementation.[124] Even 30 percent of white Georgia school administrators, almost all of whom required coercion to comply with federal mandates, believe that desegregation has improved student achievement, and 40 percent see it as beneficial to race relations.[125] More professional educators (41 percent) than other adults (30 percent) agreed that "more should be done to integrate the schools throughout the nation," even during the tumultuous year of 1973.[126] Most telling of all is the fact that white students are returning to some desegregated districts. In fifteen of fifty-two large desegregated districts, white enrollment has increased or remained stable since a plan was implemented.[127]

White parents oppose the idea of busing but find it acceptable or better; they oppose mandatory desegregation but are often pleasantly surprised with its results. Whites who participate in mandatory plans rate them more highly than whites who do not. Blacks generally endorse desegregation and even busing both before and after implementation. Thus we have strong, though not overwhelming, evidence that after the fact, many citizens accept or even endorse plans that they had initially opposed. If that is the case, our concerns about the need to ignore popular preferences in order to desegregate successfully may be mollified. If people eventually are glad of what was imposed on them, we certainly do not have popular control, but we also are far from a destructive dictatorship of arrogant judges and uncaring bureaucrats.

A final empirical reason to forge ahead with desegregation is its benefits to education in general and whites in particular. I have shown that when properly implemented, desegregation provides organizational, curricular, and pedagogical improvements for all students. It may also generate resources from outside the district that more than compensate for additional expenses. School systems that must desegregate have a justification to request more of the city budget. Courts, as in Detroit and St. Louis, may find states partially liable for segregated conditions and order them to finance educational improvements and the costs of establishing racial balance.* States may themselves pass legislation to fund new buses (as in Ohio) or to give monetary incentives to suburban districts to accept inner-city transfers (as in Massachusetts and Wisconsin). Until 1981, desegregated schools could receive a share of the $300 million ESAA budget.[128]

If properly implemented, desegregation also generates less tangible but ultimately more important benefits for whites. They learn about the role of blacks and other minorities in American history, they become accustomed to non-Anglo authority figures, they be-

*Courts may be able to hold the federal government liable for a district's segregation and order it to finance educational reforms. Federal District Judge Milton Shadur issued such a ruling in Chicago, based on a consent decree signed by the school board and the Justice Department in 1980. Congress appropriated $20 million for 1984, but the Reagan administration is resisting further grants, and it is by no means certain that this case will set a precedent.

come less fearful of blacks, they differentiate among individuals, and they learn that they can work with people who are not close friends.[129] More fancifully, desegregation may be a "purification ordeal" which "tests the community's moral fiber." After implementation, "white guilt" over racism is "expunged," and the white community is certified as "rededicated to American ideals." Desegregation reduces white "ambiguity [about] moral guidelines to structure the relationships between persons and groups," raises self-esteem, and gives "a renewed sense of purpose . . . [and a new] fit between school ideals and civic ideals."[130] More cynically, desegregation rescues white adolescents from the smug boredom of middle-class suburbia.[131] And if they are the less-favored minority in a desegregated setting, white students learn trust, endurance, courage, and humility—qualities which blacks have always developed but which "whites [too] ought to have the privilege of obtaining."[132]

When all is said and done, however, the most important reasons to desegregate schools are ethical, not empirical. Two closely related moral claims predominate. The first is President Johnson's answer to the argument that desegregation calls only for ending de jure segregation:

> Freedom is not enough. . . . You do not take a person who, for years, has been hobbled by chains and liberate him, bring him up to the starting line of a race and then say, "You are free to compete with all the others," and still justly believe that you have been completely fair. Thus it is not enough to just open the gates of opportunity. All our citizens must have the ability to walk through those gates. This is the next and the more profound stage of the battle for civil rights. We seek not just freedom but opportunity. We seek not just legal equity but human ability, not just equality as a right and a theory but equality as a fact and equality as a result.[133]

What Johnson is saying, to put it more precisely but less eloquently, is that means-regarding and prospect-regarding equal opportunity are not the same.[134] The latter exists if each person has the same prospect of attaining a goal as every other person. Prospects are not the same if one person is prohibited by law from pursuing the goal; thus de jure segregation violates this form of equal opportunity and is illegitimate in a liberal society. But mere legal equality of opportunity suffices for lotteries and poker games, and very little else. The more robust form of equal opportunity, "means-regarding," requires more than a statistical or legal equal chance. It requires that all contestants have the same resources needed to attain the goal, so that what ultimately separates winners from losers is talent, ambition, and other personal qualities—not chance, or the tools necessary to turn talents into achievements. In this view, all students must be given equally good schooling (or at least an equal chance for good schooling, so that if they remain uneducated, it is by choice); only then can they really compete fairly in the pursuit of unequal outcomes. Means-regarding equal opportunity is much harder to accomplish but much more important for a complex society than prospect-regarding equal opportunity. Thus ending de jure segregation does not suffice for moving beyond purely formal prospect-regarding equal opportunity. Only relief from the effects of prior segregation grants means-regarding equal opportunity and fulfills liberalism's promise. Or so conclude proponents of active remediation.

The catch in this logical structure is its political aura; the "ideological power" of the idea of equal opportunity "lies very largely in the prospect-regarding variant, in the wish and hope that the children of yesterday's losers may become tomorrow's winners"[135]—not in the much more stringent means-regarding variant. An insufficient remedy has strong appeal; a sufficient remedy does not—a new variant on a familiar theme in this book.

But President Johnson's justification of full and complete desegregation is incomplete. Derrick Bell and others who seek alternatives to desegregation do not disagree with it; in fact, they too insist that only active remediation can fulfill the promise of *Brown* and provide true equality of opportunity. They argue, however, that school desegregation is normatively or empirically flawed, so we must pursue means-regarding equal opportunity through other channels. It is at this point that the second moral argument for school desegregation becomes critical. It involves a vision of the ideal pluralist society. School desegregation, in this view, is an imperfect but necessary means of teaching different races and ethnicities how to live and prosper with each other. School desegregation need not—must not—"bleach" blacks and browns to look and think like Anglo-Saxons. Nor need it induce us all to join hands and sing "We shall overcome" in an access of brotherly love. Its goal is for blacks, browns, and Anglos to respect each other's autonomy, appreciate their mutual diversity, and welcome their mutual ties. Whites (and minorities) need to give up the unthinking "mindset that white is better than black, that the 'American' culture is better than any minority culture. . . . Such attitudes are . . . social dynamite."[136] Blacks and Hispanics need to learn to function in the public world dominated by Anglos' language, rules, and skills, even if they want to retreat to their private and different world at the end of a workday.[137] Children of all races need to recognize that "pluralism is the essence of urban society. . . . They must . . . develop a sense of community among heterogeneous and diversified people. This requires cosmopolitan skills of indirect communication, coordination, and negotiation."[138] If we cannot do these things, we will not have a liberal polity in the twenty-first century.[139]

Perhaps that is the point; perhaps we live not in a liberal polity, but in a race- and class-constrained polity for which equal opportunity and respectful pluralism are convenient myths. Or perhaps we place too great a burden on schools and children by asking them to spearhead the drive for equal opportunity and pluralist community. But we would be drawing those conclusions too quickly if we did not first consider whether full and complete desegregation is feasible. If the data, testimonials, and moral arguments of this section are convincing, what should we do successfully to desegregate our schools?

Desegregation succeeds if it accomplishes the goals of chapter 3: ending racial isolation, improving race relations and student achievement, ensuring equal treatment, enhancing self-esteem and opportunities, generating community support, and avoiding disorder, flight, and recurring discrimination. Because racism and American society are so tightly linked, desegregation plans will not achieve these goals through incremental policy changes following from popular control. They *can* succeed if they follow four fundamental guidelines—all nonincremental and not responsive to popular wishes. They are:

- *Wherever possible, desegregate a metropolitan region.*

The virtues of a metropolitan plan are manifold. It provides the flexibility needed for optimal ratios of race and class; it combines the resources and expectations of the suburbs with the culture and excitement of the city; it minimizes white flight and enhances stability and community support; it can simplify busing logistics; it can foster and reward integrated neighborhoods; it can break large districts down into smaller, more accessible units. Virtually every desegregation proponent gives strong reasons to incorporate a metropolitan region in a desegregation plan, and I can only underline their arguments.*

Metropolitan desegregation is in some lights not a very radical innovation. School districts have been consolidating for decades; the 115,500 districts of 1942 had become 15,000 by 1982 for reasons having nothing to do with race.[140] Local school districts are creations of state education agencies; there is no legal reason why states cannot undo what they once did. Most Southern districts are countywide anyway. In addition, metropolitan regions have consolidated transportation systems, sewer and water systems, and plans for industrial development, housing, and other public services. Planners continually urge flexible movement across city-suburb lines for virtually any policy. Metropolitan desegregation is rejected for political, not logistical or legal, reasons.

Metropolitan desegregation faces two obstacles. The first is strong public (white suburban) opposition and correspondingly weak support from elected officials and appointed education officers. But that point simply restates what I have continually argued: if we follow popular wishes, we will not desegregate successfully. To desegregate successfully, authorities must find the will to ignore (temporary, one hopes) popular opposition. The second obstacle is the Supreme Court ruling in *Milliken I* that suburbs cannot be ordered to participate in desegregation plans unless they are found to have segregated intentionally. This ruling curtails one method of overcoming the first obstacle—court-ordered consolidation.

But these obstacles, even combined, are not insurmountable. Litigators should concentrate on finding cities where they have a good legal case for a metropolitan plan, and nonlitigators should concen-

*Obviously, in some districts with a small proportion of minorities and a substantial middle class, a metropolitan plan is not necessary to achieve the goals of desegregation. In other regions a metropolitan plan may not be feasible for idiosyncratic or legal reasons. I am not insisting that metropolitan plans are necessary in all cases—only that, most of the time, metropolitan desegregation has virtues that a central-city-only plan cannot match.

trate on political rather than judicial channels. State legislators or administrators could institute plans ranging from mandatory metropolitanization to incentive systems for voluntary interdistrict transfers. Local school boards can also set up voluntary or mandatory interdistrict plans, or they can jointly sue the state to force a merger. The fact that these paths are seldom chosen is an insufficient argument against them. If we want successful desegregation, we have ways to achieve it.

- *In designing a plan, do not worry about minimizing busing times or distances; the plan should pursue desirable outcomes and let the mechanics of busing be a residual concern.*

A focus on busing per se destabilizes integrated neighborhoods, mixes races but not classes, ignores historical antipathies or sympathies, increases burdens on the already worst-off, and otherwise violates common sense and morality. Busing, by itself, is a false issue. It is not unacceptably expensive or time-consuming; it does not harm children; it involves transporting fewer than 10 percent (probably about 5 percent) additional children; fewer and fewer mothers remain at home (and therefore near neighborhood schools) during the day anyway;[141] and a majority of children are already bused to school. Plan designers should address questions of racial and class balance, geographic and demographic configurations, cultural and historical idiosyncracies, pedagogical and organizational desiderata—and let the busing chips fall where they may. Obviously, efficiency is better than inefficiency, but only if other things are equal.

Once again, the main obstacle to such nonincremental change is popular control. Most Anglos and many Hispanics and blacks will object vociferously to this rule. Whether objections to busing for racial balance stem from racism, concern about the schools at the other end, or a desire for neighborhood solidarity is, in a purely political sense, immaterial: the objections are loud and prolonged. But at the risk of sounding like a broken record, I repeat: citizens' preferences for incremental changes (at most) must be ignored if desegregation is to succeed.

The other reason to hesitate before ordering "massive busing" is normatively, if not practically, more compelling. Local schools have real virtues. Children can go to and from school together. Parents are more likely to volunteer in classes and attend PTA meetings if the school is nearby and familiar. Voters are more willing to raise taxes for "their own" schools. Most fundamentally,

> politics is always territorially based; and the neighborhood . . . is historically the first, and still the most immediate and obvious, base for democratic politics. People are most likely to be knowledgeable and concerned, active and effective, when they are close to home, among friends and familiar enemies. The democratic school, then, should be an enclosure within a neighborhood: a special environment within a known world, where children are brought together as students exactly as they will one day come together as citizens. In this setting, the school most easily realizes its mediating role [between the private world of the family and the public world of the state].[142]

Some of these virtues can be retained in an intelligently designed busing plan (for example, a mandatory plan that moves neighborhoods en masse rather than a voluntary plan that takes each child in a different direction). Other benefits of a small, participatory community can be recreated by a school system that makes determined efforts to involve parents in the new schools. Still other virtues are more fantasy than fact anyway. But in the final analysis, local schools are probably preferable—and metropolitan desegregation is the best way to generate the racially mixed housing that could lead, in turn, to desegregated neighborhood schools.

- *Change practices, personnel, and presumptions within the schools.*

There will be more mischief than merit in following the first two rules if the fact and consequences of racism continue inside the school building and classroom. David Kirp makes the point most elegantly:

> If efforts to teach whites and blacks together aim to do more than arouse the prejudices of both races, integration must become significantly fused with the educational mission of the schools. . . . Whether racial balance (or some other formula) is achieved matters far less than the subtler and more far-reaching changes in the very nature of the education that the society makes available to its children and the civic order that makes possible this education.[143]

The list of specifics here is long: desegregate faculty and staff, avoid unnecessary tracking, maintain firm and fair discipline, hold high expectations for all students, teach the skills needed to fulfill those expectations, address racial issues directly, avoid unnecessarily rewarding white, middle-class styles, promote cooperation among and imagination within students, and so on. Again, my list contains nothing new. Its only unusual element is the insistence that all of these changes are needed for any of them to have great effect, and that some disruption is an acceptable price to pay for the benefits it buys.

The main obstacle to this set of nonincremental changes is not citizens' wishes (in fact, parents eagerly seek improvements in the quality of education), but organized interests. Teachers' unions, administrators, parents of children presumed to be exceptionally talented, and possibly black and Hispanic politicians—all oppose particular changes or set conditions for their cooperation. Thus popular control, defined not as individual preferences but as interest group pluralism, once again reinforces incremental change; both must be overcome for desegregation to succeed.

- *National, local, and especially school leaders must lead.*

Effective schools have powerful principals and teachers; successful magnet programs and schools with good race relations have supportive superintendents; school districts that implement desegregation peacefully have cooperative school boards, mayors, and community elites. Leadership neither will change prejudiced attitudes nor should inhibit disgruntled parents from fleeing the system. But it will make the difference between compliance with and resistance to the law, and between schools that take advantage of the chance to improve and schools that reluctantly make a little room for the invaders. We do not need autocrats or radical transformers; we do need people who are willing to buck the tide and find opportunity in necessity.

Chapters 4 and 5 make clear what leaders need to do, and what they can hope to gain, but for this recommendation to be more than a pious hope I need also to specify where and how such leadership can emerge. Unfortunately, as chapter 4 points out, we have almost no good data or theories to tell us when leaders can afford to endorse desegregation, when they are likely to, and what the consequences will be. Nevertheless, I can make a few suggestions. If the number of minority students is low enough not to overwhelm apprehensive whites; if the leader has an external force (a court, a governor, legislation, the threat of a boycott) to use as a justification for acting; if there are new resources available so that a carrot can accompany the stick; if the leader can persuade others to join him or her so that one person need not stand alone; and if the media and other purveyors of information are not needlessly provocative—then local elites and school officials can hope to facilitate desegregation without sacrificing themselves. These variables are themselves manipulable, so it is possible for policy-makers to set up conditions under which local leadership is encouraged to surface.[144] *

Furthermore, mayors themselves can act in ways that permit them to retain office *and* implement unpopular decrees, no matter their circumstances. They can offer inducements along with threats to white neighborhoods, act as conduits for information between court and citizenry, and influence the public's view of the content and inevitability of the plan. Even in a city as riven as Boston, for example, evidence shows that the mayor had a large reservoir of goodwill, personal respect, political support for other reasons, and respect for law which he could have drawn on to "maximize coordination of desegregation and minimize the chance of a successful challenge" in the next election. More specifically:

- "The demand for public safety is so great during a time of desegregation implementation that an incumbent may gain a great deal of political respect simply by using the resources of office to ensure public order."
- "An incumbent can increase his or her political support by using the resources of office to guide public opinion in the direction of greater appreciation of the practical and legal constraints on the incumbent's position *vis à vis* the court order."

*There are, of course, factors affecting the emergence and success of leadership that are not easily subject to policy intervention. One critical factor is the racial history of the community—probably no one could have made South Boston receptive to Roxbury students. Another is the skill of opposing leaders. These points make the issue of leadership highly contingent, but not hopeless.

- "Public perceptions of public opinion can be shaped by emphasizing public support and encouraging pro-busing constituents to voice their support for the mayor and the court."

These actions and others reduce fear and uncertainty, and increase respect for the mayor and the court order, support for the plan and willingness to express it, and acceptance of the plan's inevitability. And if the evidence is compelling that Mayor White could have safely fostered desegregation success, it can be presumed to be overwhelming for any other mayor in any other city.[145]

The discussion so far assumes that desegregation is occurring in a mainly hostile community with skeptical if not resistant officials. But not all communities are like that, and the 1980s are producing new settings for potential desegregation leaders. There are now more black mayors and state legislators than at any time since Reconstruction, and their numbers are rising. Minority officials bring with them staff, police, and school administrators who are sympathetic to minority concerns.[146] We cannot assume that such sympathy translates into support for school desegregation, but at a minimum it is unlikely to generate opposition to civil rights action. Generally, black legislators and mayors lack knowledge about the benefits of, most successful techniques for, and preferred alternatives to desegregation; providing them with information, evidence of constituency support for change, and specific proposals could induce them to step forward. Finally, school officials of any race should no longer be assumed to oppose desegregation. "Defendants" in some court cases work closely with judges and plaintiffs; suburban and city school administrators in some areas work together against state and local political actors. These alliances are unusual but not unique, and policy actors would do well to pursue them as leads.

These four rules reinforce each other. Parents will accept a metropolitan plan that involves busing if the plan seems fair, sensible, and likely to improve the quality of schools. Interdistrict plans, fair and sensible methods of racial balancing, and high quality schools all require leadership. Authorities are more willing to become leaders if they sense a successful outcome to their boldness. State legislators can mandate metropolitan plans and provide resources to desegregated schools; resources, white suburbanites, and legislation are three of the elements important in generating local leadership. And so on; the cyberneticists' feedback loops can be positively as well as negatively reinforcing.

If these rules are followed, desegregation may succeed; if they are not, it probably will not.* There are no certainties in that sentence—only probabilities, based on thirty years of experience and thirty forests-worth of research reports. But the probabilities are high enough to indicate a second path away from the new American dilemma. The evidence suggests that even if racism and liberal democracy are symbiotically linked, they may not be irreversibly bonded. The symbiosis means that our preferred means of policy choice and enactment are not strong enough to break the chain; in that sense, Myrdal and the optimists of the anomaly thesis are wrong. Possibly, however, they are right in a deeper sense. Americans may believe firmly enough in the American Creed that they will be willing, if properly led, to take the steps necessary to desegregate fully and successfully. They have reached some desegregation goals in some communities, and both races have benefited therefrom. Myrdal was wrong in thinking that politics as usual and citizens' idealism would suffice, but we still have a chance to prove him right

*A second-order set of guidelines of desirable but less essential practices include: (1) simultaneous desegregation of all grades across the whole district, with brief lead times; (2) significant participation by parents and local organizations in designing, implementing, and monitoring the plan—so long as minority and poor white participants have as much influence as well-off whites, and so long as participants have a strong mandate, clear guidelines, and an independent power base; (3) wide dispersal of information about the reasons for, details of, and consequence of the plan, and channels for citizens' questions and reactions; (4) as much voluntarism as is possible without harm to nonvolunteers—for example, magnet schools coupled with other types of high quality schools, voluntary transfers that do not resegregate by race or class, and monetary incentives that do not penalize nonparticipants; (5) coordination with other programs, especially housing and jobs, to aid minorities and the poor; (6) minimizing external rules for *how* to desegregate so long as there are clear, explicit, and enforced criteria for successful outcomes at school and classroom levels.

Clever ideas and policy recommendations abound, and my list is not exhaustive. For others, see Willie, *Sociology of Urban Education*, pp. 59–76; Christine H. Rossell and Willis D. Hawley, "Policy Alternatives for Minimizing White Flight," *Educational Evaluation and Policy Analysis* 4, no. 2 (Summer 1982): 213–19; Morgan et al, *Desegregating Public Schools* and authors cited on pp. 3–5; Hawley et al., *Strategies for Effective Desegregation*.

in his assertion that Americans can reject their racist heritage if they choose to.

THE NEW AMERICAN DILEMMA, REVISITED

"I share the disappointment of many, who hoped that a simple solution would suffice for a complex problem," testified professor of education Ralph Scott.[147] He is, as he says, not alone; simple solutions proposed to the problem of racism range from emigration to benign neglect, from separatism to assimilation. But none suffice. Nor, unfortunately, do most complex solutions. How, then, can we escape the new American dilemma?

I cannot fully answer that question for myself, never mind for the American polity. But I can specify two pairs of principles that we ought carefully to weigh in making our choice.

The first pair are the competing values of diversity and freedom of movement. These are not normally thought of as competitors, and in the best of all possible worlds they would not be. But in the context of American race and ethnic relations they are. By diversity I mean cultural distinctiveness and racial separation—"ethnic purity," in President Carter's words. The United States has never been and should not be a melting pot that boils everyone down to an indistinct pseudo-Anglo-Saxon mush. Our cultural vitality is due in large part to immigrants' retaining their languages, religions, family constellations, and values; those are the things that make New York City so much more interesting than the Lynds' Middletown.[148] And from the individual's rather than the society's perspective, surely one of the fundamental rights granted by a liberal polity is the right to choose an identity and associate with like-minded people. Even this formulation is not quite right; the vocabulary here should be that of affinity, tradition, primordial loyalty, childhood absorption. It is the very nonliberal qualities embodied in a self-contained ethnic community that make it so valuable in our overwhelmingly individualistic, mobile, protean "mass society."[149] But whatever the appropriate language, if we value diversity, we should not coerce ethnic whites into lowering the barricade around their heritage any more than we should make blacks assimilate or Hispanics give up Spanish.

But diversity breeds inequality. People not only separate into in-groups and out-groups; they add a vertical dimension that creates topdogs and underdogs. Thus whites see blacks as not merely different but inferior; Princetonians are not merely different but superior. Even these psychological hierarchies would not matter much to policy-makers if they remained merely sentiments, but they have profound political and economic consequences. Blacks or Hispanics are not hired, or encouraged to move next door, or elected president; (male) WASPs are. Thus diversity turns into inequality, which inhibits freedom of movement. By freedom of movement I mean the classic liberal promise of individual opportunity, the right to pursue happiness wherever and however one desires. America does not promise happiness, let alone equal levels of happiness; in fact, liberalism glorifies inequalities resulting from individual talent, ambition, and luck. But—and it is a crucial exception—liberalism does not permit barriers of prejudice or status to produce unequal outcomes. People must have equal freedom to act in ways that will produce unequal results.

Thus racial and cultural diversity illegitimately inhibits freedom of movement. If we value the former more heavily than the latter, we will endorse neighborhood schools, black control of ghetto schools, and Hispanic control of barrio schools. If we care more about the latter, we probably must insist upon school desegregation because adulthood is likely to be too late to start seeking racial equality. If we could figure out how to make diversity mean simply difference, not inequality, we would not have to choose. Children could be schooled with others like them, then compete fairly with others unlike them for jobs, status, political positions, and so on. Separate but equal, however, has not been a notably successful formula for American race relations.

The second pair of principles to weigh in choosing our path out of the dilemma are liberalism and democracy. This is a better-known antinomy but hardly a more tractable one. By liberalism I mean rights—the guarantee by the state that all citizens can enjoy the Constitution's promises, regardless of whether other citizens want them to or not. By democracy, I mean that citizens are sovereign, that government action is shaped by citizen preference (usually defined as majority rule). The two need not conflict (as the very title of this book implies), but in American race relations they do. If we value liberalism over democracy we probably should endorse school desegregation, because it is the method in which our nation has invested the most effort in seeking to grant equal protection of the laws. Equal protection could, in theory, come by another route, but there is no reason to think that other reforms will work better than one to which so much energy and idealism have already been devoted. If we value democracy over liberalism, we probably should seek some other means of granting equal protection that does less violence to citizens' desires. Perhaps jobs, houses, good racially separate schools, or ballots can produce racial equity; the democrat will argue that at least they are worth a greater try as long as they are less abhorrent to citizens than "forced busing."

Both of these antinomies, and all four terms involved, are crude, perhaps unacceptably so; by redefining diversity, freedom of movement, liberalism, or democracy, we may be able to wriggle out of the contradictions I have posited. But no one has done so yet in a way that commands universal assent. So we continue to debate mandatory desegregation versus neighborhood schools—debates which are really over liberalism's promises of freedom of movement and basic rights on the one hand, and the older value of diversity and the newer value of democracy on the other.

This conclusion so far lacks one element—the third possible response I have outlined to the new American dilemma. We might, after all, choose neither to move full steam ahead on desegregation nor to formulate an equally effective alternative. We might, instead, continue to muddle along using conventional means of policy choice and implementation to produce a little, but not much, change in our racial hierarchy. What would that outcome imply about American society?

It would imply, I think, that we do not really want to be a liberal society. It would imply that we are willing to be either a racist society characterized by white supremacy, or a class society characterized by a structure of inherited inequalities, or both. It would imply that racism and America are profoundly and perhaps irreversibly symbiotic—that we will continue to nourish "two dissimilar organisms . . . living together . . . in close association or union, . . . where this is advantageous to both," as Webster puts it.[150]

That is a harsh and dramatic judgment. But I am not alone in making it. Judge Robert Carter, looking back on his role in litigating *Brown*, says: "It was not until *Brown I* was decided that blacks were able to understand that the fundamental vice was not legally enforced *racial segregation* itself; that this was a mere by-product, a symptom of the greater and more pernicious disease—white supremacy. . . . It . . . remains the basic virus that has debilitated blacks' efforts to secure equality in this country."[151] Segregation has as its purpose "to label or define blacks as inferior and thus exclude them from full and equal participation in society. . . . Segregation violates the equal protection clause of the fourteenth amendment not because there is no rational relationship between the classification and the purpose—it is a supremely rational system—but because its purpose is illegitimate."[152] If we grant that the real issue is white supremacy, and that segregation is merely its visible manifestation and instrument, it is no longer surprising that so much effort to end racial isolation has produced such uneven and uncertain results, or that resegregation is greatest in those regions and schools that desegregated first and most. White Americans may not, in the end, be willing to give up the racial supremacy which they certainly did not create but just as certainly benefit from.

But this last statement immediately suggests a problem with this analysis: poor and working-class whites have not benefited from white supremacy (except psychologically) and have probably been harmed by it.[153] Thus enters the class argument: desegregation remains partial at best, unsuccessful at worst, because its success would overthrow the American class structure, in which blacks disproportionately but not exclusively lose. The most subtle analysis of this sort is Alan Freeman's. To fully and completely desegregate, we would have to adopt the victim's perspective, "the core idea of [which] . . . is that doing something about the problem of racial discrimination necessarily means results." From the victim's viewpoint, racist or beneficent intent is immaterial, and individual actions are largely superfluous. What matters is whether there has been, "when the task is completed, some significant change in the conditions of life that one associates with the past practices of discrimination—segregated schools, lack of jobs, the worst jobs, lack of political power." In the 1960s, the Supreme Court inched toward the victim's perspective, which is more powerful logically and politically than the "perpetrator's," but retreated in 1974 with *Milliken I*, "an instance of law as legitimation of the existing class structure."[154]

Why the Court retreated is the key to Freeman's analysis: if "the problem [racial discrimination] will not be solved until the conditions associated with it have been eliminated,"[155] we are talking about major change. Full and complete desegregation would in the short run harm poor whites (as it has sometimes done) and in the long run displace wealthy whites. Job competition would increase, along with competition for status, suburban acreage, and political power. Most generally, "to achieve the kind of massive results demanded by the victim perspective requires suspension of the equality of opportunity ideology for a time sufficient to 'bourgeoisify' vast numbers of black people, while maintaining that ideology simultaneously for everyone else."[156] It requires, that is, that blacks be given disproportionate resources, power, and status until race would no longer affect people's life chances. The great risk is that such a massive disruption of normal patterns of reward and mobility would reveal the underlying class structure, and destroy the belief in equal opportunity that is the lynchpin of American society. Little wonder, if Freeman is right, that so many whites promote integration but flee the cities, abhor mandatory busing, and decry affirmative action.*

Analysts who focus on white supremacy do not necessarily agree with class analysts. Judge Carter insists that "class issues do have a negative impact on black and white relationships, but the race issue—the color question—remains basic."[157] William Julius Wilson

*The chief flaw in this analysis is that we *have* had some desegregation, even substantial and disruptive desegregation, because of acts by leaders of the dominant race and class. How can we explain Judges Garrity, Battisti (Cleveland), and Egly (Los Angeles), who have encountered psychological stress and physical threats because of their insistence on obeying the Constitution as they interpret it? How do Earl Warren and President Johnson fit into an argument about racial and class dominance? I relegate this issue to a footnote at least partly because I have no definitive (short) answer. Even racist and stratified societies occasionally reform themselves, perhaps to head off demands for more extensive reform. More important, these leaders show that the liberal ideology of the United States is not merely a myth. It is a powerful ideal that unquestionably leads some people to act in the public interest even when such

action violates their own narrow self-interest. There two possibilities keep my hopeful peroration from being hopelessly naive. My thanks to Alan Gewirth for focusing my attention on this issue, the greatest challenge to a race/class argument about desegregation in the United States.

counters by pointing out "the declining significance of race" but the continued significance of systemic rigidities in determining the distribution of American wealth and power.[158] I do not have a dog in that fight. Whether it is white supremacy or class supremacy that inhibits full and complete desegregation, the results are the same—harmful to many whites and some minorities, and only slightly helpful to the rest. In the end, whether we choose full desegregation or an alternative matters less than that we choose one.

We have come full circle, then, back to the original question how racism can persist for three centuries in a liberal democratic polity. Initially I proposed two answers, the anomaly thesis and the symbiosis thesis. The first implies the dilemma Myrdal described: white Americans must choose between their high ideals and their base preferences. Once they choose the former, they can use standard policy practices to rid themselves of the effects of the latter. The second implies a new and much tougher dilemma: Americans must choose between standard, apparently desirable modes of policy choice and enactment, and the goal of eradicating racism. If whites cannot bring themselves to give up the advantages that America's racial and class practices give them, they must permit elites to make that choice for them. Furthermore, they must accept that incremental, cautious, remedial change will not work—and must take disruptive, even risky actions to overcome the powerful inertia of our existing racial structure.

The history of school desegregation shows that Myrdal's formulation of the dilemma and the anomaly thesis in general are too shallow to explain the nature of American race relations. The anomaly thesis simply cannot explain why racial isolation and its effects persist even after our extended and heroic effort to desegregate schools. Do whites really not hold the ideals that Myrdal attributed to them? Why not? Is something more than politics as usual necessary to change the United States' racial structure? If so, what? The anomaly thesis has no answer to these questions, so it leaves liberals as baffled, agonized, and defensive as Senator Biden.

The history of school desegregation provides much more support for the symbiosis thesis. If racism and its psychological, structural, and behavioral consequences are deeply embedded in American society, that would explain why standard practices of incrementalism and popular control do not suffice to eradicate it. They are, after all, relatively weak weapons designed to fight small skirmishes, not major battles. Only substantial change authoritatively imposed has a chance to vanquish the well-fortified citadel of institutional racism.

This conclusion does not, I think, force us into the arms of either nihilists or radicals. We need not conclude that no change is possible, or that only complete synoptic transformation can resolve the dilemma. The United States *has* dramatically restructured its basic framework for choice and its system of policy-making at various points. The state constitutions of the 1820s, the Fifteenth Amendment, and the Nineteenth Amendment together turned a property-owners' republic into a democratic republic. The laws and regulations of the Progressive era and the New Deal turned a system of small-scale entrepreneurship and laissez-faire government into a system of corporate capitalism and business-government interaction. We can, if we choose, significantly change our racial and class structure in a peaceful, evolutionary fashion.

More specifically, the changes needed to eradicate racism through school desegregation or an alternative are not, in the end, all that risky or unprecedented. Liberal democracy has always relied on elites to save it from itself. If authoritative leaders see what is necessary to turn the semblance of democracy into real democracy, and the promise of liberal rights into their guarantee, then elitism (of a certain sort) is perfectly compatible with liberal democracy.* Earl Warren, Lyndon Johnson, and Judge Garrity emerged, after all, from the mainstream of modern American politics. Similarly, liberal

*An analyst deep in the trenches of school desegregation points out a variant on this view. Dr. Leonard Stevens, Director of Cleveland's Office on School Monitoring and Community Relations, argues:

> School desegregation, to the extent that it has occurred, is for the most part a product of law enforcement by the Federal Government (Executive Branch of Judiciary). Law enforcement, as I see it, is a necessary attribute of a working democracy, but law enforcement is not in itself a democratic process. Surely government actions to enforce the Constitution and civil rights laws manifest democratic health—but certainly enforcement actions imposed on local school systems under the force of law do not display the characteristics of participatory democracy. In short, except where school desegregation is done voluntarily on the initiative of a local school board, there is not much room in the school desegregation process for citizen control or even citizen participation. One can look for it but should not expect to find very much.

Letter from Leonard Stevens to author, November 4, 1982.

democracy has taken bold and sweeping action when necessary to save itself. The government's actions to mobilize the economy and citizenry during World War II were astonishingly coercive and far-ranging, but they did not jeopardize the American political-economic system. We invested billions of dollars in the space program in the 1950s and 1960s without any real idea of what we were doing and whether (or how) it would pay off. And once again, I would not be able to argue that certain methods of desegregative change work well if those changes had not already taken place somewhere. The accusations of white supremacy or class rigidity may, in the end, be proven wrong by Americans themselves.

If this line of argument is correct, it suggests that even my reformulation of the American dilemma does not dig deeply enough. The problem is not, at base, risky means but rather the chance that they might succeed. If they did—if substantial, authoritatively imposed change eradicated racism—the racial landscape of American politics would dramatically change. The dilemma at base is the impossibility of retaining both the benefits of racism and certainty and the virtues of liberalism. Our real choice is between change, which might benefit many but will certainly harm a few, and the status quo, which benefits a few at the expense of many. *That* is the American dilemma.

NOTES

CHAPTER 1

1. Gunnar Myrdal, *An American Dilemma: The Negro Problem and Modern Democracy* (New York: Harper & Brothers, 1944), p. xix.

2. Rough draft of Declaration of Independence, quoted in Carl L. Becker, *The Declaration of Independence* (New York: Random House, 1942), p. 147.

3. Letter of 1773, quoted in J. Franklin Jameson, *The American Revolution Considered as a Social Movement* (Princeton: Princeton University Press, 1926), p. 23.

4. William Lloyd Garrison, *An Address Delivered in Marlboro Chapel, Boston, July 4, 1838* (Boston: Issac Knapp, 1838), quoted in *American Political Thought,* ed. Larry I. Peterman and Louis F. Weschler (New York: Irvington, 1972), pp. 169–70.

5. T. Harry Williams, ed., *Abraham Lincoln: Selected Speeches, Messages, and Letters* (New York: Holt, Rinehart & Winston, 1957), pp. 72, 76.

6. Myrdal, *An American Dilemma,* p. 21.

7. Edmund S. Morgan, *American Slavery, American Freedom* (New York: Norton, 1975), pp. 380–81.

8. William Harper, "Memoir on Slavery," in *The Ideology of Slavery,* ed. Drew G. Faust (Baton Rouge: Louisiana State University Press, 1981), p. 81.

9. Thomas Roderick Dew, "Abolition of Negro Slavery," in ibid., pp. 66–67.

10. James Henry Hammond, "Letter to an English Abolitionist," in ibid., p. 177. Hammond is quoting "the much abused sentiment of Governor M'Duffie, that 'Slavery is the corner-stone of our republican edifice'" (p. 176).

11. Stanley B. Greenberg, *Race and State in Capitalist Development* (New Haven: Yale University Press, 1980), p. 26.

12. Derrick A. Bell, Jr., "Racial Remediation: An Historical Perspective on Current Conditions," *Notre Dame Lawyer* 52, no. 1 (October 1976): 16.

CHAPTER 2

1. Quoted in Richard Kluger, *Simple Justice* (New York: Knopf, 1975) 2:911.

2. See *Brown v. Board of Education (Brown I),* 347 U.S. 484 (1954); *Brown v. Board of Education (Brown II),* 349 U.S. 294 (1955); and *Plessy v. Ferguson,* 163 U.S. 537 (1896).

3. Kluger, *Simple Justice* 1:365–70; 2:662–65, 676–84.

4. Ibid. 2:671.

5. Harold J. Spaeth, *Introduction to Brown v. Board of Education,* Classic and Current Decisions of the United States Supreme Court, no. 20 (San Francisco: Freeman, 1977), p. 2.

6. "Editorial Excerpts from the Nation's Press on Segregation Ruling" and "NAACP Sets Advanced Goals," both in *New York Times,* May 18, 1954, pp. 19, 16.

7. John F. Kennedy, "Radio and Television Report to the American People on Civil Rights," June 11, 1963, in *Public Papers of the Presidents of the United States* (Washington, D.C.: U.S. Government Printing Office, 1964), pp. 468–71.

8. Note that this description was written seven years after the author left Princeton's employ. Carl A. Fields, "The Black Arrival at Princeton," *Princeton Alumni Weekly,* April 18, 1977, p. 19.

9. From "The Leverett House Forum of March 18, 1964," in *The Speeches of Malcolm X at Harvard,* ed. Archie Epps (New York: William Morrow, 1968), p. 160; James Baldwin, *The Fire Next Time* (New York: Dial, 1963), p. 108; Norman Podhoretz, "My Negro Problem—and Ours," *Commentary* 35 (February 1963): 96, 100.

10. Gordon W. Allport, *The Nature of Prejudice* (1954; reprint, Reading, Mass.: Addison-Wesley, 1979), p. 471. Note that even Allport implicitly equates "Americans" with "whites."

11. Philip E. Converse et al., *American Social Attitudes Data Sourcebook, 1947–1978* (Cambridge: Harvard University Press, 1980), p. 60.

12. Louis Harris and Associates, *A Study of Attitudes toward Racial and Religious Minorities and toward Women* (New York: Louis Harris and Associates, 1978), pp. 16–19.

13. Converse et al., *American Social Attitudes,* p. 60; Harris, *A Study of Attitudes,* pp. 14–16, 19–21.

14. In 1972, 76 percent of whites with an opinion agreed. James A. Davis, *General Social Surveys, 1972–1982: Cumulative Codebook* (Chicago: University of Chicago, National Opinion Research Center, 1982), p. 101.

15. *Statistical Abstract of the United States, 1982–1983* (Washington, D.C.: U.S. Government Printing Office, 1983), p. 488; Raymond E. Wolfinger and Steven J. Rosenstone, *Who Votes?* (New Haven: Yale University Press, 1980), pp. 90–91; Sidney Verba and Norman H. Nie, *Participation in America* (New York: Harper & Row, 1972), pp. 97–101.

16. "Largest Increase in BEOs since 1976," *Focus* 12, no. 1 (Washington, D.C.: Joint Center for Political Studies, January 1984): 8.

17. Gerald S. McDougall and Harold Bunce, "Urban Service Distributions: Some Answers to Neglected Issues" (Paper presented at the annual meeting of the Association for Public Policy Analysis and Management, Philadelphia, October 1983). Eleven of the fifty largest cities have black mayors; 27 cities with populations over 50,000 have black mayors. Milton D. Morris, "National Profile of Black Elected Officials," *Focus* 12, no. 2 (February 1984): 5.

18. Barry Sussman, "Prejudice a Factor in Choosing a President," *Washington Post,* April 17, 1983, p. A10.

19. Bernard E. Anderson, "Economic Patterns in Black America," in National Urban League, *The State of Black America* (New York: National Urban League, 1982), p. 29;

and Bureau of the Census, *The Social and Economic Status of the Black Population in the United States: An Historical View, 1790–1978*, Current Population Reports, Special Studies, series P-23, no. 80 (Washington, D.C.: U.S. Government Printing Office, 1979), pp. 42, 199.

20. Richard Freeman, "Black Economic Progress since 1964," *Public Interest* 52 (Summer 1978): 55.

21. U.S. Bureau of the Census, *Characteristics of the Population below the Poverty Level: 1981*, Current Population Reports, series P-60, no. 138 (Washington, D.C.: U.S. Government Printing Office, 1983), pp. 27–28; *Money Income and Poverty Status of Families and Persons in the United States: 1982*, Current Population Reports, series P-60, no. 140 (Washington, D.C.: U.S. Government Printing Office, 1983), p. 21.

22. Michael Reich, *Racial Inequality: A Political-Economic Analysis* (Princeton: Princeton University Press, 1981), p. 34; U.S. Bureau of the Census, *America's Black Population: 1970 to 1982*, special publication PIO/POP-83-1 (Washington, D.C.: U.S. Government Printing Office, 1983), p. 9. The employment/population ratio for the civilian labor force is about 55 percent for non-Anglo men, and 18 percent of that 55 percent is unemployed; for the male population as a whole (predominantly Anglos), the comparable figures are 67 percent in the civilian labor force, of whom 10 percent are unemployed. Data are for June 1982. In 1960, all men and non-Anglo men had similar labor force participation rates (about 75 percent). *Statistical Abstract, 1982–1983*, p. 376.

23. U.S. Bureau of the Census, *Money Income of Households, Families, and Persons in the United States: 1981*, Current Population Reports, series P-60, no. 137 (Washington, D.C.: U.S. Government Printing Office, 1983), pp. 39–40, and *Money Income: 1982*, p. 7. The absolute disparity between median incomes of the two races has also increased from $9,149 in 1967 to $10,251 in 1981 (in constant 1981 dollars).

24. Reynolds Farley, *Blacks and Whites: Narrowing the Gap* (Cambridge: Harvard University Press, 1984), figure 3-5.

25. Finis Welch, "Affirmative Action and Its Enforcement," *American Economic Review* 71, no. 2 (May 1981): 132. On wage discrimination and its changes over time, see also "Proceedings of the National Economic Association in Conjunction with the Allied Social Science Association," *Review of Black Political Economy* 10, no. 4 (special issue, Summer 1980): 354–94; Marvin M. Smith, "Industrial Racial Wage Discrimination in the U.S.," *Industrial Relations* 18, no. 1 (Winter 1979): 110–16; Edward Lazear, "The Narrowing of Black-White Wage Differentials Is Illusory," *American Economic Review* 69, no. 4 (September 1979): 553–64; James P. Smith and Finis Welch, *Race Differences in Earnings: A Survey and New Evidence* (Santa Monica, Calif.: Rand Corporation, 1978); James P. Smith, "Race and Human Capital," *American Economic Review* 74 (September 1984).

26. National Center for Education Statistics (NCES), *Digest of Education Statistics 1982* (Washington, D.C.: U.S. Government Printing Office, 1982), p. 16.

27. *Statistical Abstract, 1982–1983*, pp. 143, 145; *Historical Statistics of the United States, Colonial Times to 1970* (Washington, D.C.: U.S. Government Printing Office, 1976), p. 382.

28. Nancy Burton and Lyle Jones, "Recent Trends in Achievement Levels of Black and White Youth," *Educational Researcher* 11, no. 4 (April 1982): 11–13. These

figures, however, exclude the two tests in which black achievement has improved least, so the improvement reported in the text is somewhat exaggerated. See also Barbara Holmes, *Reading, Science, and Mathematics: A Closer Look* (Denver: Education Commission of the States, National Assessment of Educational Progress, 1982), p. 3.

29. Paul Peterson, background paper in Task Force on Federal Elementary and Secondary Education Policy, *Making the Grade* (New York: Twentieth Century Fund, 1983), pp. 54–56; Roy H. Forbes, "Test Score Advances among Southeastern Students: A Possible Bonus of Government Intervention," *Phi Delta Kappan* 62, no. 5 (January 1981): 332–34, 350.

30. Literacy is defined as the ability to read and write at all; functional literacy is defined as the ability to "read materials encountered in daily life." See National Assessment of Educational Progress, *Functional Literacy: Basic Reading Performance* (Denver: Education Commission of the States, 1976).

31. Burton and Jones, "Recent Trends in Achievement Levels," pp. 11–13.

32. Both blacks and whites improved their math scores as a consequence of remediation. Whites who received remedial help also improved their reading scores more than whites who did not; nonremediated blacks actually did better on the second reading test than blacks who had received remedial help. Robert C. Serow and James J. Davies, "Resources and Outcomes of Minimum Competency Testing as Measures of Equality of Educational Opportunity," *American Educational Research Journal* 19, no. 4 (Winter 1982): 529–39.

33. The National Center for Education Statistics reports that in 1978, 42 percent of blacks in higher education were in two-year degree programs, compared with 34 percent of whites in postsecondary education. Reginald Stuart, "New Trend in College Desegregation Emerges," *New York Times*, September 3, 1981, p. B15. Put another way, blacks composed 9.1 percent of all postsecondary enrollment in 1980, but they have more than their proportional share (10.1 percent) of enrollment in two-year public colleges, and less than their proportional share (5.4 percent) of private university enrollment. See National Center for Education Statistics, *Digest of Education Statistics 1982*, p. 104.

34. Hazel G. Erskine, "The Polls: Race Relations," *Public Opinion Quarterly* 26, no. 1 (Spring 1962): 139.

35. Converse et al., *American Social Attitudes*, p. 79.

36. Harris, *A Study of Attitudes*, p. 110.

37. CBS News/*New York Times* Poll, *The Kerner Commission—Ten Years Later* (New York: CBS News/*New York Times* Poll, 1978), appendix, p. 19.

38. Ibid., appendix, p. 9.

39. Harris, *A Study of Attitudes*, pp. 2–13, 27–33.

40. Converse et al., *American Social Attitudes*, p. 61.

41. Specifically, the poorest fifth of black families receives 3.9 percent of total black family income, whereas the poorest fifth of whites receives 5.2 percent of total white family income. Conversely, the richest 20 percent of black families receive 45.3 percent of total black family income, and the richest 20 percent of white families receives 42.1 percent of total white family income. Data are for 1982, from U.S. Bureau of the Census, *Money Income: 1982*, p. 11.

42. George Lardner, Jr., and Margot Hornblower, "Miami: Brutality Was Not Expected," *Washington Post,* May 25, 1980, pp. A1, A16.

43. *Goss v. Board of Education,* 373 U.S. 683 (1963).

44. *Griffin v. County School Board of Prince Edward County,* 377 U.S. 218 (1964); *Green v. Board of Education of New Kent County,* 391 U.S. 430 (1968); *Swann v. Charlotte-Mecklenburg Board of Education,* 402 U.S. 1 (1971).

45. *Keyes v. School District No. 1 of Denver, Colorado,* 413 U.S. 189 (1973).

46. *Milliken v. Bradley (Milliken I),* 418 U.S. 717 (1974).

47. One long-term staff member, for example, justifies OCR's recent inattention to desegregation by pointing out, "We have no constituency in Congress. . . . This all changed the day of the Detroit court order [*Milliken I*]. The Michigan delegation stopped supporting us and they had been among our strongest supporters." Charles S. Bullock III, "Implementation of Selected Equal Education Opportunity Programs" (Paper presented at the annual meeting of the American Political Science Association, Washington, D.C., 1980), pp. 46–47.

48. From 1970 to 1980, the black proportion of public school enrollment increased about 2 percent in the Northeast and Midwest. It barely changed in the other regions. Gary Orfield, *Public School Desegregation in the United States, 1968–1980* (Washington, D.C.: Joint Center for Political Studies, 1983), p. 21.

49. National Center for Education Statistics, *The Condition of Education, 1981* (Washington, D.C.: U.S. Government Printing Office, 1981), p. 60.

50. Judy L. Hanna, letter to author, October 14, 1983.

51. Charles S. Bullock III and Joseph Stewart, Jr., "Incidence and Correlates of Second-Generation Discrimination," in *Race, Sex, and Policy Problems,* ed. Marian L. Palley and Michael B. Preston (Lexington, Mass.: Lexington Books, 1979), p. 120.

52. Charles S. Bullock III, "Equal Education Opportunity," in *Implementation of Civil Rights Policy,* ed. Charles S. Bullock III and Charles M. Lamb (Monterey, Calif.: Brooks/Cole, 1984), p. 73.

53. Vincent J. Breglio, Ronald H. Hinkley, and Richard S. Beal, "Students' Economic and Educational Status and Selection for Compensatory Education" (Report prepared by Decima Research, Santa Ana, Calif., 1978), pp. 70–72. Among low achievers, for whom compensatory education programs are intended, more whites than blacks are selected. Among regular achievers, who are inappropriately placed in compensatory education classes, more blacks than whites are assigned. Hispanics have the highest selection rates, regardless of socioeconomic status or achievement levels. See also NCES, *The Condition of Education, 1983* (Washington, D.C.: U.S. Government Printing Office, 1983), p. 60.

54. NCES, *Digest of Education Statistics 1982,* p. 70 (data are for 1980), *Condition of Education, 1981,* p. 82, and *Condition of Education, 1983.*

55. Bullock and Stewart, "Incidence and Correlates of Second-Generation Discrimination," p. 120.

56. Children's Defense Fund, *School Suspensions: Are They Helping Children?* (Washington, D.C.: Washington Research Project, 1975), pp. 63–71, and *Children Out of Schools in America* (Washington, D.C.: Children's Defense Fund, 1974), pp. 130–34.

57. Orfield, *Public School Desegregation,* p. 33.

58. Bullock, "Equal Education Opportunity," pp. 70–71.

59. Orfield, *Public School Desegregation*, p. 34.
60. Bullock, "Equal Education Opportunity," pp. 70–71.
61. Ibid., p. 70.
62. Orfield, *Public School Desegregation*, appendix B.
63. For competing contentions about changes in achievement levels, see Senate Judiciary Committee, Subcommittee on Separation of Powers, *Hearings on Court-Ordered School Busing*, 97th Cong., 1st Sess., 1981, e.g., pp. 183, 552–65, 605, 615, 652, 884. On Greenville, South Carolina, see Cheryl Segal, "Students Score Better in Language, Math Testing," *Greenville Piedmont*, July 19, 1983.
64. Don Steele, "Seattle Did It," *Christian Science Monitor*, April 27, 1983, p. 22.
65. Lee A. Daniels, "In Defense of Busing," *New York Times Magazine*, April 17, 1983, p. 34.

CHAPTER 3

1. David Braybrooke and Charles E. Lindblom, *A Strategy of Decision* (New York: Free Press, 1970), p. 71.
2. Professors Braybrooke and Lindblom both commented extensively on a draft of this book and argued, independently of one another, that my use of *incrementalism* is not theirs and many even be wrong. Where relevant, I point out specific differences and argue my case, but the reader should beware that the arguments in *A Strategy of Decision* and its successors are not always applicable to my analysis.
3. David Braybrooke, comments to author, December 28, 1982.
4. Charles E. Lindblom, "Still Muddling, Not Yet Through," *Public Administration Review* 26, no. 6 (November/December 1979): 520.
5. David Braybrooke, "Some Questions about Incrementalism in Central Reviewing Agencies" (Unpublished manuscript, Dalhousie University, Halifax, Nova Scotia, 1973), p. 3; Lindblom, "Still Muddling," p. 520.
6. Charles E. Lindblom, comments to author, May 31, 1983.
7. Paul E. Peterson, comments to author, January 10, 1984.
8. *Jacobellis v. Ohio*, 378 U.S. 184, Concurring Opinion, 197 (1964).
9. Sidney Verba and Norman H. Nie, *Participation in America*, p. 2.
10. Obviously, much more can be (and has been) said about distinctions within the American electoral system among pluralism, majoritarianism, interest group liberalism, and so on. But in the case of school desegregation, all forms of popular control generate similar outcomes, so such distinctions are surprisingly unimportant here. See chapter 6 for a defense of this assertion.
11. Ronald Dworkin, *Taking Rights Seriously* (Cambridge: Harvard University Press, 1977).
12. C. Anthony Broh and Willis D. Hawley, "Clarification of the Goals of Desegregation" (Unpublished manuscript, Duke University, Institute of Policy Sciences, Durham, N.C., 1980).
13. Since researchers focus on and desegregation strategies are aimed at particular goals, I cannot systematically examine the effects of each incremental or participatory rule for action on each indicator of desegregation success.

CHAPTER 4

1. Sydney Smith, "Second Letter to Archdeacon Singleton," in *The Works of the Rev. Sydney Smith* (London: Longman, Green, Longman and Roberts, 1859), 2:286. My thanks to David Braybrooke for this quotation.

2. Larry W. Hughes, William M. Gordon, and Larry W. Hillman, *Desegregating America's Schools* (New York: Longman, 1980), p. 112.

3. J. Harvie Wilkinson III, *From Brown to Bakke: The Supreme Court and School Integration: 1954–1978* (New York: Oxford University Press, 1979), p. 75.

4. David W. Hirsch, "'We're on the Bus . . .'" (Senior thesis, Princeton University, Princeton, N.J., 1982), p. 77.

5. David A. Bennett, "The Impact of Court-Ordered Desegregation: A Defendant's View," in *Schools and the Courts: Desegregation* (Eugene, Or.: University of Oregon, ERIC Clearinghouse on Educational Management, 1979), pp. 77–120.

6. Walter M. Lee III and Samuel L. Zimmerman, "Desegregation—A Model Plan" (Unpublished report, School District of Greenville County, Greenville, S.C., 1975), foreword.

7. David J. Kirby, T. Robert Harris, Robert L. Crain, with Christine H. Rossell, *Political Strategies in Northern School Desegregation* (Lexington, Mass.: Lexington Books, 1973), p. 136.

8. Harrell R. Rodgers, Jr., and Charles S. Bullock III, *Coercion to Compliance* (Lexington, Mass.: Lexington Books, 1976), pp. 35–36.

9. Christine H. Rossell, "Assessing the Unintended Impacts of Public Policy: School Desegregation and Resegregation" (Unpublished manuscript, Boston University, 1978), pp. 26–27; and David R. Morgan with Robert E. England, "Assessing the Progress of Large City School Desegregation: A Case Survey Approach" (Unpublished report, University of Oklahoma, Bureau of Government Research, 1981), pp. 101–03, 113.

10. Christine H. Rossell, "Applied Social Science Research: What Does It Say about the Effectiveness of School Desegregation Plans?" *Journal of Legal Studies* 12 (January 1983): 89.

11. David R. Morgan, Robert E. England, and Dianna Laverents, *Desegregating Public Schools: A Handbook for Local Officials* (Norman: University of Oklahoma, Bureau of Government Research, 1982), p. 115.

12. Lillian B. Rubin, *Busing and Backlash: White against White in an Urban School District* (Berkeley: University of California Press, 1972).

13. Arthur L. Stinchcombe and D. Garth Taylor, "On Democracy and School Integration," in *School Desegregation: Past, Present, and Future,* ed. Walter G. Stephan and Joe R. Feagin (New York: Plenum, 1980), p. 181.

14. Stephen M. Weatherford, "The Politics of School Busing: Contextual Effects and Community Polarization," *Journal of Politics* 42, no. 3 (August 1980): 758, 764.

15. Christine H. Rossell, "The Effect of Community Leadership and Media on Public Behavior," *Theory into Practice* 17, no. 2 (April 1978): 134, 136; and David R. Morgan and Robert E. England, "White Enrollment Loss: The Effects of School Desegregation in Perspective" (Unpublished report, University of Oklahoma, Bureau of Government Research, 1983), table 2.

16. *Tasby v. Estes,* 412 F. Supp. 1192 (N.D. Tex., 1976).

17. For similar results in Jacksonville, see Michael W. Giles, "Racial Stability and Urban School Desegregation," *Urban Affairs Quarterly* 12 (June 1977): 503–06.

18. Willis D. Hawley, "Equity and Quality in Education: Characteristics of Effective Desegregated Schools," in *Effective School Desegregation: Equity, Quality, and Feasibility,* ed. Willis D. Hawley (Beverly Hills: Sage, 1981), p. 299. John B. McConahay, "Reducing Racial Prejudice in Desegregated Schools," in ibid., p. 43. On race relations, see also Martin Patchen, *Black-White Contact in Schools* (West Lafayette, Ind.: Purdue University Press, 1982), pp. 83–114.

19. Different methods of aggregating the data yield slightly different results. David W. Johnson, Roger T. Johnson, and Geoffrey Maruyama, "Interdependence and Interpersonal Attraction among Heterogeneous and Homogeneous Individuals: A Theoretical Formulation and a Meta-Analysis of the Research" (Unpublished manuscript, University of Minnesota, 1982), p. 32.

20. Results for parents are not statistically significant. See John H. Schweitzer and Robert J. Griffore, "A Longitudinal Study of Attitudes of Students and Parents Coincident with Court-Ordered School Desegregation," *Urban Review* 13, no. 2 (Summer 1981): 115, 117. See also Jeffrey A. Raffel, Nancy J. Colmer, and Donald L. Berry, "Public Opinion toward the Public Schools of Northern New Castle County" (Unpublished manuscript, University of Delaware, College of Urban Affairs and Public Policy, 1983), p. 37, for evidence that parents' evaluations of their children's schools decline as grade level rises.

21. Walter G. Stephan, "School Desegregation: An Evaluation of Predictions Made in *Brown v. Board of Education,*" *Psychological Bulletin* 85, no. 2 (March 1978): 226; Joel M. Moskowitz and Paul M. Wortman, "Reassessing the Impact of School Desegregation," in *Reanalyzing Program Evaluations,* ed. Robert F. Boruch, Paul M. Wortman, David S. Cordray, and Associates (San Francisco: Jossey-Bass, 1981), pp. 332, 334.

22. Robert L. Crain and Rita E. Mahard, "Minority Achievement: Policy Implications of Research," in *Effective School Desegregation,* ed. Hawley, p. 76; and Nancy H. St. John, "The Effects of School Desegregation on Children: A New Look at the Research Evidence," in *Race and Schooling in the City,* ed. Adam Yarmolinsky, Lance Liebman, and Corinne S. Schelling (Cambridge: Harvard University Press, 1981), p. 87.

This and the previous claim about race relations are contested by studies that find desegregation to have few positive outcomes at any age. No scholar, however, claims that desegregation works better for older than for younger students. A good brief review of the negative findings is in Norman Miller, *Principles Relevant to Successful School Desegregation* (Los Angeles: University of Southern California, Social Science Research Institute, 1977), in notes, pp. 1–12.

Recent data on improvements in achievement test scores for nine- and thirteen-year-olds, but not for seventeen-year-olds lead some analysts to conclude that generally grade schools do a better job of educating than high schools. See, e.g., Paul E. Peterson, background paper in Task Force on Federal Elementary and Secondary Education Policy, *Making the Grade.* If this point is correct, it is another strong argument for desegregating in the early years.

23. Hawley, "Equity and Quality," p. 299.

24. Robert L. Crain and Rita E. Mahard, "Desegregation and Black Achievement: A Review of the Research," *Law and Contemporary Problems* 42, no. 3 (Summer 1978): 37. Findings on the other grade levels accord with those reported in the text: for students desegregated in third through sixth grade, most findings are positive, some are neutral, and a few are negative. For high schoolers, there are more negative or neutral than positive findings. See, in addition, Ronald A. Krol, "A Meta Analysis of the Effects of Desegregation on Academic Achievement," *Urban Review* 12, no. 4 (1980): 217.

25. See National Institute of Education, *Violent Schools—Safe Schools: The Safe School Study Report to the Congress*, vol. 1 (Washington, D.C.: U.S. Government Printing Office, 1978), pp. 99–105, B20–B21. Data were not collected for lower grades.

26. Gary D. Gottfredson and Denise C. Daiger, *Disruption in Six Hundred Schools* (Baltimore: Johns Hopkins University, Center for the Social Organization of Schools, 1979), pp. 78–90, 153–62. This study is a reanalysis of the "Safe Schools Study" data. The original analysis finds court-ordered desegregation to be associated with increased violence in five of its six categories of schools. However, busing for desegregation is associated with violence in only two of the six sets of schools analyzed, both junior high schools. See National Institute of Education, *Violent Schools—Safe Schools*, pp. A18, A19. In both studies, the association between violence and desegregation (or busing) is weak.

27. Christine H. Rossell and Willis D. Hawley, "Understanding White Flight and Doing Something About It," in *Effective School Desegregation*, ed. Hawley, p. 170; and Morgan with England, "Assessing the Progress," pp. 99–101.

28. Braybrooke and Lindblom, *A Strategy of Decision*, p. 73.

29. The evidence is mixed on whether achievement improves as the student's (not the school's) experience with desegregation increases. For support of the proposition, see Krol, "A Meta Analysis of the Effects," p. 219; for contradictory evidence, see Crain and Mahard, "Minority Achievement," pp. 61, 66.

30. John E. Coulson, *Overview of the National Evaluation of the Emergency School Aid Act* (Santa Monica, Calif.: System Development Corporation, 1977), pp. 25–30, 50.

31. Morgan with England, "Assessing the Progress," pp. 100–01; Rossell, "Applied Social Science Research," p. 93; Rossell, "Assessing the Unintended Impacts," pp. 26–34. But see David J. Armor, "White Flight and the Future of School Desegregation," in *School Desegregation*, ed. Stephan and Feagin, pp. 193–213, for a countervailing emphasis on the extent of long-term white flight.

32. After one year of desegregation, 70 percent of the respondents cited busing as Louisville's biggest problem; after two years, 48 percent did so. Unpublished data from survey on reactions to busing in Louisville, by John B. McConahay and Willis D. Hawley (Duke University, Institute of Policy Sciences, 1978).

33. Christine H. Rossell, "The Effectiveness of Desegregation Plans in Reducing Racial Isolation, White Flight, and Achieving a Positive Community Response," in Christine H. Rossell et al., *A Review of the Empirical Research on Desegregation: Community Response, Race Relations, Academic Achievement and Resegregation* (Nashville: Vanderbilt University, Institute for Public Policy Studies, 1981), p. 14.

34. Raffel et al., "Public Opinion toward the Public Schools," pp. 10–21. A

comparison of this survey with Schweitzer and Griffore, "A Longitudinal Study," shows the dangers inherent in drawing conclusions from survey results. The latter finds that most Wilmington parents' and students' attitudes about desegregation and their schools become more negative from the first to the second year of desegregation, implying a worsening of race relations as a consequence of desegregation. Raffel et al., however, show that hostility increased after one year but largely disappeared after four or five years of desegregation, implying that race relations first worsen, then improve. A comparison of the two-year and four-year surveys induces great skepticism of studies that cover only a few years—virtually *all* attitudinal studies of school desegregation.

35. Garlie A. Forehand, Marjorie Ragosta, and Donald A. Rock, *Conditions and Processes of Effective School Desegregation* (Princeton: Educational Testing Service, 1976), pp. 164–79, 217–40.

36. B. Harold Gerard and Norman Miller, *School Desegregation: A Long Term Study* (New York: Plenum, 1975).

37. John B. McConahay, "The Effects of School Desegregation upon Students' Racial Attitudes and Behavior," *Law and Contemporary Problems* 42, no. 3 (Summer 1978): 93.

38. Robert L. Crain, Rita E. Mahard, and Ruth E. Narot, *Making Desegregation Work: How Schools Create Social Climates* (Cambridge, Mass.: Ballinger, 1982), p. 75. See also Janet W. Schofield, *Black and White in School: Trust, Tension, or Tolerance?* (New York: Praeger, 1982).

39. One can play mental games here by comparing Manhattan to Alaska—large spaces do not always imply more people. The more rigorous formulation of this proposition is: (1) Policy changes that affect a large territory are less incremental than policy changes that affect a small territory. (2) Policy changes that affect more people are less incremental than policy changes that affect fewer people. (3) Other things being equal, the larger the territory covered, the more people are affected, although of course other things are not always equal. (4) When the two conflict, the criterion regarding people dominates the criterion of space. The reason for the shorthand in the text should be obvious.

40. Hughes et al., *Desegregating America's Schools,* p. 53. Constitutionally, if a plaintiff can prove that part of a school system is segregated, the burden of proof is on school officials to show that the whole system should not be desegregated; see *Keyes v. School District No. 1 of Denver, Colorado; Dayton Board of Education v. Brinkmann,* 443 U.S. 526 (1979); *Columbus Board of Education v. Penick,* 443 U.S. 449 (1979). Thus the issue of partial desegregation is relevant only in plans that are not court ordered or in which a court permits a partial remedy.

41. Robert T. Stout and Morton Inger, *School Desegregation: Progress in Eight Cities* (Washington, D.C.: U.S. Commission on Civil Rights, 1966).

42. James S. Coleman et al., *Equality of Educational Opportunity* (Washington, D.C.: U.S. Government Printing Office, 1966); R. Gary Bridge, Charles M. Judd, and Peter R. Moock, *The Determinants of Educational Outcomes: The Impact of Families, Peers, Teachers, and Schools* (Cambridge, Mass.: Ballinger, 1979), pp. 229–31. Some dispute this claim, at least in its simple forms; see, for example, Eleanor P. Wolf,

Trial and Error: The Detroit School Segregation Case (Detroit: Wayne State University Press, 1981), pp. 126–36 and Patchen, *Black-White Contact*.

43. Ronald D. Henderson, Mary von Euler, and Jeffrey M. Schneider, "Remedies for Segregation: Some Lessons from Research," *Educational Evaluation and Policy Analysis* 3, no. 4 (July/August 1981): 68.

44. The only direct comparison of the effects of desegregation and school quality on housing preferences finds that the price of housing and possibly the rate of housing construction are more affected by the quality of schools than by their racial composition. See G. Donald Jud and James M. Watts, "Schools and Housing Values," *Land Economics* 57, no. 3 (August 1981): 459–70, and "Real Estate Values, School Quality, and the Pattern of Urban Development in Charlotte, North Carolina," *Economics of Education Review* 1, no. 1 (Winter 1981): 87–97.

45. Douglas Longshore, *The Control Threat in Desegregated Schools: Exploring the Relationship between School Racial Composition and Intergroup Hostility* (Santa Monica, Calif.: System Development Corporation, 1981), and "Race Composition and White Hostility: A Research Note on the Problem of Control in Desegregated Schools," *Social Forces* 61, no. 1 (September 1982): 73–78; Charles B. Thomas, "Race Relations in Desegregated Schools of Different Race and Social Class Composition" (Paper presented at the annual meeting of the American Educational Research Association, 1979); and Bruce A. Campbell, "The Impact of School Desegregation: An Investigation of Three Mediating Variables," *Youth and Society* 9 (September 1977): pp. 90–91, 98–100, 104. The most interesting recent discussion, which accords with my prescriptions if not precisely with my analysis, is Crain et al., *Making Desegregation Work*, pp. 64–68. However, for cautions about the negative effects on racial attitudes of mixing low-status blacks and high-status whites, without working to overcome hostility and anxiety, see Forehand et al., *Conditions and Processes*, pp. 164–73.

46. Ray C. Rist, "On the Future of School Desegregation: A New American Dilemma?" in *School Desegregation*, ed. Stephan and Feagin, p. 127.

47. Gary Orfield, "Housing Patterns and Desegregation Policy," in *Effective School Desegregation*, ed. Hawley, pp. 202–08.

48. Gary Orfield, "Why It Worked in Dixie: Southern School Desegregation and Its Implications for the North," in *Race and Schooling in the City*, ed. Yarmolinsky et al., p. 32.

49. John D. Owen, "The Distribution of Educational Resources in Large American Cities," *Journal of Human Resources* 7, no. 1 (Winter 1972): 26–38.

50. Alan K. Campbell and Philip Meranto, "The Metropolitan Educational Dilemma: Matching Resources to Needs," in *The Manipulated City*, ed. Stephen Gale and Eric Moore (Chicago: Maaroufa Press, 1975), pp. 305–18; Bill Olds, *Are Minority Pupils Shortchanged? Intra-District School Financing* (Hartford: Connecticut Civil Liberties Union, 1982).

51. J. Dennis Lord and John C. Catau, "School Desegregation Policy and Intra-School District Migration," *Social Science Quarterly* 57 (1977): 784–96.

52. Charles Clotfelter, prepared statement to Senate Judiciary Committee, Subcommittee on Separation of Powers, *Hearings on Court-Ordered School Busing*, 97th Cong., 1st Sess., 1981, p. 218.

53. Michael W. Giles, Douglas S. Gatlin, and Everett F. Cataldo, *Determinants of Resegregation: Compliance/Rejection Behavior and Policy Alternatives* (Washington, D.C.: National Science Foundation, 1976), pp. 21–39, 48–49.

54. John A. Finger, Jr., "Why Busing Plans Work," in *School Desegregation: Shadow and Substance*, ed. Florence H. Levinsohn and Benjamin D. Wright (Chicago: University of Chicago Press, 1976), p. 63.

55. Christine H. Rossell and John M. Ross, "The Long Term Effect of Court-Ordered Desegregation on Student Enrollment in Central City Public School Systems: The Case of Boston, 1974–1979" (Unpublished manuscript, Boston University, 1979).

56. Stinchcombe and Taylor, "On Democracy and School Integration," p. 175 (emphasis in original).

57. Total transportation costs ranged from 0.50 to 10.3 percent of the district budget. Costs declined slightly in the district that spent the most. See Alanson van Fleet, "Student Transportation Costs Following Desegregation," *Integrated Education* 15, no. 6 (November/December 1977): 75–77. For pre- and postdesegregation busing costs in other cities, see Gary Orfield, *Must We Bus? Segregated Schools and National Policy* (Washington, D.C.: Brookings Institution, 1978), pp. 131–43.

58. Eighty-five percent of the respondents in a 1972 Civil Rights Commission national survey agreed that "busing for desegregation adds 25 percent or more to local school costs." The greater respondents' misinformation about busing, the greater their opposition to it. Marvin Wall, "What the Public Doesn't Know Hurts," *Civil Rights Digest* 5, no. 5 (Summer 1973): 23–27. One reason for this wild misperception may be that parents are told of the costs of new buses as though they are part of the ongoing cost of desegregation. They do cost money, of course, but buses are like any capital improvement; to put all of their cost into one year's budget presentation to the public is poor accounting at best and deception at worst.

59. In 1963, student accident rates in school buses were less than 0.05 accidents per 100,000 student days; walking produced 0.3 accidents per 100,000 student days. In 1968, the figures are 0.03 and 0.14 respectively; in 1971, the figures are 0.04 and 0.12; in 1977, the figures are 0.07 and 0.08. Data are from National Safety Council, *Accident Facts*, 1965, 1970, 1975, and 1980 editions (Chicago: National Safety Council), p. 90 in each.

60. National Institute of Education, *Violent Schools—Safe Schools*, pp. A18–A19.

61. Barbara S. Zoloth, "The Impact of Busing on Student Achievement: Reanalysis," *Growth and Change* 7 (July 1976): 43–47; James A. Davis, "Busing," in *Southern Schools: An Evaluation of the Effects of the Emergency School Assistance Program and of School Desegregation*, ed. Robert L. Crain, vol. 2 (Chicago: University of Chicago, National Opinion Research Center, 1973), pp. 114–18; and Gerald L. Natkin, "The Effects of Busing on Second Grade Students' Achievement Test Scores (Jefferson County, Kentucky)" (Paper presented at the annual meeting of the American Educational Research Association, Boston, April 1980).

For a debate over the Zoloth findings, see Yao-Chi Lu and Luther Tweeten, "The

Impact of Busing on Student Achievement," *Growth and Change* 4, no. 4 (Octo. 1973): 44–46, and their further exchanges with Zoloth in *Growth and Change* 7 (July 1976): 48–52.

62. Davis, "Busing," pp. 106–14, 117–18; Crain et al., *Making Desegregation Work*, pp. 56–61.

63. Of the three surviving correlations, the strongest showed positive effects of busing, the weakest showed negative effects, and the third did not address busing at all. Davis, "Busing," pp. 117–18.

64. Michael W. Giles, Douglas S. Gatlin, and Everett F. Cataldo, "The Impact of Busing on White Flight," *Social Science Quarterly* 55 (1974): 495.

65. Ibid, pp. 496–501; Rossell, "Applied Social Science Research," p. 92; Morgan with England, "Assessing the Progress," pp. 49–53, 117.

66. Center for the Study of Law in Education, *School Transportation: Fact Sheet No. 16* (St. Louis: Washington University, 1981).

67. Charles Moody and Jeffrey Ross, "Costs of Implementing Court-Ordered Desegregation," *Breakthrough* 9, no. 1 (University of Michigan, School of Education, Fall 1980). See also *Swann v. Charlotte-Mecklenburg*, August 5, 1970 Order, 318 F. Supp. 786 (1970), pp. 792–99; Orfield, *Must We Bus?* pp. 133–41. A Civil Rights Commission survey of 1000 school superintendents found that, in the 230 districts with useable data, only 3 percent more white students and 9 percent more minority students were bused for desegregation purposes between 1966 and 1975 than had been bused beforehand. Before desegregation, more white than minority students rode buses (50 percent of whites, 47 percent of minorities); afterward, the proportions were reversed (53 percent of whites, 56 percent of minorities). "In the year of maximum desegregation, an average of 30 percent of the students were reassigned, but the average increase in busing was only five percentage points." I relegate these data to a note because Civil Rights Commission findings are academically suspect; nevertheless they suggest the degree to which busing is a bogus issue, at least for many whites. U.S. Commission on Civil Rights, *Reviewing a Decade of School Desegregation, 1966–1975: Report of a National Survey of School Superintendents* (Washington, D.C.: U.S. Government Printing Office, 1977), pp. 42–50.

68. Thomas F. Pettigrew, "The Case for Metropolitan Approaches to Public-School Desegregation," in *Race and Schooling in the City*, ed. Yarmolinsky et al., p. 174.

69. *Milliken v. Bradley*, 484 F. 2d 215 (1973).

70. Morgan with England, "Assessing the Progress," pp. 71, 75.

71. James S. Coleman, Sara Kelly, and John Moore, *Trends in School Segregation, 1968–1973* (Washington, D.C.: Urban Institute, 1975); and Reynolds Farley, Clarence Wurdock, and Toni Richards, "School Desegregation and White Flight: An Investigation of Competing Models and Their Discrepant Findings," *Sociology of Education* 53 (1980): 123; Pettigrew, "The Case for Metropolitan Approaches," pp. 166–69.

72. Orfield, *Public School Desegregation*, pp. 41–42.

73. See, for example, Nancy St. John, *School Desegregation: Outcomes for Children* (New York: Wiley, 1975). Of twenty-three studies of white achievement

after desegregation, two showed improvement, three showed harm, and eighteen showed no effects.

74. William L. Taylor, "Metropolitan Approaches to Desegregation," *Integrated Education* 13, no. 3 (May/June 1975): 133.

75. Crain and Mahard, "Minority Achievement," pp. 72–75. See also Pettigrew, "The Case for Metropolitan Approaches," p. 170; and Robert Green et al., "Metropolitan School Desegregation in New Castle County, Delaware" (Unpublished manuscript, Michigan State University, College of Urban Affairs, 1982).

76. Orfield, "Housing Patterns," p. 213, emphasis added.

77. Rossell and Hawley, "Understanding White Flight," p. 170; Farley et al., "School Desegregation and While Flight"; Armor, "White Flight"; Morgan and England, "White Enrollment Loss," table 2; and Jeffrey A. Raffel, *The Politics of School Desegregation: The Metropolitan Remedy in Delaware* (Philadelphia: Temple University Press, 1980), pp. 175–88.

78. Orfield, "Housing Patterns," p. 213.

79. Rossell and Hawley, "Understanding White Flight," p. 173; Rossell, "Applied Social Science Research," p. 92; Michael W. Giles and Douglas S. Gatlin, "Mass-Level Compliance with Public Policy: The Case of School Desegregation," *Journal of Politics* 42, no. 3 (August 1980): 734–43.

80. Morgan with England, "Assessing the Progress," p. 109; Armor, "White Flight," pp. 199–201; Rossell, "Applied Social Science Research," pp. 88–89; Rossell, "Assessing the Unintended Impacts," pp. 20–25.

81. Michael W. Giles, Everett F. Cataldo, and Douglas S. Gatlin, "White Flight and Percent Black: The Tipping Point Re-examined," *Social Science Quarterly* 56, no. 1 (June 1975): 85–92; and Michael W. Giles, "White Enrollment Stability and School Desegregation: A Two Level Analysis," *American Sociological Review* 43 (December 1978): 848–64.

82. Morgan with England, "Assessing the Progress," pp. 117–18; Rossell, "Applied Social Science Research," pp. 88–89.

83. See, for example, Crain et al., *Making Desegregation Work*, pp. 51–56, 61–65.

84. National Institute of Education, *Violent Schools—Safe Schools*, p. A16.

85. Douglas Longshore, "School Racial Composition and Blacks' Attitudes toward Desegregation," *Social Science Quarterly* 63, no. 4 (December 1982): 674–87, and "Race Composition." See also Patchen, *Black-White Contact*.

86. Albert O. Hirschman, *Exit, Voice, and Loyalty* (Cambridge: Harvard University Press, 1970); and Paul E. Peterson, "Voice, Exit, and Equity in Education" (Unpublished manuscript, Stanford University, c. 1981).

87. Center for National Policy Review et al., "School Segregation and Residential Segregation," in *School Desegregation*, ed. Stephan and Feagin, p. 235. In the murkier but authoritative language of the Supreme Court in *Swann v. Charlotte-Mecklenburg:* "People gravitate toward school facilities. . . . The location of schools may thus influence the patterns of residential development of a metropolitan area and have important impact on composition of inner-city neighborhoods." See also Karl E. Taeuber, "Housing, Schools, and Incremental Segregative Effects," *Annals of the American Academy of Political and Social Science* 441 (January 1979): 157–67.

88. Orfield, "Housing Patterns," p. 205.

89. Mark Granovetter, "The Microstructure of School Desegregation" (Unpublished manuscript, State University of New York at Stony Brook, 1982), pp. 37–39.

90. Franklin D. Wilson, *Patterns of White Avoidance* (Madison: University of Wisconsin, Institute for Research on Poverty, 1978), pp. 18–20.

91. Diana Pearce, *Breaking Down Barriers: New Evidence on the Impact of Metropolitan School Desegregation on Housing Patterns* (Washington, D.C.: Catholic University School of Law, Center for National Policy Review, 1980), p. 26. Emphasis in original.

92. Ibid., p. 42; Gary Orfield, *Toward a Strategy for Urban Integration: Lessons in School and Housing Policy from Twelve Cities* (New York: Ford Foundation, 1981); Rossell, "Applied Social Science Research," pp. 102–04.

93. Pearce, *Breaking Down Barriers*, p. 43; Orfield, *Toward a Strategy*.

94. Kentucky Commission on Human Rights, *School and Housing Desegregation Are Working Together in Louisville and Jefferson County, 1975–1983* (Louisville: Kentucky Commission on Human Rights, 1983), pp. 16–17; and Willis D. Hawley et al., *Strategies for Effective Desegregation* (Lexington, Mass.: Lexington Books, 1983), pp. 61–71.

95. Eldridge Gendron, "Busing in Florida: Before and After," *Integrated Education* (March/April 1972): 3–7.

96. Daniel U. Levine and Rayna F. Levine, "The Social and Instructional Setting for Metropolitan Integration," in National Institute of Education, *School Desegregation in Metropolitan Areas: Choices and Prospects* (Washington, D.C.: U.S. Government Printing Office, 1977), p. 94; emphasis added.

97. U.S. Commission on Civil Rights, *Statement on Metropolitan Desegregation* (Washington, D.C.: U.S. Government Printing Office, 1977), pp. 60–62; Pettigrew, "The Case for Metropolitan Approaches," pp. 169–74.

98. Brief for the Petitioners, *Bradley v. State Board of Education of the Commonwealth of Virginia*, in the Supreme Court, October 1972, no. 72–550; Integrated Education Associates, *The Richmond School Decision* (Chicago: Integrated Education Associates, 1972), pp. 137–46. See Thomas F. Pettigrew, Report to the Honorable Judge Paul Egly in Response to the Minute Order of February 7, 1978 (Pomona, Los Angeles County Superior Court, November 14, 1978) for a similar plan for the Los Angeles metropolitan region.

99. Lance Liebman, "Constitutional Values and Public Education," in *Race and Schooling in the City*, ed. Yarmolinsky et al., p. 257.

100. A 1965 survey of Bostonians found that only 10 percent of the opponents of Louise Day Hicks's antibusing campaigns were sending or expected to send their children to the Boston public schools, compared with 16 percent of her partial supporters and 25 percent of her strong supporters. These and related data provide ammunition for both sides of the busing controversy. On the one hand, many fewer anti-Hicks than pro-Hicks voters would have had to live with the direct consequences of their policy choice; if one has no children in the schools, it is relatively easy to advocate dramatic change in them. On the other hand, three-quarters of the pro-Hicks Bostonians would also not have faced direct effects on their lives if busing were

implemented. Obviously, their opposition was not based on concern for their children and was perhaps based on a general fear or dislike of blacks, general conservatism, or resistance to residential integration (Pettigrew's favored interpretation). Thomas F. Pettigrew, *Racially Separate or Together?* (New York: McGraw-Hill, 1971), pp. 211–29, esp. pp. 222–26.

101. Christine H. Rossell, "The Mayor's Role in School Desegregation Implementation," *Urban Education* 12, no. 3 (October 1977): 250. See also Thomas J. Cottle, *Busing* (Boston: Beacon Press, 1976), pp. 42–60.

102. Miller, *Principles Relevant to Successful School Desegregation*, p. 15.

103. Eugene C. Royster, D. Catherine Baltzell, and Fran C. Simmons, *Study of the Emergency School Aid Act Magnet School Program* (Cambridge, Mass.: Abt Associates, 1979): 44–73. Apparently magnet schools do not, however, lead to greater segregation in nonmagnet schools, as many people fear (pp. 47–54).

104. Rolf K. Blank et al., *Survey of Magnet Schools: Analyzing a Model for Quality Integrated Education* (Cambridge, Mass.: Abt Associates, 1983): 80–84.

105. Royster et al., *Study of the Emergency*, p. 24; Blank et al., *Survey of Magnet Schools*, p. 11.

106. Mark A. Smylie, "Reducing Racial Isolation in Large School Districts: The Comparative Effectiveness of Mandatory and Voluntary Desegregation Strategies," *Urban Education* 17, no. 4 (January 1983): pp. 485–502. See also David R. Morgan and Robert England, "Large District School Desegregation: A Preliminary Assessment of Techniques," *Social Science Quarterly* 63, no. 4 (December 1982): 694. Examples of magnet-only plans are in Orfield, *Must We Bus?* pp. 158–63; Hawley et al., *Strategies for Effective Desegregation*, pp. 31–33; and Daniel U. Levine and Robert Havighurst, eds., *The Future of Big City Schools* (Berkeley: McCutchan, 1977), pp. 85–150.

107. Christine H. Rossell and Robert L. Crain, "The Importance of Political Factors in Explaining Northern School Desegregation," *American Journal of Political Science* 26, no. 4 (November 1982): 784–87.

108. Christine H. Rossell, "Magnet Schools as a Desegregation Tool: The Importance of Contextual Factors in Explaining Their Success," *Urban Education* 14, no. 3 (October 1979): 315.

109. Royster et al., *Study of the Emergency*, tables B3, B4.

110. Smylie, "Reducing Racial Isolation," pp. 487, 495; Rossell, "Magnet Schools as a Desegregation Tool," pp. 314–17.

111. Armor, "White Flight," pp. 199–201; J. Michael Ross, prepared statement to Senate Judiciary Committee, Subcommittee on Separation of Powers, *Hearings on Court-Ordered School Busing*, 97th Cong., 1st Sess., 1981, pp. 206–07; Smylie, "Reducing Racial Isolation," pp. 492–97.

112. J. Michael Ross, "The Effectiveness of Alternative Desegregation Strategies: The Issue of Voluntary versus Mandatory Policies in Los Angeles" (Unpublished manuscript, Boston University, 1981); Armor, "White Flight," pp. 207–11; Orfield, *Public School Desegregation*, pp. 33–34; Smylie, "Reducing Racial Isolation," pp. 489–91.

113. Willis D. Hawley, "The False Promises of Anti-Busing Legislation," prepared statement to Senate Judiciary Committee, Subcommittee on Separation of Powers, *Hearings on Court-Ordered School Busing*, 97th Cong., 1st Sess., 1981, p. 127.

114. Smylie, "Reducing Racial Isolation," pp. 491–97.

115. Christine H. Rossell, "Cost-Effectiveness Analysis of School Desegregation Plans" (Paper presented at the annual meeting of the American Political Science Association, Denver, September 1982). See also Rossell, "Applied Social Science Research," p. 72.

116. Across ninety-one cities, "the proportion of reassignments that are mandatory is correlated .94 with the proportion of white students reassigned to formerly black schools." See Rossell and Crain, "The Importance of Political Factors," p. 777, note.

117. Royster et al., pp. 23–25, 59–63, 79–83, B1; Blank et al., *Survey of Magnet Schools*, pp. 78–80.

118. Daniel U. Levine and Connie Campbell, "Developing and Implementing Big-City Magnet School Programs," in *The Future of Big City Schools*, ed. Levine and Havighurst (Berkeley: McCutchan, 1977), p. 249.

119. Massachusetts Research Center, *Education and Enrollments: Boston During Phase II* (Boston: Massachusetts Research Center, 1976), p. 56.

120. Royster et al., *Study of the Emergency*, p. 40.

121. Blank et al., *Survey of Magnet Schools*, pp. 113–35. The costs of magnet schools declined in 1981–82 to about 2 percent more than nonmagnets in the cities studied. That was the year that ESAA (and its magnet school program) was folded into an education block grant, so we cannot tell whether magnet costs "really" declined, whether school districts cut back on magnet funding in anticipation of loss of federal aid, or both. Regardless of this particular question, the loss of approximately $30 million (in 1980) of ESAA funding will surely diminish the incentive for financially hard-pressed urban school districts to begin, extend, or even maintain their magnet programs. Alternatively, districts may maintain their magnet programs at 1980 or 1981 funding levels, but divert resources from other schools in order to do so. This consequence is completely counterproductive, both for those who seek to increase voluntary (in lieu of mandatory) desegregation and those who seek to retain the virtues of magnets and offset their faults by extending them to all students. See David S. Tatel, Testimony on S 1256, Emergency School Aid Extension Act, Prepared for Senate Committee on Labor and Human Resources, Subcommittee on Education, Arts, and Humanities, June 27, 1983; Statement of the National Education Association on S 1256, The Special Desegregation Activity Act, for same committee, June 27, 1983; Michael Casserly, Testimony on the Department of Education's Implementation of the Chapter 2 Block Grants, presented to House Committee on Government Operations, Subcommittee on Intergovernmental Relations and Human Resources, September 20, 1983. See also citations in chapter 6, note 128.

122. Blank et al., *Survey of Magnet Schools*, pp. 136–40. Only two of eight correlation coefficients reached statistical significance; three showed slight negative relationships between cost and educational and racial improvement; and none of the school-level (as distinguished from district-level) correlations were statistically significant. The amount of money spent, educational outcomes, and integration were each ranked from highest to lowest among the eight districts with data; no districts were similarly ranked on all three dimensions except the district that spent the most and the one that spent the least.

123. Levine and Campbell, "Developing and Implementing," in *The Future of Big*

City Schools, ed. Levine and Havighurst, pp. 247–66.

124. Blank et al., *Survey of Magnet Schools*, inter alia, e.g., 67–71, 105–06, appendix 3, pp. 8–11 and 21–31, appendix 4, pp. 9–10, and appendix 7.

125. Royster et al., *Study of the Emergency*, pp. 35–40; Blank et al., *Survey of Magnet Schools*, pp. 91–95.

126. Levine and Campbell, "Developing and Implementing," p. 264.

127. Lois Quinn, Michael Barndt, and Diane Pollard, "Relationships between School Desegregation and Government Housing Programs: A Milwaukee Case Study" (Unpublished manuscript, National Institute of Education, 1980) pp. 24–29; Los Angeles School Monitoring Commission, "Report on Enrollment Constraints at the West Valley C.E.S. Magnet as of September 5, 1979," submitted to Superior Court, County of Los Angeles, 1979.

128. Gordon Foster, "Desegregating Urban Schools: A Review of Techniques," *Harvard Educational Review* 43 (February 1973): 24.

129. Rossell, "Magnet Schools as a Desegregation Tool," p. 310. For a more positive description of the same phenomenon, see Blank et al., *Survey of Magnet Schools*, pp. 98–99.

130. "Chronicle of Race, Sex, and Schools—Wisconsin," *Integrated Education* 14 (July/August 1976): 35.

131. Royster et al., *Study of the Emergency*, pp. 84–87.

132. Blank et al., *Survey of Magnet Schools*, pp. 55–63; appendix 3, pp. 8–11; see also Daniel U. Levine, Eugene E. Eubanks, and Lois S. Roskowski, "Social Class and Home Background of Magnet and Non-Magnet Students" (Unpublished manuscript, University of Missouri, School of Education, 1980).

133. From a personal interview, cited in Levine and Campbell, "Developing and Implementing," in *The Future of Big City Schools*, ed. Levine and Havighurst, p. 467.

134. One famous early study found that city-to-suburban transfers by black Bostonians had few positive and many negative effects. David Armor, "The Evidence on Busing," *Public Interest* 28 (Summer 1972): 90–126. The study has been severely criticized, however, by Thomas F. Pettigrew et al., "Busing: A Review of 'The Evidence,'" *Public Interest* 30 (Winter 1973): 88–115 (see also the responses on pp. 116–31). Generally, the (very few) studies of such programs find good effects on minority achievement, race relations, and long-term career success of the transferred students. See Crain and Mahard, "Minority Achievement," pp. 64, 70–72.

135. The most extensive study of white students' responses to black transfers into "their" suburban schools concludes: "when reviewing these data on predictors of racial attitudes, one is struck by the complexity of the issues involved. . . . Future researchers should try to probe these issues more systematically by studying individual schools, . . . reactions to various groups of students, . . . [and] different social conditions." It finds few systematic results except that the school itself makes a great deal of difference in white students' receptivity to black transfers. Elizabeth Useem, "Correlates of White Students' Attitudes toward a Voluntary Busing Program," *Education and Urban Society* 8, no. 4 (August 1976): 441–76.

136. Royster et al., *Study of the Emergency*, pp. 36–37; Blank et al., *Survey of Magnet Schools*, inter alia., e.g., pp. 33–54, 95–104, 144–209.

137. Braybrooke and Lindblom, *A Strategy of Decision*, p. 71.

138. Lindblom, "Still Muddling," p. 521.

139. Miller, "Principles Relevant to Successful School Desegregation," p. 21.

140. Meyer Weinberg, *Minority Students: A Research Appraisal* (Washington, D.C.: U.S. Government Printing Office, 1977), pp. 330–31. Italics added when quoted by Miller, "Principles Relevant to Successful School Desegregation," notes, pp. 4–5. Miller leaves out an additional sentence, which is politically if not analytically relevant to this controversy: "Indeed, a number of experiences pointed out as demonstrating the unworkability of desegregation illustrate, instead, the inevitability of failure if nothing changes other than the racial composition of the school" (p. 331).

141. Michael Barndt, Rick Janka, and Harold Rose, "Milwaukee, Wisconsin: Mobilization for School and Community Cooperation," in *Community Politics and Educational Change: Ten School Systems under Court Order*, ed. Charles V. Willie and Susan L. Greenblatt (New York: Longman, 1981), pp. 237–59; David A. Bennett, "The Impact of Court-Ordered Desegregation," pp. 77–120; and Margery Thompson, "Milwaukee's Specialty School Plan Promotes Learning and Integration," *American School Board Journal* 166 (May 1979): 30–33. Both systematic studies of magnet schools confirm this claim. Royster et al. (*Study of the Emergency*) show that the more minority students enrolled in magnets, the closer they come to enrollment and racial balance goals, and the more supportive the community is (p. 64, table B-4). Blank et al. (*Survey of Magnet Schools*) show that as enrollment increases, the disproportionality of per-student costs decreases (p. 120). However, enrollment is negatively correlated with the "degree to which both material and symbolic features of . . . program are fully realized" (appendix 3, pp. 2, 8).

142. Two of the best, from which many of my examples come, are David L. Colton and William Berg, *Budgeting for Desegregation in Large Cities* (St. Louis: Washington University, Center for the Study of Law in Education, 1981) and David Kirp, *Just Schools* (Berkeley: University of California Press, 1983).

143. Charles B. Vergon, *The Courts and Desegregation Strategies: Ten Key Decisions* (Nashville: Vanderbilt University, Institute for Public Policy Studies, 1981), pp. 20–27.

144. E. Lutrell Bing, comments in panel presentation, "Metropolitan Desegregation: How Is It Working Today?" in National Institute of Education, *School Desegregation in Metropolitan Areas*, pp. 124–25.

145. Jeffrey A. Raffel, "The Voters Grade the Metropolitan Desegregation Plan in Delaware," *Integrated Education* 18, nos. 1–4 (January–August 1980): 64–71.

146. Forty-one findings report no difference in race relations with respect to cooperative and competitive or individualistic classroom practices. More sophisticated measures of these practices yield the same one-sided results; for example, the differences between cooperative and noncooperative techniques are statistically significant at the 0.0001 level. Articles published in the best journals find more interpersonal attraction than unpublished articles or those published in less competitive journals. Johnson et al., "Interdependence and Interpersonal Attraction," pp. 21–23, 33–34, 39–49, 95, 99–103.

Some argue that work groups must give more than equal power, status, or knowledge to minorities to compensate for the stereotypes that students (and teachers) bring to the group. See Elizabeth G. Cohen, "Design and Redesign of the Desegregated School: Problems of Status, Power, and Conflict," in *School Desegregation*, ed. Stephan and Feagin (New York: Plenum, 1980), pp. 251–80.

147. Johnson et al., "Interdependence and Interpersonal Attraction," pp. 44–47. See also Hawley et al., *Strategies for Effective Desegregation*, pp. 110–15; Garlie A. Forehand and Marjorie Ragosta, *A Handbook for Integrated Schooling* (Princeton: Educational Testing Service, 1976), pp. 36–42; Miller, "Principles Relevant to Successful School Desegregation," pp. 9–11; William B. Lacy, E. J. Mason, and Ernest Middleton, "Fostering Constructive Intergroup Contact in Desegregated Schools," *Journal of Negro Education* 52, no. 2 (1983): 130–41; Robert E. Slavin, "Cooperative Learning and Desegregation," in *Effective School Desegregation*, ed. Hawley, pp. 225–44; and Janet W. Schofield, "Desegregation, School Practices, and Student Race Relations Outcomes," in Rossell et al., *A Review of the Empirical Research on Desegregation*, pp. 112–35.

148. National Institute of Education, *Violent Schools—Safe Schools*, pp. 9, A34–A44, A52, A56.

149. David W. Johnson and Roger Johnson, *Learning Together and Alone: Cooperation, Competition, and Individualization* (Englewood Cliffs, N.J.: Prentice-Hall, 1975); and Robert E. Slavin, *Cooperative Learning* (New York: Longman, 1982).

150. Janet W. Schofield, *Black and White in School*, p. 97; see also, generally, pp. 75–97.

151. Ibid., pp. 28, 41, 50; see also, generally, pp. 39–73.

152. Chen-Lin C. Kulik and James A. Kulik, "Effects of Ability Grouping on Secondary School Students: A Meta-analysis of Evaluation Findings," *American Educational Research Journal* 19, no. 3 (Fall 1982): 415–28.

153. National Institute of Education, *Compensatory Education Study* (Washington, D.C.: U.S. Government Printing Office, 1980), p. 171.

154. Crain et al., *Making Desegregation Work*, pp. 214–20.

155. Miller, "Principles Relevant to Successful School Desegregation," p. 12.

156. Michael Rebell and Arthur R. Block, *Equality and Education: Federal Civil Rights Enforcement in the New York City School System* (Princeton: Princeton University Press, forthcoming). Warren G. Findley and Miriam Bryan, *Ability Grouping, 1970: Status, Impact, and Alternatives* (Athens: University of Georgia, Center for Educational Improvement, 1971).

157. See, for example, Schofield, *Black and White in School*, pp. 42–43.

158. Hawley et al., *Strategies for Effective Desegregation*, pp. 118–24; Gary Orfield, "How to Make Desegregation Work: The Adaptation of Schools to Their Newly-Integrated Student Bodies," *Law and Contemporary Problems* 39, no. 2 (Spring 1975): 324–28; Cassandra A. Simmons and Nelvia M. Brady, "The Impact of Ability Group Placement Decisions on the Equality of Educational Opportunity in Desegregated Elementary Schools," *Urban Review* 13, no. 2 (Summer 1981): 129–33; and Schofield, "Desegregation, School Practices," pp. 118–22.

159. Granovetter, "The Microstructure of School Desegregation."

160. Hawley et al., *Strategies for Effective Desegregation*, pp. 98–101.

161. On these and other changes, see, in addition to other works cited in this

section, Jane R. Mercer, Peter Iadicola, and Helen Moore, "Building Effective Multiethnic Schools," in *School Desegregation*, ed. Stephan and Feagin, pp. 281–307; Mark A. Smylie and Willis D. Hawley, *Increasing the Effectiveness of In-Service Training for Desegregation: A Synthesis of Current Research* (Washington, D.C.: National Education Association, 1982); Herbert J. Walberg, Diane Schiller, and Geneva D. Haertel, "The Quiet Revolution in Educational Research," *Phi Delta Kappan* 61, no. 3 (November 1979): 179–83; Robert E. Slavin and Nancy A. Madden, "School Practices That Improve Race Relations," *American Educational Research Journal* 16, no. 2 (Spring 1979): 169–80; Charles D. Moody, Sr., Junious Williams, and Charles B. Vergon, eds., *Student Rights and Discipline: Policies, Programs, and Procedures* (Ann Arbor: University of Michigan, School of Education, 1978); Boyd Bosma, *Planning for and Implementing Effective School Desegregation: The Role of Teacher Associations* (Washington, D.C.: U.S. Government Printing Office, 1980); Jere Brophy and Thomas Good, *Teacher-Student Relationships: Causes and Consequences* (New York: Holt, Rinehart, and Winston, 1974); Joyce L. Epstein, *After the Bus Arrives: Resegregation in Desegregated Schools* (Baltimore: Johns Hopkins University, Center for the Social Organization of Schools, 1983); Crain et al., *Making Desegregation Work*; William J. Genova and Herbert Walberg, *A Practitioner's Guide for Achieving Student Integration in City High Schools* (Washington, D.C.: U.S. Government Printing Office, 1981); William J. Doherty et al., *Human Relations Study: Investigations of Effective Human Relations Strategies*, vol. 2, *Technical Report* (Santa Monica, Calif.: System Development Corporation, 1981); and Henderson et al., "Remedies for Segregation."

162. Only two studies have systematically compared the effect on race relations of schools that maximize organizational reform and schools that do not. One found white students almost twice as likely to hold positive attitudes toward blacks in a fully integrated school as in a merely desegregated one (71 to 37 percent). (The integrated school met all three conditions which Gordon Allport deemed necessary for interracial contact to diminish racial prejudice: equal status, cooperation, and support from authorities for positive intergroup relations. The desegregated school did not meet these conditions.) M. Lachat, "A Description and Comparison of the Attitudes of White High School Seniors toward Black Americans in Three Suburban High Schools" (Ph.D. diss., Teachers College, Columbia University, New York, 1972). In another school, informal racial mixing increased over time in the seventh grade, which had racially heterogeneous and cooperative classrooms, and decreased over time in the eighth grade, which had racially homogeneous, tracked, and competitive classes. Janet W. Schofield and H. Andrew Sagar, "Peer Interaction Patterns in an Integrated Middle School," *Sociometry* 40 no. 2 (1977): 130–38.

163. Blank et al., *Survey of Magnet Schools*, p. 108; appendix 4, p. 9.

164. Senator Lawton Chiles, Jr., for example, tells of a ghetto school in Sarasota, Florida, which shows excellent results and has a waiting list of would-be white transfers. *Congressional Record*, S 16377, 94th Cong., 1 Sess., September 19, 1975; see also John McAdams, "Can Open Enrollment Work?" *Public Interest* 37 (Fall 1974): 69–88; and Blank et al., *Survey of Magnet Schools*, inter alia.

165. Peterson, background paper, in Task Force on Federal Elementary and Secondary Educational Policy, *Making the Grade*, p. 51.

166. See "Features" on educational partnerships, *Phi Delta Kappan* 65, no. 4 (February 1984): 383–409.

167. Susan M. Johnson, "Teacher Unions in Schools: Authority and Accommodation," *Harvard Educational Review* 53, no. 3 (August 1983): 309–26.

168. Braybrooke and Lindblom, *A Strategy of Decision*, p. 71.

169. Derrick A. Bell, Jr., "Serving Two Masters: Integration Ideals and Client Interests in School Desegregation Litigation" and "Response to December 8 Letter by Nathaniel Jones, NAACP General Counsel," both in *Limits of Justice: The Courts' Role in School Desegregation*, ed. Howard I. Kalodner and James J. Fishman (Cambridge, Mass.: Ballinger, 1978), pp. 579, 612, 618.

170. Robin M. Williams and Margaret W. Ryan, eds., *Schools in Transition: Community Experiences in Desegregation* (Chapel Hill: University of North Carolina Press, 1954).

171. Orfield, "Why It Worked," pp. 29–37.

172. Charles S. Bullock III, "The Office for Civil Rights and Implementation of Desegregation Programs in the Public Schools," *Policy Studies Journal* 8, no. 4 (special issue no. 2, 1980): 606; Orfield, *Public School Desegregation*, pp. 4, 14.

173. Rebell and Block, *Equality and Education*.

174. Forehand and Ragosta, *A Handbook for Integrated Schooling*, pp. 60–68, 83–93, 108–15; and Forehand et al., *Conditions and Processes*, pp. 80–122, inter alia.

175. Hawley et al., *Strategies for Effective Desegregation*, p. 140.

176. See Bell's extremely low-key and flexible policy recommendations, which are strikingly in contrast with his radical historical interpretation, in "Racial Remediation," p. 28.

177. F. Peter Model, "On the Cutting Edge of the Law: Thomas I. Atkins, Jr.," *Perspective* 14, no. 1 (Spring 1982): 25.

CHAPTER 5

1. Peter Flora, presentation at the annual meeting of the American Political Science Association, New York, 1981; Flora and Arnold J. Heidenheimer, *Development of the Welfare States in Europe and America* (New York: Holt, Transaction Books, 1981), p. 18.

2. We have less systematic evidence on the effects of citizen participation than on the effects of different degrees of incrementalism in policy-making. Arguments about citizen participation are also much more subjective and often rest on interpretations of complex events or on counterfactual assertions ("If only parents had really had power, . . ." or "If only leaders had been more skilled, . . . this process would have worked in city X"). Hence my arguments here are more impressionistic and less precise than in chapter 4. For the most sophisticated collection of such hypotheses about school desegregation (from, in general, strong enthusiasts) see C. Anthony Broh and William T. Trent, *Qualitative Literature and Expert Opinion on School Desegregation* (Nashville: Vanderbilt University, Institute for Public Policy Studies, 1981).

3. Don Davies, *Citizen Participation in Education: Annotated Bibliography* (New Haven: Yale University, Institution for Social and Political Studies, 1973), pp. x, xii–xiii.

4. Miller, *Principles Relevant to Successful School Desegregation,* pp. 20–21. Emphasis in original.

5. David L. Kirp, *Doing Good by Doing Little: Race and Schooling in Britain* (Berkeley and Los Angeles: University of California Press, 1979), and *Just Schools,* pp. 295, 298, 302.

6. Ben Holman, speech in Community Relations Service, Department of Justice and National Center for Quality Integrated Education, *Desegregation without Turmoil* (Washington, D.C.: U.S. Government Printing Office, 1977), p. 30.

7. Hughes et al., *Desegregating America's Schools,* p. 16.

8. Mary Davis, "Voluntary Desegregation in Michigan: Ypsilanti," *Breakthrough* 5, no. 3 (Spring 1977): 2.

9. Morgan with England, "Assessing the Progress," p. 67. They find a slight *negative* relationship between the existence of advisory groups and the amount of desegregation in elementary schools.

10. Morgan and England, "White Enrollment Loss," table 2.

11. Bullock, "Equal Education Opportunity," p. 82.

12. Rodgers and Bullock, *Coercion to Compliance,* p. 41.

13. Rossell and Crain, "The Importance of Political Factors," pp. 785–92.

14. David J. Kirby and Robert L. Crain, "The Functions of Conflict: School Desegregation in 91 Cities," *Social Science Quarterly* 53, no. 2 (September 1974): 480–90. Note that findings from this data set of ninety-one Northern cities from 1968 to 1972 may not be relevant today, because the data were collected before there was any OCR or judicial pressure to desegregate Northern districts. Thus the changes were mostly token moves voluntarily undertaken by local school boards in predominantly white cities—a situation unlikely to recur frequently in the future.

15. Los Angeles was not included in the study. See Eldon L. Wegner and Jane R. Mercer, "Dynamics of the Desegregation Process: Politics, Policies, and Community Characteristics as Factors in Change," in *The Polity of the School: New Research in Educational Politics,* ed. Frederick Wirt (Lexington, Mass.: Lexington Books, 1975), p. 134.

16. Rodgers and Bullock, *Coercion to Compliance,* pp. 41–43.

17. Kirby and Crain, "The Functions of Conflict," p. 486; Morgan with England, "Assessing the Progress," pp. 68–70, 78. It is worth stressing that nowhere has citizen protest by itself caused a plan to be rescinded or even significantly modified. That has occurred only as a consequence of judicial decisions, as in Los Angeles or metropolitan Detroit.

18. The relationship is weak and nonsignificant for postimplementation years. Morgan and England, "White Enrollment Loss," table 2; see also Christine H. Rossell, "The Effect of Community Leadership," pp. 134, 136; and Henry Jay Becker, *The Impact of Racial Composition and Public School Desegregation on Changes in Non-Public School Enrollment by White Pupils* (Baltimore: Johns Hopkins University, Center for Social Organization of Schools, 1978), table 5.

19. Hirsch, "'We're on the bus. . . ,'" p. 22.

20. Ibid.

21. Rubin, *Busing and Backlash,* p. 199. Original emphasized.

22. Morton Inger and Robert T. Stout, "School Desegregation—The Need to Govern," *Urban Review* 3 (November 1968): 35–38.

23. James Rothenberg and Mark Chesler, "Authorities' Responses to Community Challenge during Desegregation" (Paper presented at the annual meeting of the Society for the Study of Social Problems, August 1980), pp. 14–16. For a similar use of citizen groups by education authorities, see Anne Henderson, ed., *No Strings Attached: An Interim Report on the New Education Block Grant* (Columbia, Md.: National Committee for Citizens in Education, 1983). Her case studies show that "those states facing the greatest changes from Chapter 2 [of the new block grant] used their SACs [state advisory committees] to mediate and manage the upheaval that resulted. Those that were not greatly affected tended to treat their SACs as a *pro forma* exercise" (p. 30).

24. R. M. Craig, "Parent Involvement in Boston: A Perpetuation of Institutionalized Racism" (paper presented at the annual meeting of the Massachusetts Sociological Association, November 1976).

25. Myrdal was perhaps the first to point out forcefully that white Americans prefer to think of racial issues in terms of "the Negro problem," whereas in fact, "the Negro problem exists and changes because of conditions and forces operating in the larger American society." Race relations, in fact, are "a white man's problem." *An American Dilemma*, pp. li–lv.

26. The Dallas Alliance, a group of business leaders, formed an education task force to address the desegregation problem in 1975. The task force had seven Anglos, six blacks, seven Chicanos, and one Native American. It spent four months and fifteen hundred hours designing the plan which Judge Taylor accepted almost intact.

27. U.S. Commission on Civil Rights, *Fulfilling the Letter and Spirit of the Law: Desegregation of the Nation's Public Schools* (Washington, D.C.: U.S. Government Printing Office, 1976).

28. William W. Beck and Glenn M. Linden, "Anglo and Minority Perceptions of Success in Dallas School Desegregation," *Phi Delta Kappan* 60 (January 1979): 381.

29. Hirsch, "'We're on the bus. . . ,'" pp. 45–46.

30. Kirby and Crain, "The Functions of Conflict," pp. 486–89. An early study found that citizen participation in school decisions leads to conflict and low cohesion in school boards, which in turn decrease the amount of board-ordered desegregation. See Robert L. Crain and Donald B. Rosenthal, "Community Status as a Dimension of Local Decision-Making," *American Sociological Review* 32 (1967): 974–76.

31. Rodgers and Bullock, *Coercion to Compliance*, p. 42.

32. Even this oft-cited success story, however, has flaws. Because reassignment was voluntary, there has not been much student movement, most of what has occurred has been by blacks, white neighborhood schools have been retained but black schools closed, and the plan has destabilized integrated neighborhoods and schools. See Barndt et al., "Milwaukee, Wisconsin"; Quinn et al., "Relationships between School Desegregation."

33. Giles and Gatlin, "Mass-Level Compliance with Public Policy," pp. 735–39. For evidence that citizen participants in school affairs feel efficacious, regardless of their actual effects, see Robert H. Salisbury, *Citizen Participation in the Public Schools* (Lexington, Mass.: Lexington Books, 1980).

34. Douglas S. Gatlin, Michael W. Giles, and Everett F. Cataldo, "Policy Support within a Target Group: The Case of School Desegregation," *American Political Science Review* 72, no. 3 (September 1978): 990–94.

35. Blank et al., *Survey of Magnet Schools,* pp. 165–67, 188.

36. Robert E. Jennings, "School Advisory Councils in America: Frustration and Failure," in *The Politics of School Governance,* ed. George Baron (Oxford: Pergamon, 1981), p. 23.

37. The compensatory education program was incorporated as Chapter 1 of the 1981 education block grant (Education Consolidation and Improvement Act). It now suggests, but does not require, parent advisory committees, and it includes no sanctions for their absence.

38. Nevertheless, participants do feel efficacious. Over half of the PAC chairpeople report that their members observe classrooms, participate in parent-teacher conferences, and send letters to other Title I parents—all activities that give a sense of involvement, even if they produce no results. Perhaps as a consequence of all this activity, 71 percent of PAC chairs report being "very satisfied" with the planning process for Title I children, and the remaining 28 percent are "somewhat satisfied." National Institute of Education, *Compensatory Education Study,* pp. 93–105.

39. Karen M. Hult, "Citizen Organizations in Local Politics: The Minneapolis Case" (Paper presented at the annual meeting of the Midwest Political Science Association, Chicago, 1983), pp. 2, 9, 12, 15.

40. For good analyses of why advisory groups create mostly "frustration and failure," see Jennings, "School Advisory Councils in America," and George Baron, "School Councils and the Future of School Governance," both in *The Politics of School Governance,* ed. Baron, pp. 279–84; Marilyn Gittell, *Limits to Citizen Participation: The Decline of Community Organizations* (Beverley Hills: Sage, 1980); Daniel P. Moynihan, *Maximum Feasible Misunderstanding* (New York: Free Press, 1969); Don Davies et al., *Sharing the Power* (Boston: Institute for Responsive Education, 1978). For a more favorable conclusion about the effects of citizens' groups, see J. David Greenstone and Paul E. Peterson, *Race and Authority in Urban Politics* (Chicago: University of Chicago Press, 1973).

41. David K. Cohen, "Reforming School Politics," *Harvard Educational Review* 48, no. 4 (November 1978): 429–47.

42. John Larson et al., *Takoma Park Magnet School Evaluation, Part II: Final Report* (Rockville, Md.: Montgomery County Public Schools, 1981).

43. And presumably, although we have no data on this point, a higher percentage of whites than blacks were registered to vote. Lawrence W. Lezotte, "Voter Behavior as an Expression of Community Attitudes toward Desegregation" (Paper presented at the annual meeting of the American Educational Research Association, San Francisco, April 1976), p. 41.

44. Elaine B. Sharp, "Policy Innovations to Increase Citizen Access to Government: An Evaluation of the Wichita Experience" (Paper presented at the annual meeting of the American Political Science Association, New York, 1981), pp. 13, 19–20, 22–23.

45. Verba and Nie, *Participation in America,* pp. 101, 277, 162–70.

46. Ibid., pp. 336–38.

47. See, for example, Hawley et al., *Strategies for Effective Desegregation*; Hughes et al., *Desegregating America's Schools,* pp. 134–36; Forehand and Ragosta, *A Handbook for Integrated Schooling,* pp. 45–53; and Mark A. Chesler, Bunyan I.

Bryant, and James E. Crowfoot, *Making Desegregation Work: A Professional's Guide to Effecting Change* (Beverly Hills: Sage, 1981), pp. 95–143.

48. James Laue and Daniel Monti, "Intervening in School Desegregation Conflicts: The Role of the Monitor" (Unpublished manuscript, University of Missouri-St. Louis, Center for Metropolitan Studies, c. 1979), pp. 49–51.

49. Richard C. Snyder, comments in closing, in *Viewpoints and Guidelines on Court Appointed Citizens Monitoring Commissions in School Desegregation*, ed. Lila Carol (Columbus: Ohio State University, College of Education, 1977), p. 15.

50. Parents' influence on schools' decision-making (at least as perceived by teachers) has no effect on students' interracial attitudes, multicultural knowledge, attitudes toward school, or self-concept. William J. Doherty et al., *Human Relations Study*, vol. 2, *Technical Report*, pp. 61–68.

51. David J. Armor et al., *Analysis of the School Preferred Reading Program in Selected Los Angeles Minority Schools* (Santa Monica, Calif.: Rand Corporation, 1976); Jean B. Wellisch, *An In-Depth Study of Emergency School Aid Act Schools: 1974–1975* (Santa Monica, Calif.: System Development Corporation, 1976); Henry E. Hankerson, "Utilizing Parents for Paraprofessional Intervention," *Urban Review* 15, no. 2 (1983): 81–82; and Coulson, *Overview of the National Evaluation of the Emergency School Aid Act*, p. 39.

52. Royster et al., *Study of the Emergency*, pp. 36–37, 84–85; see also tables C1, C2, C14, and C15 for evidence that opportunity for parental involvement is not a strong contributor to magnets' effectiveness. Blank et al. (*Survey of Magnet Schools*) are even more enthusiastic about parent involvement; see pp. 163–66, 179–95, appendix 6, p. 4. Neither report has measures of the actual effects of parents' involvement.

53. Hawley et al., *Strategies for Effective Desegregation*, pp. 85, 117, 155. For evidence on how little support teachers get in their efforts to involve parents, see Joyce L. Epstein and Henry Jay Becker, "Teachers' Reported Practices of Parent Involvement: Problems and Possibilities," *Elementary School Journal* 88, no. 2 (November 1982): pp. 103–04, 106, 107.

54. Annette Lareau and Charles Benson, "The Economics of Home/School Relationships: A Cautionary Note," *Phi Delta Kappan* 65, no. 6 (February 1984): 401–04. These findings do not imply that parents should remain uninvolved, only that parental involvement may exacerbate problems of equity while alleviating other problems.

55. Henry Jay Becker and Joyce L. Epstein, "Parent Involvement: A Survey of Teacher Practices," *Elementary School Journal* 88, no. 2 (November 1982): 97–100.

56. Forehand et al., *Conditions and Processes*, pp. B4, B19, B20; see also appendix C.

57. However, "improving . . . schools have higher levels of parent-initiated involvement." Ronald R. Edmunds, "Some Schools Work and More Can," *Social Policy* 9 (March/April 1979): 30. See also David L. Clark, Linda S. Lotto, and Martha M. McCarthy, "Factors Associated with Success in Urban Elementary Schools," *Phi Delta Kappan* 61, no. 7 (March 1980): 470.

58. Lorraine M. McDonnell and Gail L. Zellman, *An Evaluation of the Emergency School Aid Act Nonprofit Organization Program:* vol 3, *The Role of Community Organizations in Facilitating School Desegregation* (Santa Monica, Calif.: Rand Corporation, 1978).

59. Jennifer L. Hochschild and Valerie Hadrick, "The Character and Effectiveness of Citizen Monitoring Groups in Implementing Civil Rights in Public Schools" (Unpublished manuscript, Duke University, Institute of Policy Sciences, 1981); Jennifer L. Hochschild, "If It's Worth Doing, It's Worth Doing Well: Guidelines for Effective Monitoring of Student Civil Rights" (Unpublished manuscript, Princeton University, Woodrow Wilson School of Public and International Affairs, 1981), "Local Control of School Desegregation Through Citizen Monitoring," in *New Directions for Testing and Measurement: Impact of Desegregation*, ed. Daniel J. Monti (San Francisco; Jossey-Bass, 1982): 67–82, and "Can Citizen Monitoring Groups Help Judges Implement Desegregation? It Depends," *Integrated Education* 20, no. 5 (Summer 1982): 22–31.

60. William L. Taylor, "The Meaning of the Columbus and Dayton Decisions" (Unpublished manuscript, Catholic University School of Law, Center for National Policy Review, Washington, D.C., 1979), p. 1.

61. Pamela Bullard, Joyce Grant, and Judith Stoia, "Boston, Massachusetts: Ethnic Resistance to a Comprehensive Plan," in *Community Politics and Educational Change*, ed. Willie and Greenblatt, p. 52.

62. Robert Wood, comment in faculty seminar on incrementalism and school desegregation, Wesleyan University, Middletown, Conn., September 6, 1983.

63. Wood here is citing Marion Levy's corollary to his Seven Laws for the Disillusioned Liberal: "Good intentions tend to randomize behavior." See "Professionals at Bay: Managing Boston's Public Schools," *Journal of Policy Analysis and Management* 1, no. 4 (Summer 1982): 455, 457.

64. Some writers also argue that students should be fully involved in designing and implementing the rules by which they must live. See George W. Noblit and Thomas W. Collins, "Order and Disruption in a Desegregated High School," *Crime and Delinquency* 24, no. 3 (July 1978): 277–89; Forehand and Ragosta, *A Handbook for Integrated Schooling*, pp. 75–87; Chesler et al., *Making Desegregation Work*, pp. 123–34. Monitoring bodies in Boston, Cleveland, and Los Angeles have included students; their impact has been slight. Theoretically, however, the argument is unexceptionable.

65. Leaders and citizens are not always easily distinguished; local elites are ordinary citizens in wider-than-usual arenas. Nevertheless, I use two rules of thumb for distinguishing leadership from citizen participation: leaders have elite status beyond their immediate surroundings, and leadership operates more through command and obedience than through discussion and consensus.

66. Civil Rights Commission, *Fulfilling the Letter*, p. 89.

67. Mark G. Yudof argues, however, that imposing a clear requirement works less well once the goals move beyond ending racial isolation. He calls for more participatory strategies at that point. See his "Implementing Desegregation Decrees," in *Effective School Desegregation*, ed. Hawley, p. 253.

68. Bullock, "Equal Education Opportunity"; for example, pp. 79–81, 83–85.

69. Ibid., pp. 79–81; Orfield, *Must We Bus?* pp. 233–360. Without strong support from the Secretary of HEW and the president, OCR bureaucrats by themselves either cannot or will not act effectively. See Leon Panetta and Peter Gall, *Bring us Together* (Philadelphia: Lippincott, 1971).

70. For a subtle but nontechnical analysis of the ambiguities faced by Northern district courts as a consequence of the Supreme Court's incoherence, see Tyll van Geel, "School Desegregation Doctrine and the Performance of the Judiciary," *Educational Administration Quarterly* 16, no. 3 (Fall 1980): 60–81.

71. See, for example, Willie and Greenblatt, eds., *Community Politics and Educational Change;* U.S. Commission on Civil Rights, *Fulfilling the Letter,* 1976; David Kirp et al., "Judicial Management of School Desegregation Cases" (Unpublished manuscript, University of California, Berkeley, Graduate School of Public Policy, 1979); and Gerard and Miller, *School Desegregation: A Long Term Study.*

72. Raffel, *The Politics of School Desegregation,* pp. 120–53; here, pp. 121, 122, 153.

73. William M. Berg and David Colton, "Budgeting for Desegregation in Urban School Systems," *Integrated Education* 20 (January/April 1982): 45.

74. Morgan with England, "Assessing the Progress," pp. 67, 75; Morgan and England, "White Enrollment Loss," table 2.

75. Giles and Gatlin, "Mass-Level Compliance with Public Policy," p. 746.

76. Rodgers and Bullock, *Coercion to Compliance,* pp. 59–64.

77. Rossell, "The Effect of Community Leadership."

78. Kirby and Crain, "The Functions of Conflict," p. 486.

79. Kirby et al., *Political Strategies in Northern School Desegregation,* pp. 105–32.

80. McDonnell and Zellman, "An Evaluation of the Emergency School Aid Act Nonprofit Organization Program," pp. 67–68.

81. Rossell, "The Effect of Community Leadership," pp. 134–37.

82. U.S. Commission on Civil Rights, *Fulfilling the Letter,* p. 92.

83. Miller, "Principles Relevant to Successful School Desegregation," p. 24; emphasis in original.

84. Albert S. Foley, "Mobile, Alabama: The Demise of State-Sanctioned Resistance," in *Community Politics and Educational Change,* ed. Willie and Greenblatt, pp. 174–207.

85. Rodgers and Bullock, *Coercion to Compliance,* pp. 41–44, 59–65.

86. Morgan with England, "Assessing the Progress," pp. 67, 71, 75, 77.

87. Rossell and Crain, "The Importance of Political Factors," pp. 785–91.

88. Kirby et al., *Political Strategies in Northern School Desegregation,* pp. 96–103.

89. U.S. Commission on Civil Rights, *Reviewing A Decade of School Desegregation, 1966–1975* (Washington, D.C.: U.S. Government Printing Office, 1977), p. 101.

90. Nevertheless, Gatlin et al. conclude that "our analyses lend only tenuous confirmation to the elitist assumption that public officials shape the target group's reactions to desegregation policies." I know of no better illustration of the difficulty in interpreting leaders' roles in desegregation success than this (apparent?) self-contradiction by a careful group of analysts. Gatlin et al., "Policy Support within a Target Group," pp. 991–94.

91. Giles and Gatlin, "Mass-Level Compliance with Public Policy," p. 738.

92. Morgan and England, "White Enrollment Loss," table 2.

93. Kirby et al., *Political Strategies in Northern School Desegregation,* pp. 118–19.

94. Inger and Stout, "School Desegregation—The Need to Govern," pp. 37–38.

95. Pettigrew, *Racially Separate or Together?* p. 130.

96. While not directly addressing desegregation, a recent survey of citizens' knowledge of the courts reveals considerable ignorance. Only one-fifth of the population claims to know more about the courts than about the other two branches of government; only 40 percent could identify Sandra Day O'Connor or Warren Burger as judges, and half thought it was up to the accused to prove his or her innocence in a criminal trial. See Research and Forecasts, Inc., *The American Public, The Media and the Judicial System: A National Survey on Public Awareness and Personal Experience* (New York: Hearst Corporation, 1983). However, many Bostonians seemed quite knowledgeable about their desegregation court order. See D. Garth Taylor, "Public Opinion and Political Entrepreneurship: The Mayor's Role in School Desegregation Implementation" (Unpublished manuscript, University of Chicago, 1983).

97. Rossell, "The Mayor's Role," p. 251.

98. Luckily, urban school systems, working-class or socially heterogeneous systems, systems with organized community involvement, and systems with high levels of conflict are more likely to appoint "politico" administrators than systems with less need for political and administrative skills. Dale Mann, "School Administrators as Political Representatives," in *The Polity of the School,* ed. Wirt, pp. 85–97. Nevertheless, boards and superintendents may in fact have little control over teachers (especially if they are unionized) or even over their own staffs.

99. Rossell, "The Effect of Community Leadership"; Weatherford, "The Politics of School Busing"; D. G. Hayes, "Anti-Busing Protest" (Paper presented at the annual meeting of the North Carolina Educational Research Association, Charlotte, November 1977).

100. Rossell, "Applied Social Science Research," p. 78.

101. Rossell, "The Effectiveness of Desegregation Plans," p. 9.

102. Rossell and Crain, "The Importance of Political Factors," pp. 780–91; and Laura Morlock, "Black Power and Black Influence in 91 Northern Cities" (Ph.D. diss., Johns Hopkins University, Baltimore, 1973).

103. Kirp, *Just Schools,* e.g., pp. 255–60, 264–70.

104. My thanks to Richard Nathan for directing my attention to the importance of this point.

105. Kirby et al., *Political Strategies in Northern School Desegregation,* p. 16.

106. For reviews of this literature, see Stewart Purkey and Marshall Smith, "Effective Schools: A Review," *The Elementary School Journal* 83, no. 4 (March 1983): 427–52; Jane Hannaway, "The Determinants of Academic Achievement: A Review" (Unpublished manuscript, Princeton University, Woodrow Wilson School of Public and International Affairs, 1983); Clark et al., "Factors Associated with Success in Urban Elementary Schools"; Walberg et al., "The Quiet Revolution in Educational Research," pp. 179–83; Charles D. Moody, "Effective Schools Research," *Breakthrough* 10, no. 2 (Winter 1982): 2–13; and Joan Shoemaker and Hugh W. Fraser, "What Principals Can Do: Some Implications from Studies of Effective Schooling," *Phi Delta Kappan* 63, no. 3 (November 1981): 178–82. See also National Institute of Education, *Violent Schools—Safe Schools,* pp. 127–38, 151–61, 169–247.

107. But administrator control is also associated negatively with white students' perceptions of the school's racial attitudes—perhaps because it upsets the "'status quo' position favored by those with traditional views of schooling." Superintendent and

school board influence increases interracial contact for black high school students. Forehand et al., *Conditions and Processes,* pp. 90–96, 107, 110. Blank et al., *Survey of Magnet Schools,* show that "special treatment" by the district office and leadership by the superintendent and central staff are critical to magnet schools' success. See pp. 69–71, 157–63, 167–71; appendix 3, pp. 8, 11.

108. Willis D. Hawley, "Equity and Quality," p. 301; Martha Turnage, *The Principal: Change Agent in Desegregation* (Chicago: Integrated Education Associates, 1972); George W. Noblit and Bill Johnston, eds., *The School Principal and School Desegregation* (Springfield, Il.: Charles C. Thomas, 1982); Blank et al., *Survey of Magnet Schools,* pp. 674–69, appendix 3, pp. 8, 11.

109. Teachers' attitudes, in turn, are related to the principal's racial attitudes. Forehand et al., *Conditions and Processes,* p. 201; see, generally, pp. 146–64 and 179–207. See also Crain et al., *Making Desegregation Work,* pp. 95–129.

110. See Paul Berman and Milbrey McLaughlin, "Factors Affecting the Process of Change," in *Schools, Conflict, and Change,* ed. Mike Milstein (New York: Teachers College Press, 1980); Nancy St. John, "The Effects of School Desegregation on Children: A New Look at the Research Evidence," in *Race and Schooling in the City,* ed. Yarmolinsky et al., pp. 94–96; Mark A. Chesler, James E. Crowfoot, and Bunyan I. Bryant, "Institutional Changes to Support School Desegregation: Alternative Models Underlying Research and Implementation," *Law and Contemporary Problems* 42, no. 4 (Autumn 1978): 174–213; Schofield, "Desegregation, School Practices," pp. 136–43; C. Anthony Broh and William T. Trent, *Qualitative Literature and Expert Opinion on School Desegregation,* (Nashville: Vanderbilt University, Institute for Public Policy Studies, 1981); Gary Orfield, "How to Make Desegregation Work," pp. 317–22; Miller, "Principles Relevant to Successful School Desegregation;" Hawley et al., *Strategies for Effective Desegregation;* and John Egerton, *Education and Desegregation in Eight Schools* (Evanston, Ill.: Northwestern University, Center for Equal Education, 1972).

111. David L. Kirp, "School Desegregation and the Limits of Legalism," *Public Interest* 47 (1977): 119, 126. See Kirp, *Just Schools,* e.g., pp. 292–95, for the best defense of local control of desegregation implementation.

112. Theoretically, state governments could play a strong role in desegregating local districts, which are under their jurisdiction. But again, with a few exceptions such as New Jersey and Illinois (not including Chicago), they "play either a negative role in the implementation of desegregation or a negligible role." Willie and Greenblatt, eds., *Community Politics and Educational Change,* p. 337. See also Morgan et al., *Desegregating Public Schools,* pp. 124–27; Frederick Edelstein, "Federal and State Roles in School Desegregation," *Education and Urban Policy* 9, no. 3 (May 1977): 303–26; National Project and Task Force on Desegregation Strategies, *State Leadership toward Desegregating Education: A Positive Future* (Denver: Education Commission of the States, 1980); Ben Williams and Carol Andersen, *State Strategies for Reducing Racial Isolation* (Nashville: Vanderbilt University, Institute for Public Policy Studies, 1981); and James Bolmer and Robert Shanley, *Busing: The Political and Judicial Process* (New York: Praeger, 1974), pp. 169–200.

I do not know what to infer from the vacuum of state leadership for my theoretical concern about levels of popular control; at a minimum there is certianly not a linear relationship between increasing scope of governmental activity and increasing desegregation action.

113. On Georgia, see Rodgers and Bullock, *Coercion to Compliance*, pp. 40–41. On the South, see Michael R. Fitzgerald and David R. Morgan, "Changing Patterns of Urban School Desegregation," *American Politics Quarterly* 5, no. 4 (October 1977): 437-63. On the North, see ibid.; and David Morgan and Michael Fitzgerald, "Desegregating Urban Schools: A Causal Perspective," *American Politics Quarterly* 8, no. 2 (April 1980): 187–208. On the country at large, see Reynolds Farley, "Racial Integration in the Public Schools, 1967 to 1972: Assessing the Effects of Governmental Policies," *Sociological Forces* 8 (January 1975): 3–26.

114. On high proportions of minorities, see Michael W. Giles, "Black Concentration and School District Size as Predictors of School Desegregation: the Impact of Federal Enforcement," *Sociology of Education* 48 (Fall 1975): 411–19, and Fitzgerald and Morgan, "Changing Patterns of Urban School Desegregation." On large districts, see Morgan and Fitzgerald, "Desegregating Urban Schools."

115. Rossell, "Applied Social Science Research," p. 72.

116. U.S. Commission on Civil Rights, *Reviewing a Decade of School Desegregation*. These data, especially the frequencies, are suspect for two reasons. In general, the Civil Rights Commission is a deeply political body, so its studies (at least before the early 1980s) are tinged with a strong interest in finding both that desegregation works well and that much more needs to be done. More particularly, this poll included "freedom of choice" among acceptable desegregation strategies—which is dubious at best and unconstitutional at worst. In addition, the poll does not distinguish locally initiated actions from "local actions" that were taken only to avoid a legal suit or OCR letter of noncompliance. However, since both of these flaws inflate the amount and effect of state and local plans, they make my claim that localism works poorly even stronger than these data suggest. Therefore the weaknesses of this poll strengthen rather than weaken my argument.

The same cautions apply to the analysis of these data in the section below on the role and effect of the courts.

Note also that white flight was as great with local plans (or none at all) as with federal ones (pp. 74–81).

117. McDonnell and Zellman, "An Evaluation of the Emergency School Aid Act Nonprofit Organization Program," p. 43.

118. *Human Relations Study;* vol. 2, Doherty et al., *Technical Report;* and Douglas Longshore, Judith Kaye, and Vicki Mandel, *Findings and Implications* (vol. 1 of the same series).

119. Coulson, "Overview of the National Evaluation of the Emergency School Aid Act," pp. 25–29.

120. Charles S. Bullock III, "The Office for Civil Rights," p. 601.

121. These results vary considerably by state, and the relationships are fairly weak overall. Bullock and Stewart, "Incidence and Correlates," pp. 123–24.

122. Rebell and Block, *Equality and Education.*

123. Rodgers and Bullock, *Coercion to Compliance,* pp. 62–64.

124. Charles S. Bullock III, "Implementation of Selected Equal Education Opportunity Programs," p. 56.

125. Doris Fine, "Just Schools" (Unpublished manuscript, University of California, Berkeley, 1982), pp. 3–8.

126. Rebell and Block, *Equality and Education.*

127. 411 U.S. 1 (1973).

128. Lance Liebman, "Constitutional Values and Public Education," in *Race and Schooling in the City*, ed. Yarmolinsky et al., pp. 261–65.

129. Senator John East, *Opening Statement* and *Comments in Response to Statement by Judge James B. McMillan*, Senate Judiciary Committee, Subcommittee on Separation of Powers, *Hearings on Court-Ordered School Busing*, 97th Cong., 1st Sess., 1981, pp. 109, 519.

130. Lino Graglia, *Disaster by Decree: The Supreme Court Decisions on Race and the Schools* (Ithaca, N.Y.: Cornell University Press, 1976); John Kaplan, "Segregation Litigation and the Schools—Part II: The General Northern Problem," *Northwestern University Law Review* 58 (May/June 1963): 57–214; Raoul Berger, *Government by Judiciary: The Transformation of the Fourteenth Amendment* (Cambridge: Harvard University Press, 1977), pp. 117–34, 166–245.

131. Kirp, "School Desegregation and the Limits of Legalism."

132. James R. Coleman, "The Role of Incentives in School Desegregation," in *Race and Schooling in the City*, ed. Yarmolinsky et al., pp. 182–93; Derrick Bell, "Civil Rights Commitment and the Challenge of Changing Conditions in Urban School Cases," in ibid., pp. 194–203.

133. For an academic analysis of this problem, see Iredell Jenkins, *Social Order and the Limits of Law* (Princeton: Princeton University Press, 1980). For political manifestations of this phenomenon, see Senate Judiciary Committee, *Hearings on Court-Ordered School Busing;* and Senate Judiciary Committee, Subcommmittee on the Constitution, *Hearings on the 14th Amendment and School Busing*, 97th Cong., 1st Sess., 1981.

134. Senator John East, *Comments in Response to Statement of J. Harold Flannery*, Senate Judiciary Committee, *Hearings on Court-Ordered School Busing*, p. 372.

135. Hon. Simon H. Rifkind, "Are We Asking Too Much of Our Courts?" *Federal Rules Decisions* 70 (1976): 5.

136. Donald L. Horowitz, *The Courts and Social Policy* (Washington, D.C.: Brookings Institution, 1977), pp. 22–62; here, pp. 45, 51.

137. Ibid.; Wolf, *Trial and Error;* Kirp, *Just Schools*, pp. 68–70; and Lon Fuller, "The Forms and Limits of Adjudication," *Harvard Law Review* 92 (1978): 353–409.

138. *Milliken v. Bradley (Milliken II)*, 433 U.S. 267 (1977); emphasis in original. See also Owen Fiss, "School Desegregation: The Uncertain Path of the Law," *Philosophy and Public Affairs* 4, no. 1 (Fall 1974): 3–39; Alan D. Freemen, "Legitimizing Racial Discrimination through Antidiscrimination Law: A Critical Review of Supreme Court Doctrine," *Minnesota Law Review* 62 (1978): 1049–1119; and Dworkin, *Taking Rights Seriously*, pp. 82–105, inter alia.

139. Abram Chayes, "The Role of the Judge in Public Law Litigation," *Harvard Law Review* 89, no. 7 (May 1976): 1281–1316.

140. Rossell, "Applied Social Science Research," p. 72.

141. Morgan with England, "Assessing the Progress."

142. U.S. Commission on Civil Rights, *Reviewing a Decade of School Desegregation.*

143. Brief for the United States, *Columbus v. Penick*, p. 87.

144. Morgan with England, "Assessing the Progress," pp. 67, 71, 75, 77.

145. Rossell and Crain, "The Importance of Political Factors."

146. James S. Coleman, Sara Kelly, and John Moore, *Trends in School Segregation, 1968–1973* (Washington, D.C.: The Urban Institute, 1975); and Armor, "White Flight."

147. Morgan and England, "White Enrollment Loss," table 2; and Becker, "The Impact of Racial Composition," table 5. See also U.S. Civil Rights Commission, *Reviewing a Decade of School Desegregation*, pp. 74–81.

148. Horowitz, *The Courts and Social Policy;* Wolf, *Trial and Error;* Kirp, *Just Schools*, pp. 82–116; and Kalodner and Fishman, eds., *The Limits of Justice*.

149. *Crawford v. Board of Education of Los Angeles*, 17 C. 3d 280; 130 Cal. Rptr. 724, 551 P.2d 28 (1976).

150. Ralph Cavanagh and Austin Sarat, "Thinking about Courts: Toward and Beyond a Jurisprudence of Judicial Competence," *Law and Society Review* 14, no. 2 (Winter 1980): 376. For a less well-known but convincing example of the need for judicial intervention, see Daniel J. Monti, "Administrative Foxes in Educational Chicken Coops: An Examination of the Critique of Judical Activism in School Desegregation Cases," *Law and Policy Quarterly* 2, no. 2 (April 1980): 233–56.

151. Betsy Levin and Willis D. Hawley, eds., "Symposium on the Courts, Social Science, and School Desegregation; Part I: The Legal Backdrop," *Law and Contemporary Problems* 39, no. 1 (Winter 1975): 50–162, and "Symposium on School Desegregation: Lessons of the First Twenty-Five Years: Part II: Social Science Research and the Law," *Law and Contemporary Problems* 42, no. 4 (Autumn 1978): 1–110.

152. Geoffrey Aronow, "The Special Master in School Desegregation Cases: The Evolution of Policy in the Reformation of Public Institutions through Litigation," *Hastings Constitutional Law Quarterly* 7 (Spring 1980): 739–75; "Symposium: Judicially Managed Institutional Reform," *Alabama Law Review* 32, no. 2 (Winter 1981): 267–464; "Special Project: The Remedial Process in Institutional Reform Litigation," *Columbia Law Review* 78, no. 4 (May 1978): 784–929; and "Judicial Intervention and Organization Theory: Changing Bureaucratic Behavior and Policy," *Yale Law Journal* 89, no. 3 (1980): 513–37.

153. Hochschild and Hadrick, "The Character and Effectiveness of Citizen Monitoring Groups"; and Francine Rabinovitz, "Court Supervised Implementation of Remedies" (Unpublished report, Los Angeles, 1982).

154. Chayes, "The Role of the Judge."

155. See, for example, Vergon, *The Courts and Desegregation Strategies*, pp. 25–26.

156. See also Stanley C. Brubaker, "From Incompetent Imperialism to Principled Prudence: The Role of the Courts in Restoring 'The State'" (Paper presented at the annual meeting of the American Political Science Association, New York, September 1981); Stephen L. Wasby, "Arrogation of Power or Accountability: 'Judical Imperialism' Revisited," *Judicature* 65, no. 4 (October 1981): 208–19. Theodore Eisenberg and Stephen C. Yeazell, "The Ordinary and the Extraordinary in Institutional Litigation," *Harvard Law Review* 93 (January 1980): 465–517; and Colin Diver, "The Judge as Political Powerbroker: Superintending Structural Change in Public Institutions," *Virginia Law Review* 65, no. 1 (February 1979): 43–106.

157. See *Milliken II, Crawford v. Board of Education of Los Angeles*.

158. This analysis compares sixty-five court cases with education controversies, school-related proposals in the New York and Colorado state legislatures, and OCR requirements for faculty desegregation in New York, Philadelphia, Chicago, and Los Angeles. Michael Rebell and Arthur Block, *Educational Policy Making and the Courts: An Empirical Study of Judicial Activism* (Chicago: University of Chicago Press, 1982), pp. 199–216, and *Equality and Education.*

159. Michael A. Rebell, "Judicial Activism and the Courts' New Role," *Social Policy* 12, no. 4 (1981–82): 26.

160. Howard I. Kalodner introduction to Kalodner and Fishman, eds,. *Limits of Justice*, p. 24. He follows this observation with a sobering warning; "There is probably a price that our society will pay for its decision to rest upon the federal courts the entire burden of protecting this right of the black minority. No political institution can long withstand the punishment of political isolation without an impact on its conduct. A plea to political leadership to accept its constitutional responsibilities is therefore much more than a plea in behalf of the constitutional rights of the minority; it is, rather, a plea in behalf of the survival of our governmental structure as established in Articles I, II, and III of the Constitution of the United States."

161. Kirp, "School Desegregation and the Limits of Legalism," pp. 107–16; Nathan Glazer, *Affirmative Discrimination: Ethnic Inequality and Public Policy,* (New York: Basic Books, 1975), pp. 77–129; and Jeremy Rabkin, "Office for Civil Rights," in *The Politics of Regulation,* ed. James Q. Wilson (New York: Basic Books, 1980), pp. 304–53, 436–445, notes.

162. Warren E. Miller and Donald E. Stokes, "Constituency Influence in Congress," *American Political Science Review* 57, no. 1 (March 1963): 45–56.

163. Frank Levy, *Northern Schools and Civil Rights: The Racial Imbalance Act of Massachusetts* (Chicago: Markham, 1971).

164. Frank Thompson Jr. and Daniel H. Pollitt, "Congressional Control of Judicial Remedies: President Nixon's Proposed Moratorium on 'Busing' Orders," *North Carolina Law Review* 50 (1972): 813.

165 Rossell, "Applied Social Science Research," p. 72.

166. Rodgers and Bullock, *Coercion to Compliance,* pp. 59–64, 115–19.

167. Rossell and Crain, "The Importance of Political Factors," pp. 788–91. But Fitzgerald and Morgan ("Changing Patterns of Urban School Desegregation," pp. 451–53) do not find such an association—hence the "perhaps."

168. Fitzgerald and Morgan, "Changing Patterns of Urban School Desegregation."

169. Robert England, Ted Robinson, and Kenneth J. Meier, "Black Resources and Black School Board Representation: Does Political Structure Matter?" (Paper presented at the annual meeting of the Southwestern Political Science Association, Dallas, 1981), p. 12; Ted Robinson and Robert England, "Black Representation on Central City School Boards Revisited," *Social Science Quarterly* 62, no. 3 (September 1981): 495–502; and Kenneth J. Meier and Robert England, "Black Representation and Educational Policy: Does It Make a Difference?" (Paper presented at the annual meeting of the American Political Science Association, Denver, 1982).

170. Mann, "School Administrators as Political Representatives," p. 89.

171. Thomas Dye, "Urban School Desegregation: A Comparative Analysis," *Urban Affairs Quarterly* 4 (December 1968): 141–65; and Robert L. Crain, *The Politics of School Desegregation* (Chicago: Aldine, 1968), pp. 171–73.

172. Morgan with England, "Assessing the Progress," pp. 67, 71, 75; Morgan and Fitzgerald, "Desegregating Urban Schools," pp. 196–202; and Kirby and Crain, "The Functions of Conflict," p. 486.

173. Fitzgerald and Morgan, "Changing Patterns of Urban School Desegregation."

174. Ibid., p. 453.

CHAPTER 6

1. Geraldine Kozberg and Jerome Winegar, "The South Boston Story," *Phi Delta Kappan* 62, no. 8 (April 1981): 569.

2. Margaret Mead, *New Lives for Old: Cultural Transformation—Manus, 1928–1953* (New York: Morrow, 1956), pp. 445–47; emphasis added. Machiavelli said it best, and perhaps first. See (so that I do not steal his thunder) David Braybrooke's response to this book, "Scale; Combination; Opposition—A Rethinking of Incrementalism," *Ethics* (forthcoming 1985).

3. Kenneth B. Clark, "Desegregation: An Appraisal of the Evidence," *Journal of Social Issues* 9, no. 4 (1953): 2–76. See also Herbert Hill and Jack Greenberg, *Citizen's Guide to Desegregation* (Boston: Beacon Press, 1955), pp. 123–32, 146–55; Harry Ashmore, *The Negro and the Schools* (Chapel Hill: University of North Carolina Press, 1954); and Richard Kluger, *Simple Justice* (New York: Knopf, 1975), 2:904–13.

4. Martin Luther King, Jr., *Where Do We Go from Here: Chaos or Community?* (Boston: Beacon Press, 1967).

5. Thomas L. Van Valey, Wade C. Roof, and Jerome E. Wilcox, "Trends in Residential Segregation: 1960–1970," *American Journal of Sociology* 82, no. 4 (January 1977): 826–44; and Karl E. Taeuber and Alma F. Taeuber, *Negroes in Cities: Residential Segregation and Neighborhood Change* (Chicago: Aldine, 1965).

6. Robert A. Dahl, *Pluralist Democracy in the United States* (Chicago: Rand McNally, 1967), p. 24.

7. Charles E. Lindblom, "Still Muddling," p. 520.

8. Ibid., p. 523.

9. Clarence Stone, *Economic Growth and Neighborhood Discontent* (Chapel Hill: University of North Carolina Press, 1976), p. 14.

10. Michael Lipsky, "Protest as a Political Resource," *American Political Science Review* 42, no. 4 (December 1968): 1144–58.

11. Stone, *Economic Growth and Neighborhood Discontent,* pp. 10–19, 189–214.

12. James Madison, "Federalist Paper Number 10," in Alexander Hamilton, John Jay, and James Madison, *The Federalist,* ed. with introduction by Jacob E. Cooke (Middletown, Conn.: Wesleyan University Press, 1961), p. 58.

13. Derrick Bell, "*Brown* and the Interest-Convergence Dilemma," in *Shades of*

Brown: New Perspectives on School Desegregation, ed. Derrick Bell (New York: Teachers College Press, 1980), p. 95; emphasized in original.

14. See Michael Apple, *Education and Power: Reproduction and Contradiction in Education* (Boston: Routledge & Kegan Paul, 1982); Caroline Persell, *Education and Inequality: The Roots and Results of Stratification in America's Schools* (New York: Free Press, 1977); Michael Katz, *Class, Bureaucracy, and Schools: The Illusion of Educational Change in America* (New York: Praeger, 1975); Joel H. Spring, *Education and the Rise of the Corporate State* (Boston: Beacon Press, 1973); Mario Barrera, *Race and Class in the Southwest: A Theory of Racial Inequality* (South Bend, Ind.: University of Notre Dame Press, 1979); and James Rosenbaum, *Making Inequality: The Hidden Curriculum of College Tracking* (New York; Wiley, 1976). For counterarguments, see Diane Ravitch, "On the History of Minority Group Education in the United States," *Teachers College Record* 78, no. 2 (December 1976): 213–28; Timothy L. Smith, "Immigrant Social Aspirations and American Education, 1880–1930," *American Quarterly* 21, no. 3 (Fall 1969); 523–43; Lawrence Cremin, *The Transformation of the School: Progressivism in American Education 1867–1957* (New York: Random House, 1961). For a general review of this debate, see Christopher Hurn, *The Limits and Possibilities of Schooling* (Boston: Allyn & Bacon, 1978).

15. For example, the federal government's *amicus curiae* brief stated:

> It is in the context of the present world struggle between freedom and tyranny that the problem of racial discrimination must be viewed . . . [for] discrimination against minority groups in the United States has an adverse effect upon our relations with other countries. Racial discrimination furnishes grist for the Communist propaganda mills, and it raises doubts even among friendly nations as to the intensity of our devotion to the democratic faith.

See *Brown v. Board of Education (Brown I)*, p. 6.

16. Bell, "*Brown* and the Interest-Convergence Dilemma," p. 96.

17. Alan D. Freeman, "School Desegregation Law: Promise, Contradiction, Rationalization," in *Shades of Brown*, ed. Bell, p. 85.

18. A brief, nonradical statement of this argument is in Robert Dentler, "Barriers to Northern School Desegregation," *Daedalus* 95, no. 1 (Winter 1966): 45–63.

19. Freeman, "School Desegregation Law," p. 85.

20. John A. Brittain, *The Inheritance of Economic Status* (Washington, D.C.: Brookings Institution, 1977); Reynolds Farley, *Blacks and Whites: Narrowing the Gap* (Cambridge: Harvard University Press, 1984); John Akin and Irv Garfinkel, "The Quality of Education and Cohort Variation in Black-White Earnings Differentials: Comment," *American Economic Review* 70, no. 1 (1980): 186–91; Christopher Jencks et al., *Who Gets Ahead?* (New York: Basic Books, 1979). But see also Finis Welch, "Black-White Differences in Returns to Schooling," *American Economic Review* 67 (December 1973): 893–907, for an argument that racial differences in returns to schooling are disappearing or have been eliminated; Michael R. Olneck and Ki-Seok Kim, "The Relationship between Education and Income among American Men: Some Revisions and Extensions" (Unpublished report, University of Wisconsin, Wisconsin Center for Education Research, 1983) for evidence that "high school graduation *does* have significant . . . effects on men's average incomes"; and Christopher Jencks et al., *Inequality: A Reassessment of the Effect of Family and Schooling*

in America (New York: Basic Books, 1972) for an argument that no background factors have as much effect on earnings as luck has.

21. Freeman, "School Desegregation Law," pp. 85–88.

22. Charles Silberman, *Crisis in Black and White* (New York: Random House, 1964), pp. 9–10. A fascinating argument that our purportedly liberal democracy treats school desegregation as a "ritual reform"—as a means of venting hostility about inequality without any intention of doing anything about it—is Daniel J. Monti, *A Semblance of Justice: School Desegregation and the Pursuit of Order in Urban America*. (Columbia: Univ. of Missouri Press, forthcoming). A similar argument is that whites are eager to grant blacks' rights when doing so reinforces the capitalist economic system, but unwilling to grant rights that alter the market, is W. Richard Merriman, "Citizen Attitudes toward Government, Race, Policy: The Liberal Tradition and Racial Inequality" (Paper presented at the annual meeting of the American Political Science Association, Denver, 1982).

23. Orfield, *Toward A Strategy for Urban Integration*, pp. 14–16.

24. Chesler et al., *Making Desegregation Work*, p. 22.

25. Karl Weick, "Educational Organizations as Loosely Coupled Systems," *Administrative Science Quarterly* 21 (March 1974): 1–19; and James March, "American Public School Administration," *School Review* 86, no. 2 (February 1978): 217–50.

26. Michael Lipsky, *Street-Level Bureaucracy: Dilemmas of the Individual in Public Services* (New York: Russell Sage Foundation, 1980).

27. Willis D. Hawley, "Dealing with Organizational Rigidity in Public Schools: A Theoretical Perspective," in *The Polity of the School*, ed. Wirt, pp. 187–210.

28. Dentler, "Barriers to Northern School Desegregation."

29. Jeffrey Pressman and Aaron Wildavsky, *Implementation* (Berkeley and Los Angeles: University of California Press, 1973).

30. Herbert Simon, "On the Concept of Organizational Goals," *Adminstrative Science Quarterly* 9 (1964): 1–22.

31. Alan Gaynor and Karl Clauset, Jr., "Implementing Effective School Improvement Policies: A System Dynamics Policy Analysis" (Unpublished manuscript, Boston University, School of Education, 1983).

32. Ibid.; Stewart Purkey and Marshall Smith, "Effective Schools: A Review," pp. 427–52.

33. Andrew M. Greeley, "School Desegregation and Ethnicity," in *School Desegregation*, ed. Stephan and Feagin, pp. 133–55.

34. More precisely, white support for desegregation increased 11 percent between 1964 and 1972, then declined 4 percent from 1972 to 1878. Support for segregation declined monotonically over the whole period. Philip E. Converse et al., *American Social Attitudes*, pp. 61, 91.

35. Louis Harris, "Majority of Parents Report School Busing Has Been Satisfactory Experience," *Harris Survey* no. 25, March 26, 1981. See also Orfield, *Must We Bus?* pp. 102–18.

36. Qualitative studies concur; see Wilkinson, *From Brown to Bakke;* Cottle, *Busing;* and Nicolaus Mills, ed., *The Great School Bus Controversy* (New York: Teachers College Press, 1973), pp. 233–93, and *Busing U.S.A.* (New York: Teachers

College Press, 1979), pp. 310–66.

37. Converse et al., *American Social Attitudes,* pp. 61, 91.

38. Harris, "Majority of Parents Report School Busing."

39. Greeley, "School Desegregation and Ethnicity," p. 137.

40. Center for Political Studies, *American National Election Study, 1980* (Ann Arbor: University of Michigan, Institute for Social Research, 1981).

41. In fact, "in many Hispanic communities desegregation is seen as an impediment to equal educational opportunity rather than an aid." Peter D. Roos, "Bilingual Education: The Hispanic Response to Unequal Educational Opportunity," *Law and Contemporary Problems* 42, no. 4 (Autumn 1978): 111. See also Linda Hanten, "Bilingual Education and School Desegregation," in *Race and Schooling in the City,* ed. Yarmolinsky et al., pp. 217–32; Orfield, *Must We Bus?* pp. 198–229; and Ricardo R. Fernández and Judith T. Guskin, "Hispanic Students and School Desegregation," in *Effective School Desegregation,* ed. Hawley, pp. 107–40.

42. Thomas Curtis, testimony before Senate Judiciary Committee, Subcommittee on the Constitution, *Hearings on the 14th Amendment and School Busing,* 97th Cong. 1st Sess., 1981: 221–36.

43. William Raspberry, "Why is Busing the Only Route?" *Washington Post,* September 4, 1981, p. A31; Thomas Sowell, "Government by Snobs," *Los Angeles Herald Examiner,* June 6, 1979; and Walter Williams, "Quality Education Comes in More Than One Color," in *America: A Minority Viewpoint* (Stanford, Calif.: Hoover Institution Press, 1982), pp. 12–13.

44. See, for example, *Journal of Negro Education* 47, no. 1 (Winter 1978).

45. *Tony Brown's Journal,* July–September 1983, pp. 4–15.

46. "Mrs. Gilliam Calls for End to Busing," *Dallas Morning News,* May 1981; Freedom House Institute on Schools and Education, "Critique of the Boston School Committee Plan" (Report to Judge W. Arthur Garrity, Boston, February 4, 1975); and Superintendent Constance Clayton, School District of Philadelphia, *To Educate All Our Children: Proposed Modifications to the Desegregation Plan of the School District of Philadelphia* (Philadelphia: School District of Philadelphia, 1983).

47. Morgan with England, "Assessing the Progress," pp. 159–210.

48. Ray Rist, "On the Future of School Desegregation: A New American Dilemma?" in *School Desegregation,* ed. Stephan and Feagin, p. 127.

49. Armor, "White Flight," p. 196.

50. John H. Schweitzer and Robert J. Griffore, "A Longitudinal Study," pp. 111–19 (but see note 34, chapter 4); Armor, "The Evidence on Busing"; Elizabeth Useem, "Correlates of White Students' Attitudes"; Crain et al., *Making Desegregation Work;* and Stephan, "School Desegregation: An Evaluation of Predictions," pp. 222–26.

51. Yehuda Amir, "The Role of Intergroup Contact in Change of Prejudice and Ethnic Relations," in *Towards the Elimination of Racism,* ed. Phyllis A. Katz (New York: Pergamon, 1976): 245–308; and Norman Miller, "Changing Views about the Effects of School Desegregation: *Brown* Then and Now," in *Scientific Inquiry and the Social Sciences,* ed. Marilyn Brewer and Barry Collins (San Francisco: Jossey-Bass, 1981), pp. 422–26.

52. Edgar G. Epps, "The Impact of School Desegregation on the Self-Evaluation and Achievement Orientation of Minority Children," *Law and Contemporary Problems* 42, no. 3 (Summer 1978): 75. See also Epps, "Impact of School Desegregation on Aspirations, Self-Concepts, and Other Aspects of Personality," *Law and Contemporary Problems* 39, no. 2 (Spring 1975): 300–13.

53. Miller, "Changing Views About the Effects," pp. 416–19; Stephan, "School Desegregation," pp. 227–28.

54. Roberta G. Simmons, "Black and White Self-Esteem: A Puzzle," *Social Psychology Quarterly* 41, no. 1 (1978): 56.

55. Miller, "Changing Views about the Effects," p. 425.

56. Sensitive analyses of this phenomenon are H. Andrew Sagar and Janet W. Schofield, "Integrating the Desegregated School: Problems and Possibilities," in *Advances in Motivation and Achievement*, ed. M. Maehr and D. Bartz (Greenwich, Conn.: JAI Press, 1983); Schofield, *Black and White in School;* Elizabeth G. Cohen, "Design and Redesign of the Desegregated School"; Mary H. Metz, *Classrooms and Corridors: The Crisis of Authority in Desegregated Secondary Schools* (Berkeley and Los Angeles: University of California Press, 1978); and Ray Rist, *The Invisible Children: School Integration in American Society* (Cambridge: Harvard University Press, 1978).

57. Robert C. Serow and Daniel Soloman, "Parents' Attitudes toward Desegregation: The Proximity Hypothesis," *Phi Delta Kappan* 60, no. 10 (June 1979): 753.

58. George W. Noblit and Thomas W. Collins, "Cui Bono? White Students in a Desegregating High School," *Urban Review* 13, no. 4 (Winter 1981): 205–16; Margaret T. Orr and Francis A. J. Ianni, "The Impact of Culture Contact and Desegregation on the Whites of an Urban High School," *Urban Review* 13, no. 4 (1981): 243–60.

59. Harriette P. McAdoo, "Components of Educational Achievement and Mobility in Black Families" (Paper presented at the annual meeting of the American Educational Research Association, New York, 1977), pp. 11–12.

60. *Congressional Record*, 94th Cong., 2d Sess., June 31, 1974, p. S 931.

61. Rodgers and Bullock, *Coercion to Compliance*, pp. 97–98.

62. These researchers further estimate that over twenty-five thousand additional black teachers who would have been hired under the old dual system were not hired when schools were desegregated. Assuming these teachers earned average salaries, the firing and nonhiring cost the black community about $241 million (in 1970 dollars). John Smith and Bette Smith, "Desegregation in the South and the Demise of the Black Educator," *Journal of Social and Behavioral Sciences* 20, no. 1 (Winter 1974): 33–40. These data are almost certainly inaccurate, but the evidence is so poor that we cannot even say whether they exaggerate or underestimate the harm to black teachers and principals. See also James E. Haney, "The Effects of the *Brown* Decision on Black Educators," *Journal of Negro Education* 47, no. 1 (Winter 1978): 88–95; American Friends Service Committee et al., *The Status of School Desegregation in the South, 1970* (Philadelphia: American Friends Service Committee, 1970), pp. 74–100; U.S. Commission on Civil Rights, *Twenty Years after Brown* (Washington, D.C..: U.S. Government Printing Office, 1977), pp. 56–58.

63. J. C. James, "The Black Principal: Another Vanishing American," *New Re-*

public, September 26, 1970, pp. 17–20.

64. *Singleton v. Jackson Municipal Separate School District*, 419 F. 2d 1218 (1969), en banc.

65. Bosma, *Planning for and Implementing Effective School Desegregation*, pp. 6–10.

66. Bullock and Stewart, Jr., "Incidence and Correlates of Second-Generation Discrimination," pp. 118–20.

67. More precisely, forty of the fifty largest school districts in the nation had at least 50 percent more black EMR enrollment than the proportion of black students in that district would suggest. Fifteen had 100 to 200 percent more, and an additional eight had over 200 percent more. The number of students affected by EMR placement is very small but the effect on them is very great, and the evidence suggests that it is more harmful than helpful. Bullock, "Equal Education Opportunity," pp. 70–71. For the first datum, see Bullock and Stewart, "Incidence and Correlates of Second-Generation Discrimination," pp. 116–20.

68. More precisely, thirty-five of the forty-five largest districts (among the fifty largest for which data are available) had 50 percent or more black suspensions than the proportion of black students in the school system would suggest. Sixteen had over 100 percent disproportionality, and Charlotte-Mecklenburg had 215 percent. Only districts with fewer than 7 percent or more than 70 percent black students did not show disproportionality of 50 percent or more. Bullock, "Implementation of Selected Equal Education Opportunity Programs," table 2.

We must use caution in drawing implications from the data cited in notes 67 and 68 because they have no controls for size, urbanization, socioeconomic status, and other variables besides race that could affect EMR placement and student discipline. See, however, Christine Bennett and J. John Harris III, "Suspensions and Expulsions of Male and Black Students," *Urban Education* 16, no. 4 (January 1982): 399–423, which finds disproportional black punishment to be "related to an overall orientation of white predominance which includes institutional and individual racism" (pp. 420–21).

69. National Education Association, *1971 Survey of Minority Expulsion in 2,831 Districts* (Washington, D.C.: National Education Association, 1971). For other analyses of second-generation discrimination, see National Institute of Education, *Resegregation: A Second Generation School Desegregation Issue* (Washington, D.C.: U.S. Government Printing Office, 1977), pp. 12–23; Nancy L. Arnez, "Implementation of Desegregation as a Discriminatory Process," *Journal of Negro Education* 47, no. 1 (Winter 1978): 30–39; Janet Eyler et al., "Resegregation: Segregation within Desegregated Schools," in Rossell et al., *A Review of the Empirical Research on Desegregation*, pp. 210–329; and Mark G. Yudof, "Suspension and Expulsion of Black Students from the Public Schools: Academic Capital Punishment and the Constitution," *Law and Contemporary Problems* 39, no. 2 (Spring 1975): 374–411.

70. Children's Defense Fund, *School Suspensions*, pp. 67–71, appendix B, and *Children Out of School in America*, pp. 124–34.

71. Gatlin et al., "Policy Support within a Target Group, pp. 991–93.

72. William Berg and David Colton, "*Brown* and the Distribution of School Resources," in *New Directions for Testing and Measurement*, ed. Monti, p. 86.

73. Rodgers and Bullock, *Coercion to Compliance*, pp. 95–97.

74. American Friends Service Committee et al., *The Status of School Desegregation in the South 1970* (Philadelphia: American Friends Service Committee, 1970), pp. 44–73.

75. Reginald Stuart, "Businesses Owned by Blacks Still Fighting an Uphill Battle," *New York Times*, July 26, 1981, pp. 1, 20.

76. C. Eric Lincoln, "The New Black Estate: The Coming Age of Blackamerica," in *Have We Overcome? Race Relations since Brown*, ed. Michael Namorato (Jackson: University Press of Mississippi, 1979), pp. 8–21; Reginald Stuart, "Black Colleges Survive, But Students Are Fewer," *New York Times*, February 1, 1984, p. A18.

77. Derrick Bell, "A Reassessment of Racial Balance Remedies—I," *Phi Delta Kappan* 62, no. 3 (November 1980): 177.

78. William A. Sampson and Ben Williams, "School Desegregation: The Non-Traditional Sociological Perspective," *Journal of Negro Education* 47, no. 1 (Winter 1978): 74.

79. Nathaniel R. Jones, Letter to the editors of the *Yale Law Journal*, December 8, 1976, and letter to Derrick Bell, July 31, 1975, both reprinted in *Limits of Justice*, ed. Kalodner and Fishman, pp. 614, 616, 590.

80. Herbert Wechsler, "Toward Neutral Principles of Constitutional Law," *Harvard Law Review* 73, no. 1 (November 1959): 1–33; Lino Graglia, *Disaster by Decree: The Supreme Court Decisons on Race and the Schools* (Ithaca, N.Y.: Cornell University Press, 1976); Raoul Berger, *Government by Judiciary* (Cambridge: Harvard University Press, 1977); and Philip B. Kurland, *Politics, the Constitution, and the Warren Court* (Chicago: University of Chicago Press, 1970).

81. Robert Carter, "A Reassessment of *Brown v. Board*," in *Shades of Brown*, ed. Bell, pp. 20–28.

82. Andrew Kopkind, "Banned in Boston: Busing into Southie," *Ramparts* 13 (December 1974): 37, emphasis in original.

83. Barbara L. Jackson, "Desegregation: Atlanta Style," *Theory into Practice* 17, no. 1 (February 1978): 43–53, and "Urban School Desegregation from a Black Perspective," in *Race and Schooling in the City*, ed. Yarmolinsky et al., pp. 209–14; and Benjamin Mays, "Comment: Atlanta—Living with *Brown* Twenty Years Later," *Black Law Journal* 3, no. 2 (1974): 184–92. For unusual and detailed evidence of the educational, economic, and political consequences of black school districts run by white school boards and local elites, see Southern Regional Council, *Decade of Frustration: Black Belt Schools of Georgia and Alabama in the 1970's* (Atlanta: Southern Regional Council, 1981).

84. W. E. B. DuBois, "Does the Negro Need Separate Schools?" *Journal of Negro Education* 4 (1935): 328–35.

85. A survey of parents' desires for their children's education found that black parents in general paid more attention to their children's schooling than white parents did, and wanted longer hours and stiffer requirements. But they were also twice as likely to agree strongly that "the primary purpose of education is to enable a person to achieve financial success" (28 percent of whites, 50 percent of nonwhites). Whites were more likely to agree that the purpose of education is "to add value to the general

quality of a person's life" (80 percent, compared to 69 percent of nonwhites). Research and Forecasts, *The Grolier Survey: What Parents Believe about Education* (New York: Research and Forecasts, 1983).

86. Judith Valente, "Report Calls District Schools 'Most Segregated' of Big Cities," *Washington Post*, January 25, 1983, pp. B1, B20; Brooks Jackson, "Home-Grown Answers in a Black School System," *Wall Street Journal*, March 15, 1983. See also Derrick Bell, *Race, Racism, and American Law*, 2d ed. (Boston: Little, Brown, 1980), pp. 411–43; Kirp, *Just Schools*, and "Busing," *Ramparts* 13 (December 1974): 34–48.

87. Gary Orfield, "Will Separate Be More Equal?" *Integrated Education* (January/February 1976): 3–5; see also Hawley et al., *Strategies for Effective Desegregation*, pp. 164–66. For an effort to produce the aforementioned miracle (through distinctly nonbiblical means), see Susan Chira, "Weehawken's Schools Try to Integrate Electronically," *New York Times*, January 28, 1984, pp. 25, 26: "Weehawken school officials, faced with a state [New Jersey] directive to desegregate and with parental opposition to busing, have proposed linking white and Hispanic students by computer and television while letting them stay in their own schools. . . . 'Busing is not the answer,' said . . . [the] Superintendent of Schools and the creator of the integration plan. 'This is a plan to bring about positive changes in attitude, if negative ones do exist. The state . . . should look forward to the electronic age and the space age we're entering, and this certainly is on the threshold of that age.'" The state has so far rejected the plan.

88. Thomas Sowell, "Patterns of Black Excellence," *Public Interest* 43 (Spring 1976): 26–58; J. S. Fuerst, "Report Card: Chicago's All-Black Schools," *Public Interest* 64 (Summer 1981): 79–91; Bell, *Race, Racism, and American Law*, pp. 428–31.

89. Elected officials who are morally committed to racial equity but who would also like to keep their jobs face an agonizing problem when their constituency is served a court order mandating desegregation. Such is Biden's situation as a liberal Democrat who changed his views on the mandate of *Brown* when Wilmington and New Castle County were desegregated despite much white protest. Biden now leads the Northern liberal antibusing fraction in Congress and spends much time justifying his about-face to himself and his auditors. See his comments in response to Gary Orfield's statement to Senate Judiciary Committee, Subcommittee on the Constitution, *Hearings on the 14th Amendment and School Busing*, 97th Cong. 1st Sess., 1981, pp. 276–322, esp. pp. 315–22.

90. Elizabeth Cohen makes Biden's point more elegantly when she wishes that "courts and other decison makers would come to realize that trying to change the status order of an entire society by a superficial change in the racial composition of an organization which traditionally has reflected faithfully the power and status order in society at large is not an easy thing to do either politically or practically." "The Effects of Desegregation on Race Relations," *Law and Contemporary Problems* 39, no. 2 (Spring 1975): 299.

91. Charles Lawrence, "'One More River to Cross'—Recognizing the Real Injury in *Brown*: A Prerequisite to Shaping New Remedies," in *Shades of Brown*, ed. Bell, pp. 48–68.

92. For example, white agreement with the proposition that "blacks have a right to live wherever they can afford to" rose from 53 percent in 1964 to 84 percent in 1976. However, the number of whites who live in an all or mostly white neighborhood has not changed (96 percent in 1964 and 94 percent in 1976). Converse et al., *American Social Attitudes*, pp. 66, 71. In 1982, two-thirds of blacks expressing an opinion reported that they would prefer to live in a "half black, half white" or "mostly white" neighborhood; only one-third would rather live in an "all" or "mostly black" neighborhood. Yet, in 1976 only 28 percent of blacks reported living in a mostly white or half-black, half-white neighborhood, and 72 percent were living in an all or mostly black neighborhood. These data are not precisely comparable, since they come from different polls taken six years apart, but neighborhood integration apparently did not change very much during that period and the data suggest the disparity between black preferences and reality. 1976 data from Converse et al., *American Social Attitudes*, p. 71; 1982 data from James A. Davis and Tom W. Smith, *General Social Surveys, 1972–1983: Cumulative Codebook* (Chicago: University of Chicago, National Opinion Research Center, 1983), p. 117.

93. Orfield, *Toward a Strategy for Urban Integration*. Evidence suggests that the number of blacks who purchase houses is closely related to the rise and fall of federal mortgage subsidies for the poor. See John Henretta, "Race, Housing Tenure, and the Life Course" (Unpublished manuscript, University of Florida, Gainesville, 1983); and M. L. Ladenson, "Race and Sex Discrimination in Housing: The Evidence from Probabilities of Homeownership," *Southern Economic Journal* 45 (1978): 559–75.

94. Charles V. Willie, *The Sociology of Urban Education*(Lexington, Mass.: Lexington Books, 1978), pp. 17–19; Paul Barton, Sue Bobrow, and John Walsh, *Industry/Education Community Councils* (Washington, D.C.: National Institute of Education, 1977); Susan Sherman, ed., *Education for Tomorrow's Jobs* (Washington, D.C.: National Academy of Sciences, 1983). But see Howard Ozmon, "Adopt-A-School: Definitely Not Business as Usual," *Phi Delta Kappan* 63, no. 5 (January 1982): 350–51, for appropriate cautions about business involvement in schools.

95. Peter K. Eisinger, *Black Employment in City Government, 1973–1980* (Washington, D.C.: Joint Center for Political Studies, 1983). See also Milton D. Morris, "Black Electoral Participation and the Distribution of Public Benefits," in *The Right to Vote* (New York: Rockefeller Foundation, 1981).

96. See James M. McPartland and Jomills H. Braddock II, "Going to College and Getting a Good Job: The Impact of Desegregation," in *Effective School Desegregation*, ed. Hawley, pp. 141–54; James M. McPartland, "Desegregation and Equity in Higher Education and Employment: Is Progress Related to the Desegregation of Elementary and Secondary Schools?" *Law and Contemporary Problems* 42, no. 3 (Summer 1978): 108–32; and Jomills H. Braddock II and James M. McPartland, *The Effects of Elementary-Secondary School Desegregation on Black Student Attendance and Persistence at Traditionally White Four-Year Colleges* (Baltimore: The Johns Hopkins University, Center for Social Organization of Schools, 1980).

97. Marvin Dawkins, "Black Students' Occupational Expectations: A National Study of the Impact of School Desegregation," *Urban Education* 18, no. 1 (April 1983): 98–113.

98. Robert Crain and Rita Mahard, "School Racial Composition and Black College Attendance and Achievement Test Performance," *Sociology of Education* 51 (April 1978): 81–101. Jomills H. Braddock and James M. McPartland, "Assessing School Desegregation Effects: New Directions in Research," in *Research in Sociology of Education and Socialization*, vol. 3 (Greenwich, Conn.: JAI Press, 1982), p. 276.

99. Henry Jay Becker, *Personal Networks of Opportunity in Obtaining Jobs: Racial Differences and Effects of Segregation* (Baltimore: Johns Hopkins University, Center for Social Organization of Schools, 1979).

100. Nancy Karweit, S. Hansell, and M. Ricks, *The Conditions for Peer Associations in Schools* (Baltimore: Johns Hopkins University, Center for Social Organization of Schools, 1979); and Granovetter, "The Microstructure of School Desegregation." But see also Eugene P. Erickson and William L. Yancey, "Using Connections; Antecedents and Consequences of Personal Networks in the City" (Unpublished manuscript, Temple University, Department of Sociology, 1976).

101. Katz, ed., *Toward the Elimination of Racism.*

102. Louis Harris and Associates, *A Study of Attitudes*, p. 44, emphasis added; see also Harris, *Majority of Parents Report School Busing*, p. 2.

103. Orfield, "Why It Worked in Dixie," p. 40.

104. For the 1963 data, the North shows the same results, "Northern whites living in segregated schools areas were 65 percent for integration, but in areas where there had been considerable integration, 83 percent favored the policy." Comparable data are not reported for the 1965 survey. Paul B. Sheatsley, "White Attitudes toward the Negro," *Daedalus* 95, no. 1 (Winter 1966): 221, 235, 238. Note that the "conclusion that school integration resulted in an increase in pro-integration attitudes in the desegregated school districts must be treated with some caution, however, since the stud[ies] failed within given communities to interview the same people before and after desegregation." Rossell, "Applied Social Science Research," p. 95.

105. D. Garth Taylor, Paul Sheatsley, and Andrew Greeley, "Attitudes toward Racial Integration," *Scientific American* 238, no. 6 (June 1978): 44.

106. Stanley B. Elam, *A Decade of Gallup Polls of Attitudes toward Education, 1969–1978* (Bloomington, Ind.: Phi Delta Kappa, 1978), pp. 110–11. See also pp. 163, 173–75.

107. Harris, *A Study of Attitudes*, pp. 39–40.

108. Frank Barrows, "School Busing: Charlotte, N.C.," *Atlantic* 230 (November 1972): 20.

109. Glenn Abney, "Legislating Morality: Attitude Change and Desegregation in Mississippi," *Urban Education* 11, no. 3 (October 1976): 333–38.

110. Data are not statistically significant. Serow and Solomon, "Parents' Attitudes toward Desegregation," p. 753.

111. John B. McConahay and Willis D. Hawley, *Attitudes of Louisville and Jefferson County Citizens toward Busing for Public School Desegregation: Results from the Second Year* (Unpublished report, Durham, N.C., Duke University, Institute of Policy Sciences, 1977). See also J. Michael Ross, "Resistance to Racial Change in the Urban North: 1962–1968" (Ph.D. diss., Harvard University, 1973), for the same conclusion about Boston.

112. These data do not reflect an increase in parochial school attendance. Results for public schools were not statistically significant; results for parochial schools were. Cardell Jacobson, "Desegregation Rulings and Public Attitude Changes," *American Journal of Sociology* 84, no. 3 (November 1978): 698–705.

113. McKee McClendon and Fred Pestello, "White opposition: To Busing or to Desegregation?" *Social Science Quarterly* 63, no. 1 (March 1982): 77–78.

114. In 1977, 72 percent described schools in their children's district as "good or excellent"; in 1979 (after one year of mandatory desegregation), 44 percent did; and by 1983, 62 percent did. Thirty-six percent of nonparents rated the schools as "good" or "excellent" in 1983, compared with 62 percent of public schools parents. More specific questions show similar or even more positive views—over two-thirds of public school parents rate their own child's school as "good" or "excellent" and are satisfied with their child's teacher, principal, school atmosphere, level of school work, happiness in school, and so on. Raffel et al., "Public Opinion toward the Public Schools," pp. 13–21, 29–30.

115. Ibid. See especially pp. 29-33, 48–55. in the Civil Rights Commission Poll, superintendents report that after implementation, at least 75 percent of school boards, teachers, and minority parents "support" desegregation, whereas about 40 percent of school staff and 63 percent of minority parents were supportive before the fact. Business leaders and Anglo parents began with much less support—about 20 percent endorsed desegregation—and increased their support to about 50 percent. U.S. Commission on Civil Rights, *Reviewing a Decade of School Desegregation*, pp. 87–100.

116. Edward J. Slawski, "Pontiac Parents: For Busing or Integration?" *Education and Urban Society* 8, no. 4 (August 1976): 477–98.

117. Even among opponents, however, more agreed in the second year that "busing is the law and should be followed." McConahay and Hawley, *Reactions to Busing in Louisville* (Durham, N.C.: Institute of Policy Sciences, 1978), pp. 20, 33.

118. Parents who rate desegregation negatively are more than twice as likely to believe—mistakenly—that school district test scores are dropping. The data do not permit us to say which way causation runs. However, the fact that those perceiving test score declines are also slightly more negative about blacks in general suggests that prejudice toward blacks leads to pessimism about the schools (an affective phenomenon) rather than that (mis)information about the schools leads to opposition to desegregation (a cognitive phenomenon). The inferences are mine; the data are from the New Castle County survey. On the second point in the text, 60 percent of public school parents give surburban schools an "A" or "B"; 29 percent rate the city schools as highly. The disparities are greater for nonpublic school parents and nonparents. Raffel et al., "Public Opinion toward the Public Schools," pp. 36, 75–79, 113. See, in general, Rossell, "Applied Social Science Research," pp. 95–99.

119. Daniels, "In Defense of Busing," p. 37.

120. Essie Payne, Cheryl Nowell, and Michelle Stolpa, "Student Perceptions: The Value of Little Rock," *Theory into Practice* 17, no. 2 (April 1978): 174–76.

121. Robert B. Pittman and Lewis E. Cloud, "Major Problems in Public Education from the Students' Perspective," *Phi Delta Kappan* 61, no. 6 (February 1980). By the

1980s, desegregation and busing had fallen to fifth place or below on parents' list of school problems. We cannot say, however, whether this finding is further evidence for my claim that, after the fact, desegregation is not so terrible,or whether it simply reflects the fact that very little new desegregation has taken place in the 1980s, so the issue is losing salience. See Elam, *A Decade of Gallup Polls*, p. 336, and yearly updates entitled "The –th Annual Gallup Poll of the Public's Attitudes toward the Public Schools," in *Phi Delta Kappan*.

122. Elam, *A Decade of Gallup Polls*, pp. 110–11.

123. Alexander Astin et al., ed., *The American Freshman: National Norms* (Los Angeles: American Council on Education, 1976, 1983), pp. 55 (1976), 56 (1983).

124. Charles S. Bullock III and Mary V. Braxton, "The Coming of School Desegregation: A Before and After Study of Black and White Student Perceptions," *Social Science Quarterly* 54 (June 1973): 137.

125. Rodgers and Bullock, *Coercion to Compliance*, p. 107.

126. Elam, *A Decade of Gallup Polls*, p. 164.

127. Morgan with England, "Assessing the Progress," appendix E. Whites are especially likely to return under metropolitan or token plans. See Raffel et al., "Public Opinion toward the Public Schools," pp. 86–90, for the most extensive (only?) study of "returners."

128. ESAA was folded into an education block grant in 1981, and desegregation-related aid to schools now varies widely and is significantly diminished. "The loss of ESAA funds has crippled desegregation projects. Ninety-four percent of the school districts surveyed are *not* using Chapter 2 funds [the analogous program in the new education block grant] for desegregation purposes; the funds are simply not available in the quantity necessary." American Association of School Administrators, "The Impact of Chapter 2 of the Educational Consolidation and Improvement Act on Local Education Agencies" (Arlington, Va.: American Association of School Administrators, 1983), p. 19. See also Jim Stedman, *The Consolidation of the Emergency School Aid Act—A Brief Analysis of Its Impact* (Washington, D.C.: Library of Congress, Congressional Relations Service, 1983); House Committee on Government Operations, *Block Grants Have Weakened Federal Programs for the Educationally Disadvantaged*, 98th Cong., 1st Sess., 1983; Robert Pear, "Desegregation Plans in Peril," *New York Times*, September 7, 1982, pp. A1, A16; Henderson, *No Strings Attached*. Legislation to reestablish ESAA has, as of this writing (April 1984), passed the House of Representatives, but it faces strong opposition in the Senate and the White House.

129. Schofield, *Black and White in School*, esp. pp. 155–82.

130. Jacqueline Scherer and Edward Slawski, "Desegregation: Advantages to Whites," *Urban Review* 13, no. 4 (Winter 1981): 217–25.

131. Edward A. Wynne, *Growing Up Suburban* (Austin: University of Texas Press, 1977), esp. pp. 56–58, 156–59.

132. Willie, *The Sociology of Urban Education*, pp. 8, 68–69.

133. Lyndon Baines Johnson, "Commencement Address at Howard University: 'To Fulfill These Rights,' June 4, 1965," *Public Papers of the Presidents*, pp. 635–40.

134. Douglas Rae et al., *Equalities* (Cambridge: Harvard University Press, 1981), pp. 64–81.

135. Ibid., p. 67.

136. Leonard B. Stevens, Letter to the editor, "In School, Separate Is Still Unequal," *New York Times*, May 9, 1983, p. A18.

137. Richard Rodriguez, *Hunger of Memory* (Boston: Godine, 1982).

138. Willie, *The Sociology of Urban Education*, pp. ix, 3.

139. Minorities now comprise 17 percent of the total United States population and more than 26 percent of the school-aged population. By 1990, they will comprise 20 to 25 and 30 percent respectively. C. Emily Feistritzer, *The Condition of Teaching* (Princeton, N.J.: Carnegie Foundation for the Advancement of Teaching, 1983), p. 14.

140. *Historical Statistics* 1:368; and *Statistical Abstract, 1982*–1983, p. 294.

141. Over two-thirds of women aged twenty to forty-five (the age of most women when their children are young) work outside the home; between 48 and 84 percent of women with children at home are in the labor force, with variations acording to their marital status and the age of their children. *Statistical Abstract, 1982*–1983, pp. 377, 382.

142. Michael Walzer, *Spheres of Justice: A Defense of Pluralism and Equality* (New York: Basic Books, 1983), p. 225.

143. Kirp, "School Desegregation and the Limits of Legalism," p. 118.

144. My thanks to Paul E. Peterson for urging the need for policy proposals, not merely exhortation, to induce leadership.

145. Taylor, "Public Opinion and Political Entrepreneurship."

146. My thanks to David Tatel for pointing out the significance of the increasing numbers of black mayors and state legislators. In 1983, there were 2700 elected black municipal officials and 380 elected black state officials (compared to 620 and 170, respectively, in 1970). Also in 1983, 1400 blacks held elected posts in education, 600 in the judiciary and law enforcement agencies, and 500 in county government (compared with 360, 210, and 90, respectively, in 1970). The numbers are small, but probably a disproportionate share of elected black officials (and their staff) are in large Northern cities where the most change—whether desegregation or something else—remains to be accomplished. "Largest Increase in BEOs since 1976," *Focus* 12, no. 1 (January 1984): 8. See also "A National Profile of Black Elected Officials," *Focus* 12, no. 2 (February 1984).

147. Ralph Scott, Jr., Statement to Senate Judiciary Committee, Subcommittee on the Constitution, *Hearings on Court-Ordered School Busing*, 97th Cong., 1st Sess., 1981, p. 165.

148. Robert J. Lynd and Helen M. Lynd, *Middletown: A Study in Contemporary American Culture* (New York: Harcourt, Brace, 1929).

149. From a conservative perspective, Alexis de Tocqueville is clearly the best advocate of nonliberal communities in the United States. See *Democracy in America*, trans. George Lawrence, ed. J. P. Mayer (New York: Doubleday, 1969). From a social democratic perspective, Michael Walzer gives the best defense of nonliberal communities in a liberal society, in *Spheres of Justice*.

150. *Webster's New World Dictionary, College Edition* (Cleveland: World Publishing Co., 1959), p. 1477.

151. Carter, "Reassessment of *Brown v. Board*," in *Shades of Brown*, ed. Bell pp. 23–24; emphasis in original.

152. Lawrence, "'One More River to Cross,'" in ibid., pp. 50–51.

153. Reich, *Racial Inequality*.

154. Freeman, "School Desegregation Law," in *Shades of Brown*, ed. Bell pp. 73–74.

155. Freeman, "Legitimizing Racial Discrimination," p. 1053.

156. Freeman, "School Desegregation Law," p. 88.

157. Carter, "A Reassessment of *Brown v. Board*," in *Shades of Brown*, ed. Bell p. 25.

158. William Julius Wilson, *The Declining Significance of Race: Blacks and Changing American Institutions* (Chicago: University of Chicago Press, 1978). See also Charles V. Willie, *The Caste and Class Controversy* (New York: General Hall, 1979); John C. Leggett, *Class, Race, and Labor* (London: Oxford University Press, 1968); James A. Geschwender, *Class, Race, and Worker Insurgency* (Cambridge: Cambridge University Press, 1977); Oliver Cox, *Caste, Class, and Race* (New York: Monthly Review Press, 1948); Manning Marable, *How Capitalism Underdeveloped Black America* (Boston: South End Press, 1983); and George Fredrickson, *White Supremacy: A Comparative Study in American and South African Histories* (New York: Oxford University Press, 1981). For a contrasting argument, see Thomas Sowell, *Race and Economics* (New York: Longman, 1975).

INDEX